MW01194773

EISENHOWER REPUBLICANISM

Eisenhower Republicanism

Pursuing the Middle Way

Steven Wagner

NORTHERN

ILLINOIS

UNIVERSITY

PRESS

DeKalb

Library of Congress Cataloging-in-Publication Data

Wagner, Steven (Steven T.)

Eisenhower Republicanism : pursuing the middle way / Steven Wagner.

   p.   cm.

Includes bibliographical references and index.

ISBN-13: 978-0-87580-362-3 (clothbound : alk. paper)

ISBN-10: 0-87580-362-8 (clothbound : alk. paper)

1. Eisenhower, Dwight D. (Dwight David), 1890–1969—Political and social views.

2. United States—Politics and government—1953–1961. 3. Republican Party

(U.S. : 1854–)—History—20th century. I. Title.

E836.W34 2006

973.921—dc22

2006001576

Contents

Acknowledgments

The successful completion of this book would not have been possible without the help and support of many individuals and institutions. The following list includes only a few of those to whom I owe a debt of gratitude. The history department at Purdue University provided financial and professional support for the early stages of this project. Purdue historians Patrick Hearden, Michael Morrison, Randy Roberts, and Donald Parman read early versions of the manuscript and offered valuable suggestions. I am grateful to the Purdue Research Foundation for two summer research grants. Archival research was facilitated by the generous support of the Eisenhower World Affairs Institute in Washington, D.C.—for research at the Eisenhower Presidential Library (DDEL) in Abilene, Kansas, and the Rockefeller Archive Center (RAC) in Sleepy Hollow, New York. The helpful and dedicated archivists there, particularly Thomas Branigar (DDEL) and Harold Oakhill (RAC), made my research more productive. My colleagues in the social science department at Missouri Southern State University, particularly Robert Markman who read a portion of the manuscript, created a supportive environment that made my work on the final stages of this project much easier. The students in my Modern America course at Missouri Southern, by serving as a sounding board for my material on the "middle way," also made a valuable contribution. Melody Herr, my editor at Northern Illinois University Press, was very supportive of this project and offered timely encouragement. Her suggestions, along with those of the anonymous readers she commissioned, have greatly strengthened this book.

A project like this is not possible without the support of friends and family. I especially want to thank my parents, Paul and Donna Wagner, and my friend Matt Loayza for providing that support. Finally, I would like to thank my wife, Angela Firkus. A fellow scholar, her involvement went beyond that of wife and friend; she read every word of the manuscript, discussed it with me at every stage, and offered invaluable suggestions for improvement. All of those mentioned above, and many others, have made important contributions to this book. Any shortcomings that remain are mine alone.

Abbreviations

ACW Diary	Ann C. Whitman Diary Series, DDE Papers as President, DDEL
ADA	Americans for Democratic Action
AFL	American Federation of Labor
AIA	Aid to Impacted Areas
AMA	American Medical Association
CBS	Columbia Broadcasting System
CIO	Congress of Industrial Organizations
CUOHROC	Columbia University Oral History Research Office Collection
DDE	Dwight D. Eisenhower
DDE Papers as President	Dwight D. Eisenhower Papers as President of the United States, 1953–1961
DDE Postpresidential Papers	Dwight D. Eisenhower Postpresidential Papers, 1961–1969
DDE Records as President	Dwight D. Eisenhower Records as President, White House Central Files, 1953–1961
DDEL	Dwight D. Eisenhower Library, Abilene, Kansas
DLF	Development Loan Fund
FSA	Federal Security Agency
GATT	General Agreement on Tariffs and Trade
GPO	Government Printing Office

HEW	Health, Education, and Welfare (in the notes, HEW refers to the Health, Education, and Welfare, Record Group 4, Nelson A. Rockefeller Personal, Rockefeller Archive Center, North Tarrytown, New York)
HUAC	House Un-American Activities Committee
IDAB	International Development Advisory Board
IMF	International Monetary Fund
NAACP	National Association for the Advancement of Colored People
NAM	National Association of Manufacturers
NAR	Nelson A. Rockefeller
NATO	North Atlantic Treaty Organization
NDEA	National Defense Education Act
NLRB	National Labor Relations Board
NSF	National Science Foundation
OAA	Old-Age Assistance
OASI	Old-Age and Survivors Insurance
PACGO	President's Advisory Committee on Government Organization
PL	Public Law
PPP	*Public Papers of the Presidents; Containing the Public Messages, Speeches, and Statements of the President* (Washington, D.C.: GPO, 1958–1961)
RAC	Rockefeller Archive Center, North Tarrytown, New York
REAC	Reorganization Advisory Committee, Washington, D.C., files, RG4, NAR Personal, RAC
RG	Record Group
RRPL	Ronald Reagan Presidential Library
RTAA	Reciprocal Trade Agreements Act of 1934
SAP	Special Assistant to the President, Washington, D.C., files, RG4, NAR Personal, RAC
SCGO	Special Committee on Government Organization
UN	United Nations
World Bank	International Bank for Reconstruction and Development

EISENHOWER REPUBLICANISM

Introduction

Theodore White, historian, journalist, and astute observer of American politics, described the Republican Party as "fratricidal" twin brothers. One brother represented American idealism; the other, American enterprise. It has been this way since the beginning, he pointed out, when "Pure New England abolitionists let their conscience be joined with the skills of some of the most practical veterans of the old Whigs to form a party that would end slavery."[1] In 1952, conditions were favorable for a long-delayed battle between these twin brothers for control of the party. Franklin D. Roosevelt's immense popularity had led to a string of liberal Republican presidential nominations: Alf Landon (1936), a former Bull Moose Progressive who had endorsed many New Deal programs; Wendell Willkie (1940), a former Democrat who had voted for Roosevelt in 1932; and Thomas Dewey (1944 and 1948), who supported the New Deal but thought that Republicans could administer it more efficiently. These candidates' failure to defeat Roosevelt, and Dewey's particularly embarrassing loss to Harry S. Truman in 1948, made party conservatives determined to run one of their own—Ohio Senator Robert Taft—in 1952. Liberal Republicans, however, would not give up easily. Their support remained strong in the large industrial states of the North and East, which had more electoral clout than the conservative states of the South and West. Ties to big business also promised liberals a greater share of the campaign funds. What ultimately assured liberal Republicans another nomination, however, was General Dwight D. Eisenhower's decision to enter the race.

Before 1952, most people did not know Eisenhower's political affiliation. In 1948, members of both parties had tried to convince the popular general to run for president. In 1952, Truman himself had offered to endorse him for the Democratic nomination. Eisenhower's beliefs, however, were more in line with the liberal wing of the Republican Party. He was reluctant to enter politics, but the ground swell of public support, his sense of duty to his country, and his dissatisfaction with Taft ultimately persuaded him to enter the presidential race in 1952.[2] James C. Hagerty, Eisenhower's campaign advisor and later his press secretary, put it more bluntly: Eisenhower "made up his mind to run because he feared [the] Taft wing of [the] G. O. P. and Truman incompetence."[3]

Eisenhower's enormous popularity ensured his election, but the victory masked intense factionalism within the Republican Party. The first Republican president in twenty years, Eisenhower was at odds with a growing faction of his own party. Conservatives, who had developed a considerable base of power on Capitol Hill, were eager to overturn a generation of liberal domestic policies and internationalist foreign policies. Central to the factional differences was the role of the federal government. Conservatives preferred free enterprise and individual initiative to federal programs and the taxes necessary to support them. When government action was unavoidable, they favored state or local control in areas where the federal government had no explicit power. In foreign policy, conservatives had not reverted back to the isolationism they espoused before World War II, but they had not completely converted to internationalism either. Many wanted to limit the president's power to conduct foreign policy, hoping to prevent the sort of diplomacy practiced by Roosevelt during the war. Conservatives virulently opposed communism, but they did not see the "mutual security" benefits of foreign aid "giveaway" programs. Most were also protectionists who were opposed to lowering foreign trade barriers.

Eisenhower, in contrast, supported a more active role for the federal government in both domestic and foreign policy. He supported the continuation and, in some cases, the expansion of popular New Deal programs. When new programs were necessary, however, he supported those that would allow the federal government to act as a catalyst for change without adding significantly to its responsibilities. This would allow government to look after the welfare of individuals and still maintain fiscal responsibility. It was, according to Eisenhower, "a liberal program in all of those things that bring the federal government in contact with the individual," but conservative when it came to "the economy of this country."[4] Somewhat less enthusiastically, Eisenhower also supported federal legislation that would protect the economic interests of farmers and organized labor and the civil rights of African Americans. On foreign policy issues, he was a committed internationalist. He opposed any effort to limit the president's power to conduct foreign policy. He also favored free trade and considered foreign aid a vital component of America's defense.

The promotion of active government, both at home and abroad, may initially seem to have been a mere continuation of the Democratic policies of the previous twenty years, but this was not Eisenhower's intention. The key to understanding how he distinguished his policies from those of the liberal Democrats and the conservative Republicans is his philosophy of the "middle way." After he had secured the Republican nomination in 1952, Eisenhower began to speak more frequently about the "middle way." In an October campaign speech, he warned his audience about the dangers of going too far to the political left or right. Those on the left, he said, believed people were "so weak, so irresponsible, that an all-powerful government must direct and protect" them. The end of that road, he warned, was "dictatorship." On the right were those "who deny the obligation of government to intervene on behalf of the people even when the complexities of modern life demand it." The end of that road was "anarchy." To avoid these extremes, he said, "government should proceed along the middle way."[5]

In American political culture those who describe themselves as "middle of the road" are often portrayed as unwilling to take a stand or lacking in political sophistication. This was not the case with Eisenhower. The "middle way" was a carefully considered political philosophy similar to Theodore Roosevelt's cautious progressivism. Fearing an upheaval of the working class if the excesses of monopoly capitalism were not curbed, Roosevelt embraced social and economic programs that he believed would alleviate class conflict and promote economic stability. He believed that if such reforms were not willingly undertaken by "rational" men, then socialists—the "lunatic fringe"—would force a more radical agenda on the country. His motive, therefore, was not to undermine capitalism but, rather, to preserve and protect it through necessary reforms.[6]

Eisenhower's philosophy was similar. Conservatives referred to many of the domestic programs he proposed as "creeping socialism," but Eisenhower believed that, by addressing the problems that threatened American society, his programs would stem—not encourage—the impetus toward socialism. Eisenhower saw his domestic programs as a safety net, or as "a floor over the pit of personal disaster in our complex modern society." Unlike socialism, however, these programs did not create a "ceiling" that limited initiative and industry.[7] They did not interfere with "the right . . . to build the most glorious structure on top of that floor."[8]

Eisenhower hoped his policies would change the direction of the Republican Party. This would allow him to retire, confident that the party would continue along the "middle way." This was not to be. More often than not, Eisenhower's legislative proposals were defeated by an unwitting alliance of conservatives, who sought to limit the role of the federal government, and liberals, who wanted the federal government to do more than Eisenhower proposed. Eisenhower's legislative failures had political consequences as well. By 1958, Republican congressional representation had sunk to its lowest level since 1936 and Vice President Richard Nixon's hope of becoming president in 1960 was all but lost.

Nixon's place within the Republican Party was ambiguous. Eisenhower had chosen him as running mate with the hope that his strong ties to the party's conservative wing would help secure passage of his legislative agenda. As a presidential candidate, however, Nixon could not very well repudiate the policies of the man under whom he had served for eight years. His attempt to satisfy conservatives and liberals contributed to his defeat and led each faction to blame it on a lack of adherence to their own philosophy.

The result of Nixon's defeat was open factional warfare over the party's 1964 presidential nomination. For the liberal wing, Nelson Rockefeller was the leading candidate. His political philosophy and belief in active government placed him squarely in the liberal camp; his victory in the 1958 New York gubernatorial race had been one of the few bright spots for the party in that otherwise dark year. Conservatives, who had supported liberal presidential candidates for seven straight elections, believed that their time had come and began a grassroots campaign to nominate Barry Goldwater, the leading conservative since Robert Taft's death.

Goldwater's nomination, despite his devastating defeat in the general election, signaled a major victory for the conservatives in the factional struggle for control of the Republican Party. In the early twenty-first century, when the word "liberal" is used with contempt by Republicans, it is easy to forget that a liberal wing influenced the direction of the Republican Party throughout much of its history. Eisenhower's pursuit of the "middle way" was his unsuccessful attempt to perpetuate that influence.

A Floor over the
Pit of Personal Disaster

Early in his presidency, Eisenhower wrote a letter to his good friend Brigadier General Bradford G. Chynoweth in which he explained how his "middle way" philosophy applied to social welfare. Chynoweth, like many of Eisenhower's former associates, disagreed with his stand on this issue. "It seems to me that no great intelligence is required in order to discern the practical necessity of establishing some kind of security for individuals in a specialized and highly industrialized age," Eisenhower wrote. "At one time such security was provided by the existence of free land and a great mass of untouched and valuable resources throughout our country. These are no longer to be had for the asking." On the other hand, he continued, it was a mistake to "push further and further into the socialistic experiment," which impaired the self-respect, initiative, and incentive of individuals to provide for themselves. "Excluding the field of moral values," Eisenhower concluded, "anything that affects or is proposed for masses of humans is wrong if the position it seeks is at either end of possible argument."[1]

Searching for the "middle way" in the field of social welfare, Eisenhower attempted to provide for the general welfare, as called for in the Constitution, without taking on the enormous financial burdens of an ever-expanding welfare state or significantly encroaching on the responsibilities of local government. He was continually frustrated when his moderate programs were opposed by conservative Republicans anxious to overturn the legacy of the New Deal and by liberal Democrats unwilling to settle for less federal intervention than they would like. Eisenhower's only first-term social welfare success came in Social Security, an area where a program was already in place. His initiatives in health care and education, which both required new programs, failed at the hands of an unlikely alliance of conservative Republicans and liberal Democrats. Leading the way in the formation of policy in this field was the new Department of Health, Education, and Welfare.

The Department of Health, Education, and Welfare

During the 1952 campaign, Eisenhower promised to study the problem of federal waste and mismanagement and, if elected, make recommendations for government reorganization.[2] Eisenhower asked Nelson A. Rockefeller, grandson of John D. Rockefeller, to begin the process. Rockefeller financed a study at Temple University whose president, Robert L. Johnson, had a special interest in the subject. In 1947 President Truman had appointed Johnson to a panel, headed by former President Herbert Hoover, that was charged with making recommendations for increasing the efficiency of the federal bureaucracy. These recommendations went largely unfulfilled due to Truman's poor relationship with Congress. After Eisenhower's election victory, he made Rockefeller's role official by appointing him chairman of a new Special Committee on Government Organization (SCGO). The other members of the committee were the president's brother Milton Eisenhower, the president of Pennsylvania State University; and Arthur Flemming, president of Ohio Wesleyan University and former director of the Office of Defense Mobilization. The SCGO had a broad mandate to study and recommend changes in the organization and activities of the executive branch in order to promote economy and efficiency. The starting point for the SCGO's studies were the reports produced by the Hoover Commission and Temple University, but Eisenhower's "middle way" served as the blueprint for the committee's recommendations. "We have been guided by your own expressed determination to avoid any actions which tend to make people ever more dependent upon the government and yet to make certain that the human side of our national problems is not forgotten," noted the committee's report.[3]

The first recommendation of the SCGO was the creation of a new cabinet-level department to absorb the functions of the Federal Security Agency (FSA), which had been created by Franklin D. Roosevelt in 1939. The FSA had thirty-eight thousand employees representing the Social Security System, the Food and Drug Administration, the Public Health Service, and the Office of Education. Despite a budget of $4.6 billion, the FSA lacked cabinet status. The creation of a new department, the committee believed, would be "an important milestone on the road to social progress," making clear that the Republican Party recognized that the government responsibilities embodied by the FSA were permanent, providing "an excellent example of the beneficial functioning of our two-party system."[4] Eisenhower accepted the recommendation and on March 12, 1953, delivered a special message to Congress requesting approval for the creation of the Department of Health, Education, and Welfare (HEW).[5]

Republicans had opposed President Truman's attempts to elevate the FSA to cabinet status in both 1949 and 1950. For many Republicans, health and education were not legitimate areas of federal concern. Placing the Public Health Service and the Office of Education under the supervision of a cabinet department, particularly one oriented toward welfare, would only strengthen the federal bureaucracy's claim to legitimacy in these areas. The SCGO overcame these objections through decentralization. The HEW plan did not place all the department's powers in the hands of the secretary. The functions of the Public Health Service and the Office of Education remained in those agencies, which were subordinate divisions of the new department; the secretary would have only supervisory control. The plan also called for the creation of a special assistant to the secretary for health and medical affairs, to be appointed by the president from outside of government. The secretary had the authority to administer Social Security and welfare programs, but the president would also appoint a commissioner of Social Security to assist with these matters.

There was very little opposition from either party to the creation of HEW. The measure won bipartisan support, and Eisenhower signed the bill creating the new department on April 11, 1953. Although Republican congressmen participated in the creation of HEW, they were not acquiescing in the creation of a permanent welfare state. Rather, they were admitting that Social Security, the Food and Drug Administration, and the other HEW components were an accepted and popular part of American society. Only the most conservative Republicans still favored their elimination.

Oveta Culp Hobby became HEW's first secretary. Hobby was a registered Democrat from Texas, but she had backed Eisenhower against Robert Taft and endorsed Eisenhower for president on the front page of her newspaper, the *Houston Post*. Her appointment would reward the many southern Democrats who had crossed over to vote for Eisenhower and would solidify the bipartisan credentials of the new department. Choosing a prominent Democrat for his cabinet was an astute political move, but Eisenhower had concerns about Hobby's ability to handle the job and believed she would need an able assistant.[6] He offered Nelson Rockefeller, who had served in the Roosevelt and Truman administrations, the job of undersecretary. Rockefeller's advisors recommended that he turn down the offer because they believed his interests would not be served by accepting the number two position in an upstart department so far removed from his primary interest of foreign affairs. Rockefeller, however, rejected this advice, claiming he had been interested in health, education, and welfare all his life. Furthermore, he felt obligated to the new department he had helped to create. "I'm responsible for creating this baby," he said, "I have a responsibility for seeing to it that it succeeds."[7] Rockefeller also believed it was important for the Republican Party, so often associated with preserving the status quo, to demonstrate that the social gains of the New Deal era had bipartisan support and would be not only retained but improved upon by the Republican Party. "A Republican administration couldn't be seen to be trying to turn back the clock," he later recalled.[8]

Social Security

As Eisenhower asserted in his campaign statements, he was definitely not in favor of turning back the clock. "I believe that the social gains achieved by the people of the United States, whether they were enacted by a Republican or a Democratic administration, are not only here to stay but are to be improved and expanded," Eisenhower noted during an October campaign stop. "Anyone who says it is my purpose to cut down Social Security, unemployment insurance, to leave the ill and aged destitute, is lying."[9] Despite these general principles, however, it was unclear to Hobby and Rockefeller where Eisenhower stood on the specific domestic policy debates that concerned HEW.

Among the issues up for immediate consideration was the expansion of the Social Security system. Throughout the campaign, Eisenhower had promised that if he was elected, he would extend coverage to groups not currently eligible for benefits. He repeated this pledge in his first State of the Union message on February 3, 1953.[10] He made good on these promises in August 1953 when, in a special message to Congress, he proposed extending Social Security protection to 10.5 million people not currently covered. Among the groups made eligible by the proposal were self-employed professionals, farmers, agricultural and domestic workers, state and local government employees, and clergymen.[11]

What was unclear was whether Eisenhower favored expansion of the system in its current form, or if he preferred the "pay-as-you-go" plan that the 1952 Republican platform said deserved a "thorough study."[12] Under the current system, benefits for the elderly were paid using the same framework that had been established by the Social Security Act of 1935. This act created a federally operated, compulsory, Old-Age and Survivors Insurance (OASI) program. Qualified workers paid for OASI with a payroll tax matched by their employer. Proceeds were placed in a federal trust account. At the age of sixty-five, those workers, or their survivors, became eligible for monthly payments relative to the amount they had contributed to the program over the years. The act also created an Old-Age Assistance (OAA) program that reimbursed the states for part of the money they spent supporting the indigent elderly who had not contributed to the system.[13]

The "pay-as-you-go" plan, promoted by the U.S. Chamber of Commerce, and endorsed by many conservatives, was an attempt to collapse the two programs created by the Social Security Act of 1935 into a single, universal coverage, old-age pension funded by current revenues. Under this plan, all employed workers would be subject to the existing OASI payroll tax and all elderly persons would be eligible for a flat-rate pension, regardless of their employment history. This would allow for the elimination of OAA. The cost of starting up the program would be paid for with the existing trust account, and all future benefits would be paid from that year's contributions. In his 1953 budget message, Eisenhower stated that "From now on, the old-age tax [OASI] and trust accounts, while maintaining the contributory principle, should be handled more nearly on a pay-as-you-go basis."[14]

Fulfilling the Republican platform promise to conduct a "thorough study" of "pay-as-you-go," the chair of the House Ways and Means Committee, Daniel A. Reed (R-NY), established a special subcommittee under Carl T. Curtis (R-NE) in February 1953 to study Social Security. House Republicans' desire for the Curtis Committee to complete its ambitious survey before they acted prevented any Social Security legislation from reaching the floor in 1953. Throughout the session Curtis clashed with House Democrats led by John D. Dingell (D-MI) and Herman Eberharter (D-PA) who accused the Curtis subcommittee of undermining the American people's confidence in Social Security and claimed the hearings were "nothing but an attempt to discredit and smash the present Social Security system."[15] In December Curtis reported his findings, calling for a system nearly identical to the Chamber of Commerce's "pay-as-you-go" plan.

In the meantime, Rockefeller and Assistant Secretary Roswell B. "Rod" Perkins conducted their own study of Social Security and came to the opposite conclusion. Much to the satisfaction of Secretary Hobby, Rockefeller and Perkins recommended expanding the system based on the current model. Like organized labor and other groups that opposed "pay-as-you-go," they argued that under a current financing system (such as the one proposed by Curtis and the Chamber of Commerce) business interests and others seeking lower taxes would pressure Congress to keep the program's costs down, preventing future benefits from keeping pace with inflation. Eliminating OAA, they argued, would place the burden of providing for indigent persons who did not contribute to the system more squarely on the working class, since funds would come from the payroll tax rather than the progressive income tax. Furthermore, eliminating the trust-fund aspect of Social Security created the possibility that it could be dismantled by future politicians who did not want the responsibility of collecting taxes to pay for it.

On November 20, 1953, Hobby and Rockefeller outlined HEW's proposal for expanding the current system to Eisenhower and the cabinet. Following the presentation the cabinet broke into applause, and the president stated that the proposal had his approval.[16] This meeting is often credited with convincing Eisenhower to abandon "pay-as-you-go" plans and endorse expansion of the current system.[17] Other evidence, however, suggests that by this time Eisenhower may have already changed his mind. On October 7, 1953, in a letter to financier E. F. Hutton, Eisenhower anticipated HEW's contention that eliminating the trust fund would ultimately lead to the dismantling of the system. "It would appear logical to build upon the system that has been in place for almost 20 years," he wrote, "rather than embark upon the radical course of turning it completely upside down and running the very real danger that we would end up with no system at all."[18]

On January 14, 1954, Eisenhower submitted the HEW plan to Congress as the administration's proposal for changes to Social Security.[19] He reiterated this support in a number of public speeches. "We want to preserve and strengthen its [the Social Security System's] reliance on a contributory system, in which workers and their employers share the obligation to make payments and in which the self[-]employed also contribute to provide for their own retirement," Eisenhower said the following month in New York City. "Equally firm in our thinking is the belief that the benefits paid to workers and self[-]employed persons after retirement should bear a definite relation to their earnings in their years of activity. To scrap either of these underlying principles would move the system in the direction of charity and undermine the social insurance concept."[20] Statements such as this introduced an element of irony into the debate. Eisenhower characterized the "pay-as-you-go" plan, favored by conservatives, as a government charity, while presenting the administration's plan, the continuation of a liberal "New Deal" program, as something workers were entitled to.

The president's public endorsement of HEW's proposal was certainly helpful, but other circumstances also contributed to getting the Republican Congress to go along with expanding the program that, perhaps more than any other, defined the New Deal. Representative Curtis's preoccupation with a run for the Senate in 1954 effectively killed the momentum of his "pay-as-you-go" proposal. Meanwhile, Rockefeller, displaying the great persuasive abilities he would later put to use as governor of New York, convinced House Ways and Means Chairman Daniel Reed, once a supporter of Curtis, to back the administration's proposal.[21] Without any alternative scheme or the backing of prominent figures, the Republican Congress could not very well vote against expanding one of the most popular government programs. The administration's proposal was, therefore, overwhelmingly approved by both houses, and Eisenhower signed it into law as the Social Security Amendments Act on September 1, 1954.

This act brought nearly ten million additional people under the protection of Social Security. These included self-employed professionals such as accountants, engineers, architects, and funeral directors (but not doctors, dentists, optometrists, chiropractors, veterinarians, or lawyers); self-employed farmers; and clergymen and members of religious orders. Others brought under the law in greater numbers than before included agricultural and domestic workers, fishermen, employees of state and local governments and employees of the federal government not covered by other retirement plans, and U.S. citizens employed outside the United States. Other important provisions of the law included an average increase in benefits of 16 percent for those already receiving checks; higher benefits for those who would begin receiving checks in the future; a provision allowing workers to drop four or five years of low income from those years averaged to compute the amount of benefits; a provision for "freezing" one's earning record during a period of six months or more of disability; and an increase in the amount of money that could be earned while benefits checks were being received. The *New York Times* proclaimed, "In strictly human terms this was perhaps the most significant achievement of the administration in the 1954 session of Congress."[22]

Health Insurance

During the 1952 campaign, Eisenhower continually stated his opposition to any form of federal compulsory health insurance, such as that proposed by President Truman in 1949 and 1950. These plans he condemned as examples of "creeping socialism."[23] Eisenhower believed that plans offered by commercial and nonprofit insurance carriers, together with locally administered programs for those unable to afford insurance, could best meet the needs of the American people. "Any move toward socialized medicine is sure to have one result," he said. "Instead of the patient getting more and better medical care for less, he will get less and poorer medical care for more. . . . We must preserve the completely voluntary relationship between doctor and patient." Eisenhower's stand clearly reflected the Republican Party line as stated in the 1952 platform.[24]

Eisenhower did admit that the existing system was in need of improvement, but during the campaign he did not offer any specific suggestions. HEW brought the problem into sharper focus. In 1952 only 17 percent ($1.6 billion) of all private expenditures for medical care ($9.4 billion) were paid by insurance.[25] Insurance carriers were, understandably, reluctant to offer policies that would place them at great financial risk. Some of the specific shortcomings in coverage identified by HEW included age restrictions that prevented elderly Americans from getting insurance (only 26 percent of Americans aged sixty-five or older were insured); inadequate coverage of low-income families and those who lived in rural areas (only 25 percent of individuals in families with annual incomes below two thousand dollars were insured); the characterization of certain individuals as "uninsurable" based on a preexisting condition; total benefit limits that fell short in cases of catastrophic illness; limits on the number of days of hospitalization covered; exclusions that limited coverage to specific procedures and treatments; and coverage for early diagnosis and treatment of chronic disease.[26] With the help of HEW, Eisenhower sought a "middle way" between federally sponsored health insurance, a system he thought of as "socialized medicine," and the existing system, where insurance carriers covered only a small percentage of health-care costs.[27]

Once again Rockefeller played an important role in Eisenhower's pursuit of the "middle way." The answer to bringing adequate medical care within the means of all Americans, he argued, was not to institute federally sponsored health insurance but to provide incentives for health insurance companies to expand their coverage. With the help of his assistant Oscar Ruebhausen, Rockefeller came up with a plan to do this without committing the federal government to a predominant role. The plan was known as health reinsurance.

Under Rockefeller's reinsurance plan, the federal government would insure commercial insurance companies and nonprofit associations such as Blue Cross and Blue Shield against "abnormal losses" associated with offering policies to individuals not adequately covered by health insurance, or for costs not widely covered by insurance policies.[28] The plan would not pay benefits to individuals or reimburse companies for benefits paid to any individual policyholder. Nor would the plan reimburse companies for their overall losses. Rather, insurance companies would propose that a particular type of policy be eligible for reinsurance. If the policy promoted the overall goals of the plan, reinsurance would be offered at premiums set by the secretary of HEW. Insurance carriers could then offer these policies without fear that doing so would financially jeopardize the company. If the company did experience an "abnormal loss" associated with a reinsured policy, then they could file a claim with HEW. The plan was meant to be self-supporting. An initial appropriation of $25 million would be necessary to get the program started, but after that it would be paid for by the premiums. To protect the principle of free enterprise, the plan was subject to a "no competition" provision. Reinsurance would be offered only if it was not available commercially at a premium rate comparable to that offered by HEW at an extent sufficient to achieve the plan's goals. Regulation of the insurance industry was not the purpose of the plan. Participants need only demonstrate that they were financially sound and operating according to the law and in a manner entitling them to public confidence.[29]

Eisenhower approved the reinsurance plan. Its delicate balance between government involvement and private enterprise appealed to his sense of the "middle way." As he would later say, it allowed the federal government to "fulfill its responsibility for leadership in these matters but in such a way that demagogues could not make the government responsible for all activity in them."[30] He began preparing the way for an administration-backed health-care bill with a special message to Congress in January 1954 and a series of public speeches emphasizing that health care should be accessible to Americans of all classes and races and in both rural and metropolitan areas.[31]

The health reinsurance plan had the administration's backing, but it was not without its detractors in the cabinet. Secretary of the Treasury George Humphrey, the administration's most dedicated conservative and chief penny-pincher, and his undersecretary, Marion Folsom, along with Budget director Joseph Dodge were all against the plan. They consoled themselves in the belief that it would not pass.[32]

The Department of the Treasury and the Budget Bureau were not the only opponents of the health reinsurance plan. Like many "middle way" initiatives, an unlikely coalition of the right and left wings of the political spectrum opposed the administration's health-care plan. Conservative groups such as the American Medical Association (AMA) opposed the plan on the grounds that it was an "opening wedge" for socialized medicine and would lead to a decrease in the quality of medical care.[33] On the other hand, liberal groups such as organized labor and Americans for Democratic Action (ADA) opposed the plan out of fear that it might prevent passage of compulsory national health insurance.

In an effort to win support for the bill, Eisenhower hosted a luncheon for insurance company executives on May 17, 1954. In his address the president emphasized that the majority of Americans believed that the insurance industry was doing an inadequate job of meeting their needs. Of these, he pointed out, a substantial number, including organized labor and the ADA, were in favor of a national compulsory health insurance system. The reinsurance plan, he argued, was a way to help the insurance industry better meet the demands of the people. By stemming the tide of support for a compulsory system, reinsurance would save the insurance industry and, indirectly, the health-care providers represented by the AMA.[34]

Secretary Hobby, in addition to making a national television address, also met with AMA executives in an attempt to win them over with Eisenhower's "lesser of two evils" approach.[35] Hobby tried to convince the AMA representatives that reinsurance was in the interests of the doctors because it would provide a buffer against compulsory health insurance and because better insurance coverage would ensure payment of doctor's bills.[36] The AMA continued to be intransigent, however. Dr. Walter B. Martin, its president, reiterated the association's fears that comprehensive care would lead to a decrease in the quality of medical care.[37]

Despite Eisenhower's personal backing, on July 13, 1954, the House rejected the health reinsurance plan by a vote of 238 to 134. Seventy-five of those who voted against the bill were Republicans.[38] Eisenhower did not take the defeat lightly. He asked his press secretary, James Hagerty, to get a breakdown of the roll call vote and bring him the names of Republicans who had voted against it. "If any of those fellows who voted against that bill expect me to do anything for them in this campaign they are going to be very much surprised," Eisenhower told him, referring to the 1954 congressional election campaigns. "This was a major part of our liberal program and anyone who voted against it will not have one iota of support from me."[39] The next day he went public with his criticism. "The people that voted against this bill just don't understand what are the facts of American life," Eisenhower told the White House press corps. "There is nothing to be gained, as I see it, by shutting our eyes to the fact that all of our people are not getting the kind of health care to which they are entitled."[40]

Eisenhower did not limit his anger to House members. He blamed the AMA for waging a campaign to portray the bill as "socialized" medicine. When Senate Majority Leader William Knowland (R-CA) tried to defend the AMA position at a legislative leaders meeting, Eisenhower cut him off: "Listen, Bill. . . . We said during the campaign that we were against socialized medicine. . . . As far as I'm concerned the American Medical Association is just plain stupid. This plan of ours would have shown the people how we could improve their health care and stay out of socialized medicine."[41]

Health reinsurance was an excellent example of Eisenhower's "middle way." By using government resources to encourage the insurance industry to expand health coverage, it would have acted as a catalyst for improving the system without assuming primary responsibility for it. Eisenhower vowed to continue the fight: "I am trying to redeem my campaign promises, and I will never cease trying. This is only a temporary defeat; this thing will be carried forward as long as I am in office."[42] The Eisenhower administration's attempts to revive the reinsurance plan in the Eighty-fourth congressional session also failed, however.

Education

The field of education was especially suited to Eisenhower's "middle way" approach. Local control of schools was jealously guarded by proponents of states' rights and limited federal government. Resistance to interference in this area was further bolstered in the southern states after the Supreme Court's 1954 ruling in *Brown v. The Board of Education of Topeka, Kansas,* which overturned the doctrine allowing "separate but equal" facilities for blacks. Further complicating this issue was the importance of education for the future security of an America caught up in a Cold War with the Soviet Union. Eisenhower sought to balance these various concerns, allowing the federal government to serve its own interests in solving the nation's education crisis while preventing it from getting permanently involved in an area he believed to be of local concern. This was a battle he would fight throughout his presidency.

When Eisenhower took office, the only major area of federal involvement in education was Aid to Impacted Areas (AIA), which authorized federal aid for school construction that was necessary because of shortages caused by the war or overcrowding because of defense-related activities. Although the law had lapsed in June 1952, sufficient funds existed to carry the program through to June 1953, when the Eighty-third Congress extended it for another year.[43]

By the early 1950s, a number of factors had converged to elevate the shortage of classroom space in America's schools to the level of a crisis. During World War II the proliferation of defense-related industries in certain areas of the country greatly overburdened the school systems. Additionally, the war effort took precedence over the construction of schools. Compounding these problems, by the early 1950s, children comprising what had become known as the baby boom began to reach school age.

The urgency of the situation caused even some conservative Republicans to rethink the role of the federal government in an area so important to the nation's future. Senator Robert Taft (R-OH), the voice of conservatism in America until his death in 1953, stood more in line with his Democratic colleagues on the issue of education. In May 1949, Taft sponsored the Aid to Education Act. This act provided $270 million a year to the states to enable them to improve their grade schools and high schools. The purpose was to make minimum educational opportunities available to every child, no matter how poor his or her state or district.[44] Taft believed the federal government had an "interest to see that there is a basic floor . . . no child can have an equal opportunity unless he has a basic minimum education." Many of Taft's conservative colleagues disagreed. "I hear the socialists have gotten to Bob Taft," complained Senator John Bricker (R-OH).[45]

Eisenhower was also reluctant to commit the federal government in the field of education. His early public stands on this issue indicate that in times of emergency, or in areas where taxes could not provide an adequate level of education, he would "heartily support" federal aid. He would "flatly oppose," however, "any grant by the federal government to all states in the Union for educational purposes." In situations where aid was warranted, Eisenhower believed there should be no direct interference of federal authority in the process of education.[46]

Nonetheless, Eisenhower did want the federal government to play a role in alleviating the classroom shortage. During an August 1953 cabinet discussion on the budget, Secretary Hobby announced that HEW could make cuts. This pleased Eisenhower until he heard that school construction was the area where she hoped to save money. "This is the most important thing in our society," he told her, "every liberal—including me—will disapprove."[47] Referring to himself as a liberal was a tactic Eisenhower often used when defending his position on "human issues," particularly when in the presence of conservatives.

Eisenhower insisted that aid to the states for education be tied to need. This necessitated several administration-sponsored bills to determine where and how much federal aid was needed. These bills included authorization for a White House Conference on Education and $1 million for preparatory conferences in the states and territories; authorization for the Office of Education (a part of HEW) to make arrangements with universities for joint studies of educational problems; and creation of a nine-person National Advisory Committee on Education to advise the secretary of HEW on educational matters.[48] Each of these bills was passed, although the National Advisory Committee was never created because of a lack of enthusiasm in both Congress and HEW. Advocates of school aid were dismayed by these "puny bills," which they viewed as a stalling technique. The necessary information to determine need, one congressman complained, could be obtained "just by picking up the phone."[49]

Congress, impatient for tangible action during an election year, proposed its own school aid bill in 1954. In July, the Senate Labor and Welfare Committee reported a bill sponsored by twenty-four prominent Democratic senators authorizing emergency school construction aid with a grant of $500 million, payable to the states over a two-year period, for as much as 40 percent of school construction costs. The Eisenhower administration took a negative stand on the bill, reiterating a desire to wait until after the state and national conferences. Secretary Hobby also convinced the cabinet that the hope of future aid might lead some states to postpone pending projects. No further action was taken on the Senate bill before the conclusion of the Eighty-third congressional session.[50]

By the time the Eighty-fourth Congress convened in 1955, the Eisenhower administration could no longer avoid supporting a bill to aid school construction. Information submitted by the states to the Office of Education indicated a deficit of more than three hundred thousand classrooms. At the rate of sixty thousand new classrooms per year, the states were preventing the deficit from increasing but were not making up the ground they had already lost.[51] Although the White House Conference on Education was still ten months away, the administration would have to act or let Congress steal the initiative.[52]

HEW's proposal for federal aid for school construction was, like the reinsurance plan, an attempt by the Eisenhower administration to use federal resources to alleviate a domestic crisis without significantly overstepping its perception of the bounds of limited government. Again, Nelson Rockefeller played an important role in choreographing the balancing act. With the help of HEW official Roswell Perkins, former New York Lieutenant Governor Frank Moore, and Wall Street attorney John Mitchell, Rockefeller devised a variation of the public authority concept used in New York City, where the Triborough Bridge and Tunnel Authority had allowed the city to build bridges and tunnels with bonds backed by toll revenues.

Many school districts, because of debt restrictions placed on them by local communities, did not have the authority to issue bonds. Under the Rockefeller plan, states would set up school building authorities. These building authorities would then issue bonds and construct schools, which they could then rent to the local school districts. When the bonds were paid off, ownership of the buildings would be transferred to the school districts. The debts would not be a direct obligation of the states, but they would contribute one-half of a reserve fund to guarantee the bonds. The federal government would contribute the other half, thereby stimulating action without spending too much money or assuming primary responsibility. This would also allow the states to avoid constitutional debt limits.[53]

The proposal was not a break from Eisenhower's belief in limited federal involvement since the proposal did not eliminate state responsibility, but he had mixed feelings about the plan. He believed that neglecting education was just as bad as neglecting military security, but he worried that the opposition Congress would go too far. The political implications of such a program were not lost on him either. Vice President Richard Nixon reminded him that former California Governor Earl Warren (R) had established his reputation as a liberal based on his attention to roads and schools. Nixon believed it was "essential that the president be identified with a school construction program."[54]

Eisenhower decided to adopt HEW's recommendations, but his continued reluctance was apparent in his speech introducing the plan on February 8, 1955. He downplayed the new aspects of the proposed legislation, explaining it as "an effort to widen the accepted channels of financing school construction . . . to increase materially the flow of public and private lending through them." This, he argued, could be done "without interference with the responsibility of state and local school systems." He also emphasized that the proposal was "for the purpose of meeting the emergency only."[55]

The administration's first recommendation was that Congress authorize $750 million over three years to purchase school bonds from local communities unable to sell bonds at a reasonable interest rate (later established as 3.5 percent). Second, it recommended that the states establish school building agencies that could issue bonds to build schools, which they would then lease to local school districts unable to borrow money on their own. The state and federal government would contribute to a reserve fund for the building authority equal to one year's payment on principle and interest. Lease payments by the schools would cover installments on the principle and interest of the bonds, repayment of the reserve fund, and a share of the administrative costs. When all the financial obligations to the agency were met, the school districts would take over ownership of the buildings.[56]

Third, the proposal recommended appropriating $200 million over three years for school districts where the amount of taxable property and local income was so low it was impossible for the district either to repay borrowed money or to rent a satisfactory school building. The money would have to be matched with state-appropriated funds. Finally, the plan recommended $20 million to cover one-half of the administrative costs of state programs designed to overcome obstacles to local financing or to provide additional state aid. In all, the plan recommended spending more than $1 billion over a three-year period. All but $200 million, however, would be subject to repayment.[57]

Eisenhower's fear that Congress would want to go further was well founded. Congressional Democrats considered the administration's plan a "gimmick," just as they had the reinsurance plan; this one they believed was "conceived by investment bankers and dedicated to money lenders."[58] Encouraged by education lobbies, they urged direct federal grants and substantially higher sums. They also wanted to add federal assistance for teachers' salaries.

The Eisenhower administration recognized that insufficient teachers' salaries were causing a shortage of qualified teachers, but the president opposed federal involvement in the operation of schools, believing it would lead to federal control of education. "With every teacher and school administrator looking to the national government for any future pay increases," Eisenhower later wrote, "it would almost inevitably follow that partisanship and the education of our young people would be inextricably mixed. . . . The final result would be the loss of true academic freedom and variety in education."[59]

In July, the House Education and Labor Committee countered the administration bill with one of its own. The House bill authorized direct grants of $1.6 billion over four years, to be matched by the states; $750 million for federal purchase of local school construction bonds; and $150 million for debt servicing of school construction bonds. Lack of consensus on the issue, however, relegated the bill to the Rules Committee for the remainder of the 1955 session.[60]

When Congress reconvened in 1956, Eisenhower revised his school aid plan by increasing the amount of grant money for districts unable to finance or rent school buildings. Democrats initially stuck behind their own bill, but the dividing lines were about to change. Congressman Adam Clayton Powell (D-NY) added an amendment to the House bill, denying school construction funds to any state that did not comply with the 1954 Supreme Court decision on segregation.[61] The amendment caused a realignment on the issue of aid to education. Many who opposed the amendment— such as the National Education Association, the American Federation of Labor–Congress of Industrial Organizations (AFL-CIO), and the president and his supporters—did so on the grounds that it would destroy any chance of getting a school aid bill passed. They believed southern Democrats would surely filibuster to death any bill to which the amendment was attached. Because of the Supreme Court decision, however, a vote against the Powell amendment would seem to be a vote against the Constitution.[62] The Powell amendment was, therefore, approved 225 to 192, with Republicans voting 148 to 46 in favor of it. A last-ditch effort to recommit the amended House bill and substitute the administration's bill was favored by nearly the same number of Republicans (149) but failed 158 to 262. The House bill with the Powell amendment attached then failed 194 to 224, with Republicans voting 75 to 119 against.[63] As predicted by those who did not want to link antisegregation measures to school aid, the Powell amendment united southern Democrats against integration with Republicans who opposed federal aid to education in general, leading to the bill's defeat and a failure to pass legislation to aid schools.

Eisenhower's 1957 proposal was similar to the one he had put forward the previous year. It would have authorized a $1.3 billion program of federal grants to the states for school construction based on the number of school-aged children. It would also have provided $750 million to purchase bonds issued by school districts and authority to back the credit of school district bonds. Eisenhower asked that it be "enacted on its own merits, uncomplicated by provisions dealing with the complex problems of integration."[64]

Eisenhower attempted to get congressional Republicans behind his proposal, reminding them that "Education is vital to a free government" and that the federal government could do things that state and local governments could not without becoming a "controlling factor" in the field of education. He reminded them of one application of this philosophy nearly one hundred years earlier, the Morrill Land Grant Act of 1862, sponsored by Representative Justin Morrill of Vermont, one of the organizers of the Republican Party. "That federal act," Eisenhower told his fellow Republicans, "made possible the growth of higher education in many places where it otherwise could not have been begun or would have had great difficulty in starting." The equivalent in 1957, Eisenhower told them, would be "emergency Federal help to assist the states to knock out a schoolroom deficit resulting from the national—not local—disasters of depression and war."[65]

Despite this plea and despite the fact that the 1956 Republican platform promised to renew its efforts to enact a need-based program to relieve the nation's classroom shortage, many Republican congressional leaders still balked at the idea of federal aid to education.[66] Senate Minority Leader William Knowland said that he would oppose any proposal for grants but would not object to loans to needy areas. House Minority Leader Joseph Martin (MA) and former Majority Leader Charles Halleck (IN) also voiced their objections to the president.[67] When Representative Clarence J. Brown (R-OH), who claimed to be extending the legacy of the late Ohio Senator Robert Taft, claimed that he could not go home if he voted for a school program, Eisenhower reminded him that in 1950, the year after he had sponsored the Aid to Education Act, Taft was reelected by the largest majority he ever received.[68]

In an address to the 1957 Governors' Conference, Eisenhower scolded governors who opposed his education program on the grounds of states' rights. As a rule, he assured them, he was opposed to federal expansion, but in cases of undeniable national need coupled with state inaction or inadequate action he found it necessary for the federal government to intervene in areas traditionally reserved to the states. Urging them to substitute action for rhetoric, Eisenhower asserted, "It is idle to champion states' rights without upholding states' responsibilities as well."[69]

The House Education and Labor Committee reported out a bill that combined the administration's proposals with those favored by Democrats. As in the previous year, the bill was complicated by an antisegregation amendment, this time offered by Stuyvesant Wainwright, a Republican (NY). Hoping to get some kind of aid to education bill passed and realizing that the antisegregation amendment would prevent the House bill from passing, Democrats Stewart L. Udall (AZ) and Lee Metcalf (MT) said they were willing to compromise and support amendments to return the bill to the president's original requests. Before this could be worked out, however, southern Democrat Howard Smith (VA) moved to strike the enacting clause, killing the bill. This motion passed 208–203, with 111 Republicans voting in favor of it. A switch of three votes would have saved the bill and probably gotten the administration's program through the House. Eisenhower's reluctance to use his influence to effect the outcome of such a close vote led some supporters of school aid to question his commitment to the cause.[70]

Two unrelated events contributed to a major change in the proposal that Eisenhower made in the field of education in 1958. The first was the decision by Governor Orval Faubus in September 1957 to use the Arkansas National Guard to prevent the integration of Little Rock Central High School, an act that openly defied the 1954 Supreme Court decision in *Brown v. Board.* Eisenhower's school aid proposals had been complicated in the two previous years by desegregation amendments, and the heightened tensions caused by the Little Rock crisis made it very unlikely that such a bill could be passed in 1958. The second event was the launch of *Sputnik,* the first man-made earth satellite, by the Soviet Union on October 4, 1957. Although *Sputnik* was of relatively little scientific value and did not represent a significant lead over the United States in technology, it created the perception that the United States had fallen behind in the "space race."[71]

Marion B. Folsom, HEW's new secretary, later recalled that the decision to shift the emphasis of the education program predated the launch of *Sputnik:* "Our efforts failed in 1957 by only five votes, due to the combination of the conservative Republicans, who didn't follow the President's wish, and the southern Democrats who were against it because of integration." After that, Folsom recalled, "We both felt it would be unlikely that we could get any classroom construction legislation through. . . . The President said 'why can't we get up something to step up the teaching of mathematics and science, and put that in?'"[72]

Folsom decided to work up a complete package of proposals designed to attend to all deficiencies in the field of education. By the time Folsom presented his plan to the cabinet, *Sputnik* had been launched, giving added emphasis to the need for the program.[73] The plan was adopted by the administration, and Eisenhower presented it to Congress on January 27, 1958. It focused primarily on math and science education. For the National Science Foundation (NSF), Eisenhower recommended an increase in funds for the supplementary training of math and science teachers and to support teacher fellowships; an increase in funds to improve the content of science courses at all levels; an increase in the NSF's graduate fellowship program; and funds to allow the NSF to initiate new programs to provide fellowships for secondary school science teachers, graduate teaching assistants, and those who aspired to become high school math and science teachers. Other programs to be administered by the HEW included a program of ten thousand federal scholarships a year for four years for qualified high school graduates who lacked the financial resources to go to college; federal matching grants to the states to improve and expand the teaching of science and math; graduate fellowships for students to prepare for college teaching careers; federal matching grants to help universities to expand their graduate programs; and support for universities to expand and improve the teaching of modern foreign languages. Eisenhower emphasized that "this emergency program stems from national need, and its fruits will bear directly on national security. The method of accomplishment is sound: the keystone is state, local, and private effort; the federal role is to assist—not control or supplant—those efforts." In total the requested program would cost $1.6 billion over four years.[74]

The administration's bill, the National Defense Education Act (NDEA), made it through Congress relatively easily. The national hysteria generated by the news media coverage of *Sputnik* made every congressman anxious to contribute to the United States' effort to "catch up" with the Soviets in technology; and training more students in math and science seemed, to many, a good way to start. The main controversy regarding the bill was over Eisenhower's request for ten thousand federal scholarships a year for four years. Congressman Walter Judd (R-MN) introduced an amendment to strip the bill of its scholarship provisions and place the $120 million to finance them into a low interest college loan fund. Although the scholarship fund was considered by many to be the key provision of the bill, Eisenhower was not disappointed when it was eliminated. Convinced of their necessity by Folsom, Eisenhower was still uncomfortable with the scholarships. The loans, Eisenhower believed, would "make an education available to the student while encouraging self reliance."[75]

Once the scholarship provision was eliminated, the NDEA passed the House easily, although ninety-five Republicans voted to recommit before the final vote was taken. The Senate passed a version of the bill that included twenty-three thousand federal scholarships—more than twice the number requested by the administration—but accepted the House of Representatives' substitutions in conference committee. Eisenhower signed the NDEA into law on September 2, 1958.[76]

With the NDEA successfully passed, the administration's focus, under the direction of Secretary Arthur Flemming, once again turned toward federal aid for school construction. Eisenhower had become reluctant to support these programs, however, even voicing a distaste for such well-established programs as Aid to Impacted Areas. He had backed a request to continue AIA in 1958, even though consideration of the proposal had prompted him "into a discussion of where 'socialism' will stop."[77] While he considered the NDEA an appropriate response to a national need, he felt that school construction should remain a local responsibility. Eisenhower does not seem to have recognized the irony—that NDEA, with its emphasis on content, represented more of a government intrusion into education than AIA. When Eisenhower signed the bill continuing school construction aid in federally affected areas, he recommended a four-year phasing out of the program, saying that the federal presence in affected communities had stabilized and was an economic benefit to the areas, no longer an emergency burden as it had been during and immediately after the war.[78]

Even if Eisenhower had been more excited about federal aid to education, it would have been difficult for the administration to get a bill through Congress in 1958–1959. After landslide victories in the 1958 congressional elections, Democrats were in no mood to compromise with a "lame-duck" president. Northern Democrats wanted immediate large-scale grants to the states for both public school construction and teachers' salaries. Southern Democrats, fearing antisegregation amendments on school aid bills, joined with Republicans who objected to federal aid to education in general, creating a "conservative coalition" that made legislation difficult. With opposition so strong on both sides, it was very difficult for Eisenhower to achieve the "middle way."

When Secretary Flemming presented his plans for a school construction bill to the cabinet in January 1959, Eisenhower voiced his reluctance, noting that he did not want to inspire a reliance on the federal government in this area. He believed that federal assistance should go only to those states that had a demonstrated need. In regard to the other states, he asked, "Why don't they do their job? They claim 'states' rights,' but what about states' responsibilities?" Furthermore, the president was concerned that, if such a plan were made a part of the administration's program, "it would split wide open the small group of Republicans that remains."[79]

Secretary of Agriculture Ezra Taft Benson agreed with Eisenhower: "It is my conviction that large grants of federal funds are not the answer to our educational needs. . . . A program of federal aid to education in the form of assistance for school construction would likely provide a great disservice to our public school system and tend to stymie initiative on the part of the local people." Furthermore, Benson believed, "such a program cannot be justified on the grounds that state and local governments cannot afford school improvements when the federal debt is several times larger than the combined debt of all state and local governments."[80]

Despite all his reservations, however, Eisenhower decided that the administration had to make the proposal. "I don't know of anything I hate as much, but I guess we must," he said. Eisenhower later explained his decision to Bryce Harlow: "You come to the middle of the road on problems such as this because they are human problems." While Eisenhower had never been an enthusiastic supporter of federal aid for education, his reluctance here stands in stark contrast to his 1953 remark that school construction was the "most important thing in our society."[81]

The administration submitted its proposal in 1959 requesting federal payments to help local school districts pay off the interest and principle of $3 billion in long-term school construction bonds, which were to be issued within five years of enactment of the legislation. The cost of the bill was estimated at $85 million per year over the life of the bonds, with an eventual cost of about $2 billion. The proposal made no provision for aid for teachers' salaries or direct federal grants to needy areas.[82] Congress took no final action on the proposal in 1959 but defeated it the following year. Charles Halleck had been correct in his prediction that Congress would kill the bill "with only a bare nod in its direction."[83]

In 1960 the House passed a $1.3 billion bill providing grants for school construction that contained a Powell antisegregation amendment. The "conservative coalition" in the House as a whole had not been large enough to defeat it, but the coalition of southern Democrats and conservative Republicans in the Rules Committee prevented it from emerging from the House. A presidential veto was expected if the bill survived. Meanwhile, the Senate passed a bill authorizing $1.8 billion in federal grants for school construction and teachers' salaries, with payments weighted toward poorer states. Only nine Republican senators voted in favor. When asked about federal aid for teachers' salaries, Eisenhower responded: "I do not believe the Federal government ought to be in the business of paying a local official. . . . I can't imagine anything worse for the government to get into."[84]

Conclusion

Eisenhower's attempt to find a "middle way" for social welfare policy was only partially successful. Like the majority of Americans, Eisenhower accepted the contributions made by presidents Roosevelt and Truman to social welfare. In these areas, where programs were already in place, he sought to strengthen and expand upon them. In this he was successful. His creation of the Department of Health, Education, and Welfare gave cabinet status to the Federal Security Agency; and his amendments to the Social Security Act gave more than ten million additional workers access to retirement insurance. Where new programs were necessary, however, Eisenhower was far less successful. Eisenhower's proposals for health reinsurance and school construction were attempts to use the resources of the federal government to encourage progress in these areas. In the health reinsurance proposal, the government would have encouraged insurance companies to expand their health-care coverage by reinsuring their high-risk policies. In the school construction proposal, the government would have encouraged the construction of new schools by expediting their financing. In both cases the federal government would have avoided primary responsibility. Eisenhower was seeking a "middle way" between conservatives, who believed that health-care and education were outside the scope of federal responsibility, and liberals, who would have preferred that the federal government accept primary responsibility for them. Both programs failed. Eisenhower's only successful new program in the area of social welfare was the NDEA, but this success can be attributed primarily to the Cold War.

Secretary Hobby blamed congressional Democrats for the failure of Eisenhower's social welfare proposals. She believed they were "attempting to insure that this administration got no glory for any legislative accomplishments in this field."[85] Eisenhower, expecting no help from Democrats, blamed conservatives in his own party. Many of these Republicans were, indeed, unhappy with the policies proposed by their president. Senator Barry Goldwater (R-AZ), who had become a leading conservative spokesman since the death of Robert Taft in 1953, wrote: "It is obvious that the administration has succumbed to the principle that we owe some sort of living . . . to the citizens of this country, and I am beginning to wonder if we haven't gone a lot further than many of us think on this road we happily call socialism." He later recalled that he was "deeply disappointed when the Republican administration under President Eisenhower, with a working majority in both houses of Congress, proposed to continue the old New Deal, Fair Deal schemes, offering only a modification in scale and no change in direction."[86]

The president could not even get a word of support from his brother, Edgar Eisenhower, who wrote that many of his friends could see "very little difference between the policy of your administration and that of the former administration." The president replied: "Should any political party attempt to abolish social security, unemployment insurance, and eliminate labor laws and farm programs, you would not hear of that party again in our political history. There is a tiny splinter group, of course, that believes you can do these things. . . . Their number is negligible and they are stupid." Eisenhower's experiences in the field of social policy gave added meaning to a remark he had made to his secretary, Ann Whitman: "You don't have very many friends when you're walking a decent middle way."[87]

Giving Labor
an Equal Voice

On July 31, 1954, just eighteen months into Eisenhower's first term as president, Republican Senator Robert Taft of Ohio died. In the years following the senator's death, conservatives misrepresented his role in the early years of the Eisenhower administration. Seeking to take over Taft's title of "Mr. Conservative," later conservatives like Barry Goldwater invoked Taft's name in support of positions that Taft himself would never have supported. Based on his prewar isolationism and his staunch fiscal responsibility, Taft had earned the label "conservative," but Eisenhower later recalled, "In some things I found him unexpectedly 'liberal,' specifically in his attitude on old-age pensions, school aid, and public housing—attitudes, incidentally, which were miles away from those of some self-described 'Taft stalwarts.'" One day after a legislative leaders' meeting, Taft walked into Eisenhower's office to continue a discussion on welfare policy. "You know, I hate federal bureaucracy," he said. "The best way I can think of to combat its growth and at the same time help people would be to have the federal government pay a flat fee to the states for every child in school, and automatically to send out a monthly pension check, also of a fixed amount, to every man and woman who reached the age of sixty-five." When Eisenhower heard this suggestion, he laughed. "Why, Bob," he said "with those views you're twice as liberal as I am. How did you ever come to be called a conservative?" Taft replied, "Oh, you know how it is. . . . A label like that gets applied to you, and afterwards you just have to live with it."[1]

Taft was a more loyal backer of the administration than Eisenhower expected after the heated contest between the two men in the 1952 Republican presidential primaries. "Of all the legislative leaders with whom I thought, in advance, that I would have constant trouble, there was none with whom incessant difficulty seemed more probable than with Senator Taft," Eisenhower later recalled. "For many weeks before he died . . . I considered him my ablest associate on the hill, and indeed one of the stalwarts of the administration. . . . I found him to be far less reactionary than I had judged him to be from a reading of his speeches and public statements. In some things I found him extraordinarily 'leftish.'"[2]

During the Eisenhower administration, debate on labor policy revolved primarily around amending a law that Senator Taft had cosponsored, the Labor Management Relations Act of 1947 (Taft-Hartley Act). In his final years, Senator Taft had come to believe that some of the provisions of this act were too hard on labor and needed amending. Eisenhower believed that, had Taft lived, his influence would have helped prevent the rift that occurred in the Republican Party over this issue. It is likely that, in the process, he would have gone a long way toward healing the overall divisions in the party as well.

Eisenhower's views on labor-management relations reflected his belief in the "middle way." He did not favor repeal of the Taft-Hartley Act as organized labor advocated, but he did feel (as Taft did) that some of its provisions were too harsh and needed amending. During the 1952 campaign, when speaking to members of the American Federation of Labor (AFL) at their annual convention, Eisenhower said he would not support amendments that would weaken the rights of working people. "In seeking desirable amendments," he promised, "I will ask the advice and suggestions of all groups—public, management, and labor. . . . If I have any executive responsibility, labor will have an equal voice with all others."[3] As with social welfare, Eisenhower sought a "middle way" for labor policy. He wanted to move beyond the belief that one had to be either prolabor or probusiness and find a position that was fair to both parties and beneficial to the economy.

Existing Labor Law

The National Labor Relations Act of 1935 (Wagner Act) was the most important labor law in American history. It was a major impetus for the growth of labor organizations and earned the nickname "labor's bill of rights." It covered all firms and employees in activities affecting interstate commerce except agricultural workers, railroad workers, and government employees. It gave workers the right to organize and join labor unions, to bargain collectively through representatives of their own choosing, and to strike. It also set up the National Labor Relations Board (NLRB), an independent federal agency with three members appointed by the president, to administer the act and gave it the power to certify that a union represented a particular group of employees.

The Wagner Act also forbade employers from engaging in specific types of labor practices: interfering with or restraining employees exercising their right to organize and bargain collectively; attempting to dominate or influence a labor union; refusing to bargain collectively and in "good faith" with unions representing their employees; and, finally, encouraging or discouraging union membership through any special conditions of employment or through discrimination against union or nonunion members in hiring. The law stated, however, that this last provision could not be used to prohibit closed shops, where an employer agrees to hire only union members, or union shops, where an employer agrees to require anyone hired to join the union.[4] There were no provisions in the Wagner Act that prohibited union practices that employers might deem unfair. Another omission, according to the act's opponents, was a provision that would allow the government to delay or block a strike that threatened national interests.

In the midterm elections of 1946, the Republican Party won control of the upcoming Eightieth Congress, gaining majorities in both houses for the first time since 1931. The "Class of 1946," as the first-term Republicans were called, was dominated by conservatives: John Bricker (OH), William Jenner (IN), Charles Kersten (WI), William Knowland (CA), George Malone (NE), Joseph McCarthy (WI), Karl Mundt (SD), Richard Nixon (CA), Arthur Watkins (UT), and John Williams (DE). These freshmen congressmen were eager to overturn as much New Deal legislation as possible, and one of their first priorities was to amend the Wagner Act.[5]

On June 23, 1947, the Republican-controlled Congress passed the Taft-Hartley Act over President Truman's veto. The Taft-Hartley Act was the first major revision of a New Deal act passed by a postwar Congress. It retained the features of the earlier Wagner Act but added to it in ways widely interpreted as antilabor. Labor leaders dubbed it a "slave labor" bill, and twenty-eight Democratic members of Congress declared it a "new guarantee of industrial slavery."[6]

The act allowed the president, when he believed that a strike would endanger national health or safety, to appoint a board of inquiry to investigate the dispute. After receiving the report of the investigation, the president could ask the attorney general to seek a federal court injunction to block or prevent the continuation of the strike. If the court found that the strike was endangering the nation's health or safety, it would grant the injunction, requiring the parties in the dispute to attempt to settle their differences within the next sixty days. Other provisions extended the negotiating period by twenty days, in effect creating an eighty-day cooling-off period during which the law would prohibit a "national emergency strike."

To the Wagner Act's list of prohibited employer practices, the Taft-Hartley Act added a list of prohibited labor-union practices. Among these were the secondary boycott and "blackmail" picketing. In a secondary boycott, a union induces one company's workers to strike in an attempt to convince their employer to stop doing business with another company, with whom the real dispute exists. Blackmail picketing is when a union demonstrates at a workplace whose workers it does not represent, in an attempt to compel an employer to recognize or bargain with it. Taft-Hartley made this illegal, but only if the employer had already recognized another union following an NLRB-sponsored election. The Taft-Hartley Act also outlawed the closed shop and the union-hiring halls that discriminated against nonunion members. Union shops were allowed as long as state law did not forbid them. This caveat led several states to pass "right-to-work" laws, outlawing union shops. Other provisions of Taft-Hartley that would become contentious prevented employees in economic strikes (meaning the strike was about wages rather than unfair practices) from voting in union representation elections and required union officers to file a non-communist affidavit and take an oath that they were not a communist.

Secretary Durkin and the Shanley Report

Eisenhower followed up on his AFL campaign promise to give labor an "equal voice with all others" by appointing Martin Durkin secretary of Labor. Durkin was head of the AFL plumbers' union and former secretary of the Illinois Department of Labor. Eisenhower's logic was that since the Department of Commerce was traditionally headed by a man from the ranks of business, someone with firsthand experience in the labor movement should head the Labor Department. Durkin, a Democrat and an active supporter of Democratic nominee Adlai Stevenson during the 1952 campaign, was understandably hesitant to accept the position. Eisenhower explained that while he would expect Durkin to represent labor's viewpoint, his loyalty would be to the nation rather than the labor movement itself. Durkin was concerned that such a stance would make it difficult for him to return to his field of work once he left government service. He finally decided to accept the cabinet post after his union agreed to hold his position open for one year, should he decide to return.[7]

During the course of his search for a secretary of Labor, Eisenhower kept his desire to nominate someone from the ranks of labor a secret, fearing that if his intentions became known it would be difficult for him to make the appointment.[8] Eisenhower's fears were well founded. When Taft heard of the nomination of the partisan labor leader, he declared it "incredible." The *New Republic*, a liberal publication that Eisenhower might have expected to applaud his choice of a Labor secretary, was more cynical, commenting that Eisenhower had picked a cabinet consisting of "eight millionaires and one plumber."[9]

Eisenhower repeated his promises to the AFL in his first State of the Union message: "We have now had five years experience with the Labor Management Act of 1947, commonly known as the Taft-Hartley Act. That experience has shown the need for some corrective action, and we should promptly proceed to amend that act." Eisenhower made no specific proposals as to the nature of those amendments, merely charging Congress and the Labor Department to "conduct their arguments in the overpowering light of national interest," and to "remember that the institutions of trade unionism and collective bargaining are monuments to the freedom that must prevail in our industrial life."[10]

Despite the vagueness of this charge, Eisenhower did have specific items in Taft-Hartley that he wished to address. Employers could use the law's provision that prevented employees who struck for economic reasons from voting for their collective bargaining representatives in such as way as to "bust the union" by provoking a strike and then replacing the strikers with new permanent employees. These employees could then hold an election in which the strikers could not vote. Eisenhower was in favor of eliminating this possibility, by amending the law to prohibit union representation elections for four months after the beginning of a strike.[11] Another provision of the law that Eisenhower favored amending was the one that required union officers to file an affidavit and take an oath that they were not members of the Communist Party. Eisenhower believed this to be unfair since management representatives were not required to take the same oath.[12]

Following the State of the Union message, Eisenhower set up a committee to study Taft-Hartley and submit back to him recommended changes that could then possibly be transmitted to Congress. His hope was that the committee would develop amendments that Congress would consider fair to business, labor, and the general public. The committee included Secretary of Labor Martin Durkin, Secretary of Commerce Sinclair Weeks, presidential aide Bernard Shanley, Senator Robert Taft, and two other congressmen.[13] The inclusion of Senator Taft, cosponsor of the original act, would be crucial to getting changes through the Republican Congress. *Fortune* magazine reported that Taft supported the changes suggested by the president, plus other changes generally favorable to labor that lacked the support of congressional conservatives.[14]

The main source of conflict in the committee was between Secretary of Labor Durkin and Secretary of Commerce Weeks. The difference in background between these two men—Durkin was a labor union president and active Democrat; Weeks was a metal products manufacturer Eisenhower described in his diary as "so completely conservative in his views that at times he seems to be illogical"—made it very unlikely they would agree on labor policy.[15] The committee's impasse led to the final report being written by Bernard Shanley, who drafted proposals for Eisenhower that clearly reflected the sympathies of labor. Steve Dunn, counsel for the Department of Commerce, after seeing the proposals asked, "Who won the election?"[16]

The report recommended nineteen amendments to the Taft-Hartley Act. Among them were the two amendments proposed by Eisenhower. One prohibited union representation elections for four months after the beginning of a strike. The prohibition would remain in effect even if all the strikers had been replaced by employees who wanted to be represented by a different union or no union at all. This amendment was intended to prevent employers from provoking strikes for the sake of "union busting." The other amendment recommended eliminating the requirement that labor union officers file affidavits and take oaths they were not members of the Communist Party.

Another amendment would reduce the number of prohibitions against secondary boycotts. Under Taft-Hartley, employees of one company were prohibited from striking in sympathy with the employees of another company. On construction sites, labor is often contracted to a number of different companies. The Shanley Report recommended that employees of one company be allowed to strike in support of employees of another company working on the same site. Similarly, in certain industries, such as the garment industry, it is common for components to be "farmed out," that is, made by another company and purchased by the producer of the finished product. The Shanley Report recommended that employees of two different companies making components of the same finished product be allowed to strike in support of each another.

Other proposed amendments strengthened the union shop and moved toward reestablishing the closed shop. One took away the right of states to prohibit agreements making union membership a condition of employment. This would prevent states from passing "right-to-work" laws prohibiting union shops. This amendment also clarified the jurisdictions of the states and the federal government in labor matters in such a way as to recognize the higher authority of federal law. Both of these amendments would significantly strengthen the union shop. Another amendment would permit employers to notify unions of job vacancies, giving them the opportunity to refer qualified applicants. It also authorized employers to agree with unions on the minimum training and experience required for employment. Finally, it allowed employers in industries where employment is temporary or intermittent, such as construction, to require employees to join the union within seven days of being hired. These three provisions all tended toward the reestablishment of closed shops.[17]

Shanley informed Durkin that Eisenhower planned to send the proposed Taft-Hartley amendments to Congress on July 31. When Robert Taft died on that day, however, Shanley told Durkin that Eisenhower had decided to delay the message since it would be in poor taste to propose amendments to Taft's law on the day of his death. Shanley promised, however, that Eisenhower would send the message shortly. On August 3, the *Wall Street Journal* published the nineteen proposed amendments, describing them as a proposed presidential message to Congress.[18] The most likely source of the story was Sinclair Weeks, or one of his subordinates in the Department of Commerce, in an attempt to rally opposition to the proposals. If so, the leak had the desired effect. The White House quickly emphasized that the text was not definite, and that work on the draft had not yet approached even the "semi-final stage."[19]

Based on Shanley's earlier assurances, Durkin felt that Eisenhower was going back on his commitment to amend Taft-Hartley. In his next meeting with the president, Durkin said that unless he could be assured of Eisenhower's support on the committee's nineteen proposed amendments, that he would lose the support of organized labor and be unable to return to his AFL position. Eisenhower told Durkin that if he would work with the administration "in a common effort to develop fair amendments to the law," his success would assure him a good position in the future. Durkin was not to be mollified. He explained that he felt Shanley had broken faith in the process of "collective bargaining." Eisenhower was offended by Durkin's use of the term "collective bargaining," and he told the secretary that the discussions of the committee were not contract negotiations. He went on to say that, while Durkin was perfectly free to make "such recommendations and offer such advice as his own convictions and wisdom dictated," he was concerned that Durkin "regarded himself in the Cabinet as a special pleader for labor" rather than as the president's "principle labor advisor."[20]

Eisenhower's failure to get behind the committee's proposals, as Shanley had promised he would, made Durkin feel he had been double-crossed. Within two weeks of this meeting, Durkin tendered his resignation, expressing his desire to return to his position at the AFL. When word got out that duplicity on his part may have led to Durkin's resignation, the president went on the offensive, turning legitimate inquiries about Durkin's resignation into statements on his personal integrity. "To my knowledge, I have never broken an agreement," he said at a press conference. "If there is anyone here who has contrary evidence, he can have the floor and make his speech."[21] No one being present who wished to call the president a liar, the issue was dropped. Eisenhower later claimed that he had never told Shanley he would support the committee's recommendations. According to Eisenhower, "Secretary Durkin was the only case in my eight years in the White House in which a resignation was tendered because of failure to achieve a meeting of minds between me and a principal subordinate." To replace Durkin, Eisenhower chose James P. Mitchell, vice president in charge of labor relations for Bloomingdale's department stores. Mitchell measured up, in Eisenhower's opinion, "to the caliber of the other members of the Cabinet."[22]

Durkin may have been justified in feeling betrayed by the president and his advisors, but he was being unrealistic if he believed that Eisenhower's support for the nineteen proposed amendments to the Taft-Hartley Act would have assured their passage. This was particularly true after the death of Robert Taft. Although Taft had been a member of the committee that produced the proposed amendments and did advocate prolabor changes to the law that bore his name, it is unlikely he would have agreed with some of the suggested provisions. Particularly objectionable to him would have been the provision that took away the states' authority to pass "right-to-work" laws. The chance of getting any progressive labor legislation past the conservative wing of the Republican Party in Congress, however, died with Senator Taft.

Eisenhower believed that had Taft lived, his ability to persuade conservative congressmen to agree with the administration would have helped the Republican Party develop into a stronger and more unified organization.[23] Shortly before his death, Taft chose William Knowland (R-CA) to replace him as Senate majority leader. Eisenhower went along with this choice despite the fact that Knowland was a conservative who often opposed the administration. Eisenhower believed that if he supported a candidate other than the one chosen by Taft, he would alienate senators that Taft had worked hard to keep in line. Knowland proved far less able than Taft to generate support for Eisenhower in the Senate, prompting Eisenhower to confide to Attorney General Herbert Brownell that Knowland was the biggest disappointment he had found since entering politics." Eisenhower would later write in his diary that in Knowland's case, "There seems to be no final answer to the question 'How stupid can you get?'"[24]

Taft's death also put Republican control of the Senate in a precarious position. To replace Taft, the governor of Ohio appointed a Democrat, leaving forty-seven Republicans, forty-eight Democrats, and one independent. This brought to an end what little honeymoon Eisenhower had experienced with Congress. The situation would further erode after the 1954 elections when Republicans formally lost control of both houses of Congress.

The Attempt to Amend Taft-Hartley

Over the next several months Eisenhower refrained from comment on Taft-Hartley revisions, taking the advice of Treasury Secretary George Humphrey that he should not recommend detailed amendments to the Taft-Hartley Act except in the areas in which he had promised amendments during the campaign. According to Humphrey, he should attempt to define the limits within which he could accept the law and not find it necessary to oppose it. Eisenhower practiced doing this in his diary. "I am personally opposed to the principle of the closed shop and would not find it possible to approve a federal bill containing such a provision," he wrote. "At the same time I believe . . . unions to be an absolutely essential factor of modern industrial life in order that men who work may be assured of fair wages, proper working conditions, and other benefits that flow to them as a body. The present law recognizes and authorizes the so-called 'right-to-work' clause, the federal authority shall not attempt to override the states' decision in this matter."[25]

Other cabinet members agreed that the president should restrict his participation in this controversial matter.[26] Keeping with this belief,

Eisenhower had Vice President Nixon read the presidential message to the annual AFL convention in 1953, expressing his disappointment at losing the knowledge and experience of Durkin and promising that the Shanley Committee would continue its work and soon make recommendations.[27]

In his 1954 State of the Union message, Eisenhower was finally able to announce that on January 11 he would forward to Congress proposed changes to the Taft-Hartley Act.[28] The preamble to this message had a tone significantly different from his campaign promises demanding immediate changes to Taft-Hartley; the call for amendments was considerably less urgent and more calculated. "Although the process is not and perhaps never will be complete," he wrote, "we have now achieved a measure of practical experience and emotional maturity in this field which, I do not doubt, is responsible for the relatively peaceful character of recent industrial relations." Because of this, Eisenhower concluded, "[N]o drastic legislative innovations in this field are therefore desirable at this time. . . . The Labor Management Relations Act, 1947, is sound legislation. Experience gained in the operation of the Act, however, indicates that changes can be made to reinforce its basic objectives."[29]

The fourteen amendments Eisenhower went on to recommended closely paralleled the nineteen proposals over which Durkin had resigned. Several of the more controversial proposals, however, were left out. One was the amendment that would have eliminated the right of states to pass "right-to-work" laws. Also left out was the proposal to authorize employers to negotiate with unions as to the minimum training and experience required for employment. Opponents of this suggestion believed it would open the way for a return of the closed shop.[30] Believing that "there is nothing which so vitally affects the individual employee as the loss of his pay when he is called on strike," Eisenhower also included a new proposal. He suggested that employees facing the decision to strike should have an opportunity to vote by secret ballot under NLRB auspices.[31]

Although labor unions favored many of the changes suggested by Eisenhower, they were disappointed he had left out some of the more prolabor amendments originally proposed by the Shanley Committee; particularly the prohibition of state "right-to-work" laws. Union leaders also strongly opposed the new provision on strike balloting.[32] Vice President Nixon downplayed the labor objections, commenting, "Regardless of what we do, [we] won't get labor leaders for us." The important thing, he said, was what the voters thought. Nixon believed that the proposed legislation would set "the tone to this whole administration in regard to it being liberal, middle-of-the-road, or conservative. People will see we are liberalizing Taft-Hartley."[33]

Some conservative Republicans thought that the proposed legislation was too "prolabor," particularly after the administration eliminated the proposal to require an NLRB-sponsored prestrike vote. Among the most vocal dissenters was Barry Goldwater, who introduced an unsuccessful amendment that would have given states jurisdiction over labor disputes in a wide range of situations. In the end, however, most Republicans, including Goldwater, sided with the administration. The Senate's vote to kill the bill by recommitting it to committee without instructions was nearly a straight party one. Only three Republicans voted with the forty-six Democrats in favor of killing the bill (D 46–0, R 3–42, I 1–0).[34]

In this case, however, the nearly straight party vote did not represent an ideological divide between the two parties. The three Republicans who voted to kill the bill—William Langer (ND), Milton Young (ND) and George Malone—were conservatives who, along with like-minded southern Democrats, thought the bill was too prolabor. This interparty conservative alliance voted with liberal Democrats, who believed the bill was not prolabor enough, forming an unlikely coalition that was successful in defeating the "middle way." Although their participation was not decisive, the defection of the three Republicans angered Eisenhower. They are "not Republicans anyway," he said when he heard the news.[35] After the Senate's defeat of the bill, the House took no further action.

With the 1954 administration-sponsored bill died any serious attempt to amend the Taft-Hartley Act until 1958. In his State of the Union messages of 1955 and 1956, Eisenhower renewed his request that Congress amend Taft-Hartley, but Congress took no action on these requests. Eisenhower blamed the Democrats in Congress for not following through on his campaign promises, but other than that he let the issue drop. Eisenhower was heeding the advice of Secretary of Labor Mitchell who recommended that, given the relative harmony of labor-management relations and the current attitude of Congress, he had little to gain from pressing the issue. The prosperity of the 1950s had calmed fears that the law would adversely affect wages, hours, and working conditions, and labor-management relations were steadily improving. According to the administration's own estimates, the percentage of working time lost because of strikes between 1949 and 1952 was 60 percent higher than that lost between January 1953 and August 1956.[36]

Eisenhower and Congress had also bought time with labor by amending the Fair Labor Standards Act of 1939, raising the minimum wage. In his State of the Union message of 1955, Eisenhower had recommended that Congress raise the minimum wage from seventy-five cents to ninety cents and extend the coverage to include about two million workers in interstate chain stores, hotels, and movie theaters. Congress failed to extend the coverage of the act but, on September 12, with very little debate increased the minimum wage to one dollar, more than what was requested by Eisenhower but less than the one dollar and twenty-five cents favored by the AFL, the Congress of Industrial Organizations (CIO), and other labor groups. The Chamber of Commerce, National Association of Manufacturers (NAM), and other probusiness groups opposed the action.[37]

The McClellan Committee

Complacency regarding labor legislation came to an abrupt halt in 1957, as a result of the work of the Senate's Select Committee on Improper Activities in the Labor and Management Field, headed by Senator John J. McClellan (D-AR). The Senate had formed the committee in response to a 1956 report by the Subcommittee on Welfare and Pension Plans, which concluded that "an unscrupulous minority" had "preyed upon" employee welfare and pension funds. The committee's report stated there had been "shocking abuses such as embezzlement, collusion, kickbacks, exorbitant insurance charges and various other forms of malfeasance." Additionally, "mismanagement, lack of know-how, waste, extravagance, indifference, nepotism and a lack of criteria for sound operation" had contributed to a drain of funds with serious losses for the employee beneficiaries. "The fact that looting and dishonesty exists at all," the committee concluded, "points up the opportunity for abuse under the existing absence of controls."[38] The committee's hearings, led by its chief counsel Robert F. Kennedy, revealed widespread corruption within certain unions, particularly James R. Hoffa's International Brotherhood of Teamsters, whose infractions resulted in their expulsion from the AFL-CIO.

These hearings convinced Eisenhower that the time was right to move ahead on labor legislation.[39] On January 23, 1958, he made public his proposals to deal with labor corruption in a message to Congress on labor-management relations.[40] These proposals recommended anticorruption provisions to safeguard union dues and welfare and pension funds against misuse by union officials. They also recommended several Taft-Hartley amendments, but these were less union-friendly than his past proposals, intending to end certain union practices that the administration believed had contributed to the corruption. Examples of these amendments included tightening the restrictions against secondary boycotts and blackmail picketing. Secondary boycotts had been outlawed by Taft-Hartley, but the practice continued, taking advantage of loopholes in the law. Blackmail picketing was prohibited only in specific situations. The Shanley Committee report had actually recommended easing prohibitions on both. Eisenhower also recommended that states be allowed to assert jurisdiction in "no man's land" cases—those cases that would normally fall under NLRB jurisdiction but which the NLRB declined to handle because the firms involved were too small. Unions were against state jurisdiction since most state laws took a tougher stand against labor than federal laws. In an attempt to include some prolabor provisions, Eisenhower used this opportunity to reintroduce the proposal to eliminate the requirement that union officers sign noncommunist affidavits. He also proposed a new solution to "union busting" during an economic strike. Rather than preventing representation elections for four months following the beginning of a strike, he proposed that striking workers be allowed to vote in such elections, even if they had been replaced.[41]

After the McClellan Committee findings, however, the Senate was in no mood to become bogged down in an attempt to pass a sweeping labor reform bill complete with Taft-Hartley amendments. Rather, it wanted to react to the most serious of the committee findings—welfare and pension fund tampering—and quickly pass a relatively uncontroversial bill. The Welfare and Pensions Act, sent to the floor by the Labor and Public Welfare Committee, safeguarded employee welfare and pension plans, regardless of whether management or labor administered them, by requiring that they be registered with the Labor Department, make their financial records available to the public, and give annual reports on their funding and operation. The act also provided criminal penalties for violation of its provisions. Several Republican senators attempted to amend the bill by inserting provisions based on the administration's recommendations, but these attempts were defeated when Senator John F. Kennedy (D-MA), one of the bill's sponsors, promised to hold hearings on more broadly based anticorruption legislation later. The bill then passed the Senate without dissent. In the House, the provision for criminal penalties was dropped. Eisenhower signed the House version into law on August 28, 1958.

Following through on his promise, in June 1958 Senator Kennedy and Senator Irving Ives (R-NY) sponsored a labor and anticorruption bill. The bill contained many of the anticorruption provisions and Taft-Hartley amendments favored by the administration, including the provision allowing economic strikers to vote in representation elections, but it excluded the administration's recommendations on secondary boycotts, blackmail picketing, and "no-man's-land." Eisenhower and Secretary Mitchell opposed passage of the bill, but it moved through the Senate nearly as easily as the Welfare and Pensions Act had. Opposition to the bill became more acute in the House, however, and conservative Republicans and southern Democrats were able to defeat it. House Speaker Sam Rayburn (D-TX) aided their cause by allowing the bill to lie on his desk for over a month before referring it to committee. Northern Democrats charged that Republicans in league with the NAM and the Chamber of Commerce had "sabotaged" the bill because they wanted a harsh antilabor bill. Eisenhower responded that Republicans had gone all out for a good anticorruption bill but that "radical" Democratic opposition had killed it and offered "a substitute far too weak to do the job."[42]

Passage of so-called right-to-work laws was also a critical issue in 1958, an election year. As of 1958, twenty states had "right-to-work" legislation.[43] Republicans in many states without such legislation were running on platforms that promoted it. Because of the importance of this issue, Eisenhower was called upon to give his opinion on the subject, with union backers urging him to denounce the section of the Taft-Hartley Act that authorized such laws (14-b), and antiunion conservatives urging him to either favor national "right-to-work" legislation or encourage states to exercise their rights under section 14-b. Eisenhower refused to do either, stating merely that the section authorized each state to settle this matter as it saw fit.[44]

Eisenhower was concerned that Republicans, particularly William Knowland who had resigned his Senate seat to run for the governorship of California, were using his name in connection with "right-to-work." He asked Vice President Nixon, who was in California campaigning, to "set the record straight."[45] Nixon's position was similar to Eisenhower's. He told the *Los Angeles Times* that he had voted for the Taft-Hartley Act, which left the decision on "right-to-work" up to the states, and that it would be improper for a federal official to take a position other than that. Nixon was afraid that if he said he was against "right-to-work," voters would think he was against Knowland.[46] Knowland later admitted that his defeat in 1958 probably had a great deal to do with his stand on "right-to-work."[47]

Landrum-Griffin

With all the publicity about union corruption that surrounded the continuing McClellan Committee hearings, neither party was willing to let the issue drop without the passage of major reform legislation. In a January 28, 1959, message to Congress on labor-management relations, Eisenhower made essentially the same recommendations for labor reform and Taft-Hartley amendments that he had made the previous year.[48] Senator Kennedy, who had become his party's leading spokesman on labor, did not agree with the president's approach. Legislation was needed, he said, to clean up the kind of labor racketeering and collusion that the McClellan Committee had revealed. Attempting to deal with controversial collective bargaining issues in the same bill with anticorruption measures that had broad support would only endanger the passage of needed legislation. This, Kennedy believed, had been the fate of his 1958 legislation. Keeping with this belief, on March 25, Kennedy along with Sam Ervin (D-NC) introduced an anticorruption bill that concentrated on barring misuse of union funds, required annual reports by unions on their finances, and imposed rules to encourage democracy in the running of unions. The bill did include some provisions that amended Taft-Hartley, but they were ones generally favored by unions rather than the tougher ones that Eisenhower had begun to ask for.

Republican leadership did not oppose what was in the Kennedy-Ervin bill, but they criticized it for what it did not contain. This included, specifically, provisions further restricting secondary boycotts, blackmail picketing, and "hot cargo" contracts—those between a union and an employer stating that employees were not required to handle goods emanating from or headed to a nonunion shop, a sweat shop, or a shop on strike. These practices, they contended, contributed to union corruption. On the floor, senators amended the Kennedy-Ervin bill to include a ban on "hot-cargo" contracts and a worker's "bill of rights." Unions opposed both amendments. On April 25, 1959, the Senate passed the bill ninety to one. Barry

Goldwater cast the lone dissenting vote, calling it a "panty-waist bill" and a "weak gesture . . . largely written by unions. It contains none of the real reforms recommended by the President." Goldwater called his "nay" vote "one of the proudest I ever made."[49]

Eisenhower was not pleased with the Senate bill either. On August 6, while the House was preparing to debate the merits of several competing labor bills, Eisenhower went on national radio and television to address the people on the need for an effective labor bill. Calling the corruption that had been uncovered by the McClellan Committee a "national disgrace," he urged passage of legislation to "protect the American people from the gangsters, racketeers, and other corrupt elements who have invaded the labor-management field." For such legislation to be effective, he told them, it would need to end "coercive" practices such as blackmail picketing and secondary boycotts. It would also have to give the states jurisdiction in "no-man's land" cases. The Kennedy-Ervin bill had not met these "minimum requirements," he said, and therefore would not be effective.[50]

Eisenhower did make a few prolabor proposals in his speech, allowing him to argue that his program was nonpartisan and free of any special interest, but compared to the time he spent on the "coercive" union practices these proposals seemed almost an afterthought.[51] Overall, Eisenhower's speech demonstrates how the focus of his labor proposals had shifted since 1953–1954. Originally presented as an attempt to give labor "an equal voice with all others," the president's proposals were now more antiunion in tone. Several factors—Robert Taft's death, Martin Durkin's resignation, and the McClellan Committee hearings—had all contributed to Eisenhower's shift on this issue. The McClellan Committee hearings, however, had made nearly everyone tougher on organized labor, so, despite Eisenhower's shift, he still found himself in the middle.

Much preferable to Eisenhower than Kennedy-Ervin was a bill sponsored by Phil Landrum (D-GA) and Robert Griffin (R-MI), both members of the House Labor Committee. Landrum-Griffin sections 1–6, the anticorruption provisions, were nearly identical to the Kennedy-Ervin bill. Landrum-Griffin section 7, however, was a list of Taft-Hartley amendments favored by the president. It included provisions on blackmail picketing, secondary boycotts, and "no-man's-land," three issues Eisenhower had specifically mentioned in his television address. Also included were a few prolabor "sweeteners," which, like the president's comments, allowed Landrum-Griffin's supporters, including many Democrats, to refer to their bill as a moderate alternative to Kennedy-Ervin, but one that was still tough enough to end corruption.

Tensions ran high from August 11 to August 13 as the House debated three competing labor bills under complicated parliamentary rules. In addition to Landrum-Griffin and Kennedy-Ervin, which in the House was sponsored by Carl Elliot (D-AL), there was a bill sponsored by John Shelly (D-CA) and James Roosevelt (D-CA). Shelly-Roosevelt, while favored by liberal Democrats, was condemned by most as too "soft" on corruption.

Representatives, who were spending extended periods on the House floor to avoid confrontations with labor and business lobbyists, were quick to anger. One congressman had to be physically restrained from attacking a colleague. In a blatant attempt to sway southern voters, supporters of Kennedy-Ervin argued that Landrum-Griffin was a pro–civil rights bill, but the conservative coalition held.[52] On August 13, in perhaps the most important labor vote since the passage of Taft-Hartley in 1947, the House voted 229–201 (D 95–184, R 134–17) to substitute the Landrum-Griffin bill for the Kennedy-Ervin bill. Landrum-Griffin then passed 303–125. The momentum of the House votes carried over into conference committee, and despite the senators' preference for their own bill, Landrum-Griffin emerged with relatively few compromises. Both houses overwhelmingly accepted the conference report, and President Eisenhower signed it into law on September 14 as the Labor-Management Reporting and Disclosure Act of 1959.[53]

The new law made eleven changes to the Taft-Harley Act. Among them were the three recommended by Eisenhower in his television address: tougher restrictions on blackmail picketing and on secondary boycotts and jurisdiction for states in "no-man's-land" cases. An exemption for the construction and garment industries in the secondary boycott amendment, recommended by Senator Kennedy, had been the only significant concession by House members in conference committee. This would allow "same site" construction strikes and sympathy strikes against the makers of "farmed out" components in the garment industry. This exemption, along with other amendments such as the removal of the noncommunist affidavit requirement for union officials and permission for economic strikers to vote in union representation elections for one year after the beginning of a strike, were prounion and had, in fact, been supported by Secretary Durkin during Eisenhower's first year in office.[54]

Eisenhower was pleased with the new legislation, which included most of the recommendations he had made over the past two years. Landrum-Griffin also represented a personal and political victory for the president since, at the time of his television address, its passage did not seem likely.[55] Labor representatives on the other hand, while grateful for the few Taft-Hartley amendments that benefited unions, were not pleased. An AFL-CIO spokesman said the law was "worse" for labor than the Taft-Hartley Act. One union sent a letter to the 229 House members who had voted for Landrum-Griffin promising to do everything in their power to prove to the working people in their districts that their representative had voted against them and urged them to retaliate at the polls.[56]

Conclusion

Despite Eisenhower's satisfaction with Landrum-Griffin, his attempts to find a "middle way" in the field of labor-management relations were, on the whole, unsuccessful. His appointment of Martin Durkin as secretary of

Labor and his apparent approval of Bernard Shanley's original plan for amending Taft-Hartley in 1954 show that he was attempting to follow through on his promise to give labor "an equal voice with all others." When his early attempts failed, largely because of the death of Senator Robert Taft, he gave in to his more conservative advisors such as Sinclair Weeks and George Humphrey. These men convinced him to avoid the issue, supporting only those amendments to Taft-Hartley that he had committed to in the campaign. Eisenhower's own convictions were so attuned with those of management that, without an advisor sympathetic to the cause, he was unable to put himself in the shoes of labor except on those provisions of the law that had proved blatantly unfair.

If there had been any hope for a comprehensive list of prolabor amendments to the Taft-Hartley Act during the Eisenhower administration, it was crushed by the findings of the McClellan Committee in 1957. Accusations of rampant corruption in the labor union movement shifted the focus of the administration's proposals away from prounion revisions to Taft-Hartley and toward primarily antiunion measures to prevent corruption.

Nixon may have been right when he downplayed the objections of labor, saying that no matter what the administration did it would not get the support of union leaders. Unfortunately for Eisenhower, however, by pursuing the "middle way" he had also failed to get the support of business leaders. Inability to win the support of either group severely limited Eisenhower's achievements in the field of labor-management relations.

A Program
for All Farmers and
for All America

Ezra Taft Benson noted in his memoir, "The first time I ever saw Dwight Eisenhower, he offered me a job."[1] Benson was an unlikely choice for secretary of Agriculture. Although he had been around farms for much of his life, had served as a county agent and state extension worker for the Department of Agriculture, and had served as the executive secretary of the National Council of Farmer Cooperatives from 1939 to 1944, he was not active in politics. In fact, he had devoted his life to his work as member of the Council of Twelve of the Church of Jesus Christ of Latter-day Saints. His home state of Idaho and his adopted state of Utah were not as important agriculturally as the Farm Belt states from which secretaries of Agriculture were traditionally drawn. Finally, he adhered to a philosophy considerably more conservative than Eisenhower's; in fact, he had supported his distant cousin Robert Taft over Eisenhower in the Republican primaries.

Besides his general uncertainty about accepting a government position that would take him away from his home and his church, Benson was concerned about having to defend policies he did not agree with, and he was apprehensive about becoming engaged in political struggles. At his first meeting with the president, Benson expressed some of these concerns. He gave Eisenhower what seemed to him compelling reasons why he should appoint someone else secretary of Agriculture, including the fact that he had been a Taft supporter. "I believe that farmers should be permitted to make their own decisions on their own farms with a minimum of government interference," he told Eisenhower, alluding to his belief that the federal government should not interfere with the price of agricultural commodities. "Now, that's in conflict with the philosophy of the New Deal and it may be in conflict with some of the Republicans in Congress, but that's the way I feel. And I'd find it very difficult to be in Washington supporting a program I didn't believe in." Eisenhower responded, "Mr. Benson, you'll never be asked to support a program you don't believe in."[2]

Agriculture was the one area of domestic policy where Eisenhower favored an overturn of New Deal programs. In other fields he was willing to accept these programs where they already existed or, as in the case of Social Security, even extend them. When it came to the system of price supports that the Agricultural Adjustment Act of 1938 had created, however, Eisenhower refused. What makes this issue particularly interesting is that, while taking farm products off government price supports and returning them to the free market is "conservative" policy, Eisenhower did not receive support for it from many of the conservative congressmen who opposed his more liberal social policies. The reason for this ideological contradiction was that many of these conservative congressmen came from "farm states," and they feared that eliminating or cutting back government farm programs would cost them votes. Eisenhower was under great pressure from the more politically minded members of his staff to do the more expedient thing and back away from the principle of free-market agriculture.

Benson, therefore, found that he and Eisenhower agreed on the basic principles that should guide agricultural policy. While Eisenhower agreed with Benson in principle, however, he did impress upon his secretary of Agriculture the need to find a "middle way." The "middle way," while aiming toward the long-term goal of a free market for agriculture, would allow price supports already in effect to continue until their legislative mandate had run out, at which time they would be gradually scaled back. In the meantime the government would sponsor programs to correct the root cause of the farmers' problem, the surplus of key agricultural products. Like reinsuring health insurance policies and guaranteeing the bond issues of school building authorities, the programs were designed to allow the federal government to act as a catalyst for progress without accepting permanent responsibility.

Eisenhower and Benson both knew that returning agriculture to a free market, even gradually, would be a hotly contested political issue. Liberal Democrats would fight hard to retain the programs put in place by Roosevelt and Truman. They would be joined by southern Democrats and farm-state Republicans who feared reprisals at the ballot box if they supported changes to programs that benefited their constituents. Meanwhile, conservatives who did not come from farm states and, therefore, had the luxury of ideological consistency, like Arizona Senator Barry Goldwater, argued for "prompt and final termination of the farm subsidy program," with "no equivocation."[3] Foreseeing the potential political difficulties, Eisenhower and Benson came to an agreement. Once they had determined the proper course, they should pursue it without regard to the political consequences. "If it was right in principle," Benson said, "in the long run it would be good politically."[4] Benson would have occasion to remind

Eisenhower of this agreement several times over the next eight years. Eisenhower kept his word, backing his secretary of Agriculture despite much political fallout.

The Agricultural Adjustment Act

The Agricultural Adjustment Act of 1938 established a price support and a production control system for several agricultural commodities. This act allowed the secretary of Agriculture to take certain countermeasures, when it appeared that a crop covered by the act would be in surplus, causing the price to fall. These countermeasures could include both price supports and acreage allotments. Under price supports, the government would support prices by purchasing from farmers all supplies of a given commodity when the market price fell below a certain agreed-upon level. Acreage allotments had to be planned further in advance. Under this system, the secretary of Agriculture would determine the number of acres necessary to meet the anticipated demand for a certain crop for the coming year. These acres would then be allotted among existing farmers on the basis of their production history.[5]

The support price on a given product was based on the concept of parity. According to this concept, at some time in the past, farmers' labors and efforts had brought them a "fair" return in terms of production cost, purchasing power, and standards of living. The aim of the parity concept was to determine what prices farmers would have to receive currently to enjoy the same relative purchasing power as during a period when farm prices were "fair." For most crops this baseline period was 1910–1914. Parity for a particular good was expressed as a percentage of the fair situation that supposedly existed in these periods. If, for instance, the government supported corn at 75 percent of parity, it was guaranteeing that the economic situation for corn farmers would be no worse than 75 percent of what it had been during the fair period.[6]

Based on this standard, farm prices as a whole were below parity for the entire period from 1921 to 1940, reaching the level of 90 percent in only six of those years. The onset of World War II changed this. Accelerated need for farm products by the U.S. armed forces and its allies, combined with increased domestic purchasing power caused by the virtual elimination of unemployment, wiped out farm surpluses and even created shortages of some goods, causing prices to rise. The government relaxed acreage controls on most commodities to encourage production. It also raised the parity level for price supports on the "basic" crops—cotton, corn, wheat, rice, tobacco, and peanuts—to 90 percent so that farmers would not be discouraged from increasing production out of fear that the market would collapse when the demand dropped off.[7]

Demand for agricultural products remained high until 1948, when market prices for many goods began to fall below support prices, forcing the government to buy and store the surplus. With the wartime support of "basic" crops set to expire at the end of the year, Congress once again began debating agricultural policy. The question was whether to continue to support the prices of agricultural products, and if so, how and at what level. President Truman favored a permanent support system that would be based on flexible (rather than high, rigid) support prices. Instead of supports being fixed at 90 percent of parity, they would range between certain levels based on supply. If the supply of a particular commodity were high, the price support would be lowered to discourage production. If supply were low, the support could be raised to encourage an increase in production.

This was the basis of a bill put forth in 1948 by Representative Clifford Hope (KS) and Senator George Aiken (VT), both Republicans. The Hope-Aiken bill included a range of 60–90 percent of parity for support of each of the "basic" crops (except tobacco, which would stay at 90 percent). Other commodities would be supported at 0–90 percent of parity. The exact level of support, within these ranges, would be determined by the secretary of Agriculture. Most Republicans favored this system of flexible support, often referred to as the "sliding scale," but some from the West and Midwest joined with a solid bloc of southern Democrats in opposition to measures they believed would hurt their constituents. This opposition necessitated a compromise. Support for "basic" crops, plus several other important agricultural commodities, would remain at 90 percent of parity until January 1, 1950, when the flexible support system would go into effect. Support for other commodities would be set between 60 and 90 percent, at the discretion of the secretary of Agriculture. The Hope-Aiken Act, with these compromises, passed on June 20, 1948.[8]

When the Eighty-first Congress, with its majority of Democrats, took office in January 1949, they began to take measures to prevent the Hope-Aiken Act from being fully implemented. Debate in the House on this matter centered around three proposals. The first plan, put forth by the new secretary of Agriculture, Charles Brannan, proposed to maintain federal price supports at a high level of parity, 90–100 percent, but only on a portion of each farmer's production, the first $25,700. This, he believed, would ensure that the benefits would go primarily to small farmers. The plan was not limited to the "basic" crops but would apply to other important commodities, such as livestock and perishables, as well. Brannan's plan divided House Democrats.[9]

The House Agriculture Committee sent to the floor a plan offered by Democratic Representative Stephen Pace of Georgia. The Pace plan eliminated Brannan's restrictions on the amount of goods eligible for price supports and authorized a permanent system of price supports at 100 percent parity for the basic crops plus several other important commodities. Opponents of the Brannan plan who did not favor the high, permanent supports offered by Pace supported Albert Gore's (D-TN) proposal to extend, for one year, the existing price supports for basic crops at 90 percent, with other commodities supported at 60–90 percent. The vast majority of Republicans preferred Gore's proposal, which passed 239–170 (R 160–4).[10]

In the Senate, former Secretary of Agriculture Clinton Anderson (D-NM) sponsored a bill that more closely resembled the Hope-Aiken Act. The Anderson bill would maintain support of the "basic" crops at 90 percent through 1950. After that it instituted a flexible support system, but with a range of 75–90 percent for the basic crops, it was more favorable to farmers than the Hope-Aiken Act. Tobacco would remain at 90 percent, as in Hope-Aiken. Other commodities would be supported at a price between 60 and 90 percent of parity. After a great deal of debate, the Anderson bill narrowly passed the Senate. After clearing the conference committee on October 19, the last day of the congressional session, Truman signed it into law as the Agricultural Act of 1949.[11]

When the Korean War began in June 1950 the demand for agricultural goods rose once again. This caused prices to rise above parity levels, so the government did not have to purchase them. The Defense Production Acts of 1951 and 1952 relaxed acreage restrictions, and price supports were left in place to encourage production as they had been during World War II. This wartime legislation prevented the flexible support system called for in the Agricultural Act of 1949 from going into effect until 1954. Demand for agricultural products during the Korean War was not as extraordinary as it had been during World War II, however, and prices began to fall as early as 1952.[12]

The Agriculture Act of 1954

During the presidential campaign, despite the advice of his brother Milton, Dwight Eisenhower came out in favor of maintaining price supports at a high level of parity. In a speech in Kasson, Minnesota, in September 1952 he stated, "I firmly believe that agriculture is entitled to a fair, full share of the national income. . . . And a fair share is not merely 90 percent of parity—it is full parity."[13] Fortunately for his soon-to-be secretary of Agriculture, however, he hedged: "Here and now, without any 'ifs' or 'buts,' I say to you that I stand behind—and the Republican Party stands behind—the price support laws now on the books."[14] This allowed Eisenhower to later claim that, although he did not agree with them in principle, he would, as president, continue price supports on basic commodities at 90 percent of parity through 1954.

During his confirmation hearings, Benson was pressed by those who supported high, rigid price supports on whether he would support the pledge made by Eisenhower at Kasson. Asked by Senator Milton Young (R-ND) whether he supported price supports at 90 percent parity, he answered, "Yes, if it's on the books," meaning only that, as secretary, he would be obligated to carry out the law, but he added, "supports are no substitute for parity on the market." When pressed as to whether he would support the maintenance of price supports at 90 percent beyond 1954, Benson refused to commit to it.[15]

Senator Young and others who supported high, rigid price supports had good reason to feel that the appointment of Benson as secretary of Agriculture was a threat to this policy. It did not take long for their fears to be justified. On February 5, fifteen days after taking office, Secretary Benson held his first press conference. At this conference he distributed a statement that made clear his position on the long-term continuation of price supports. "Our agricultural policy," Benson's statement read, "should aim to obtain in the market place full parity prices of farm products and parity incomes for farm people so that farmers will have freedom to operate efficiently and to adjust their production to changing consumer demands in an expanding economy." This objective, however, could not be ensured by government programs alone. While enforcing the price support laws currently on the books, Benson stated, he would formulate long-term programs to more fully and effectively address the problems of American farmers. "Price supports," he said "should provide insurance against disaster to the farm-producing plant and help to stabilize national food supplies." Price supports that encouraged surpluses should be avoided. "Inefficiency," he concluded, "should not be subsidized in Agriculture or in any other segment of our economy."[16]

This statement and a speech along similar lines made several days later in St. Paul, Minnesota, were attacked by members of Congress who supported the policy of high, rigid price supports. They found particularly offensive the phrase "insurance against disaster," which they took to mean that the federal government would not step in until such time that disaster was imminent, and the term "inefficiency," which they took as a statement on Benson's part that American farmers were inefficient. Senator James Murray (D-MT) called the St. Paul speech "shocking" and "an insult to the farmer. . . . If this be the end of the Administration's honeymoon, so be it. It is far better to end the honeymoon than to end the farmer." Senator Richard Russell (D-GA) concurred, "After the election I promised to cooperate with this Administration, but I'm not going to follow it down the road to disaster." Senator Burnet Maybank (D-SC) said that the speech showed a "lack of common sense." He went on to attack Benson personally. "If this is an indication of the policy thinking of the new Secretary, then God help the poor and working dirt farmers of this country," he said. "I do not intend to stand idly by and see men who have no basic knowledge of our farm problems cut the heart out of the basic segment of our economy." Democrats were not alone in attacking the secretary's policies. Senator Milton Young, who had opposed Benson's confirmation, proposed to some of his colleagues in the U.S. Senate that they form a committee to "straighten out Benson."[17]

When Benson's critics began to urge Eisenhower to fire him, Benson was not sure that his job was safe. Despite the president's past assurances that they were in agreement on agricultural policy, Benson knew that cabinet secretaries were often dismissed out of political necessity. So, when Eisenhower asked to see him in the Oval Office just a month after the inauguration, Benson thought his time was up. "Ezra," the president said, "I believe every word you said at St. Paul." He laughed and then added, "I'm not sure you should have said it quite so soon."[18] Once again the president affirmed his support for Benson's policies, this time in the face of a storm of political protest. Benson could now set about implementing his policies with the knowledge that Eisenhower would back him.

The question of price supports, temporarily postponed by the need for increased production during the Korean War, was once again an urgent concern and would remain so throughout the Eisenhower years. The Korean War had not created the demand for agricultural products that World War II had. In 1952 farm prices began to fall and continued to do so in 1953. Under the rigid price support system, the federal government began to acquire huge surpluses of agricultural goods. "Agriculture was at a crossroad," Benson believed. "Either it would rush headlong down the road of socialistic controls and regimentation—the road of 'letting the government do it'—or it would turn gradually toward a kind of freedom and responsibility, freedom to plant, freedom to market, freedom to compete and make its own decisions."[19]

Since it would mean disaster for farmers to eliminate price supports entirely, Benson set his sights on converting to a flexible system of support, such as that called for in the Hope-Aiken Act of 1948 and the Agricultural Act of 1949, neither of which had ever been fully implemented. The ability to set price supports within a parity range would give the secretary some measure of control over the surplus. By lowering the price support on goods already in great supply, he could deter their production. The long-term effect of such a policy would be to put supply more in line with demand, preparing agriculture for a conversion to the free market.

Although Benson was convinced that Eisenhower agreed with him on general principles, the president still had not confirmed that he was in favor of converting to a flexible support system after the Defense Production Act, and with it the "Kasson pledge" expired at the end of 1953. This was, after all, a decision that would have political ramifications, and 1954 was an election year. Benson was counting on Eisenhower's belief that what was right in principle would, in the long term, be right politically. The breakthrough, in Benson's opinion, came on October 22, 1953, when Benson gave a cabinet paper on the agricultural situation in preparation for his legislative proposals for 1954. At this meeting Eisenhower came out in favor of a flexible price support system and against high, rigid price supports.[20]

On December 11, 1953, Secretary Benson presented the Department of Agriculture's legislative program to Eisenhower and the cabinet.[21] The most important proposal was the conversion to a flexible scale for the support of the "basic" crops, ranging from 75 to 90 percent of parity. Another feature of the program was the conversion to a "modern" method of calculating parity. The old method was based on price relationships, buying habits, and methods of farm production from forty years earlier. "Modern parity" would take account of these factors during only the last ten years, permitting "changes in farm technology and in consumer demand to express themselves in the level of price support." Congress had already adopted "modern parity" on some commodities; but to prevent losses on crops for which the "modern" parity level was lower than it would have been under the old method of computation, Congress had adopted the policy of giving the higher of the two, a practice called "dual parity." Benson's proposal would put an end to dual parity, easing farmers into the new system by instructing the secretary to prevent the parity level from dropping by more than 5 percent in any one year. To further cushion the transition for farmers, $2.5 billion of the existing surplus held by the federal government would be used for charitable purposes and not counted for computing price supports. Finally, the government would spend $1 billion over the next three years to remove surpluses from the market. These would be donated to nations experiencing food shortages or sold abroad in exchange for foreign currencies. Eisenhower accepted the proposals and sent them to Congress on January 11, 1954.[22]

In a radio broadcast the evening that Eisenhower sent the agricultural proposals to Congress, Benson made the case that the administration's program addressed the roots of the farm problem in America, rather than just treating its symptoms. This was consistent with what he called an "old American principle." When something is wrong, he said, "Find the basic cause and do something about it." When a fence is down, "Don't make a career out of chasing stray cows. . . . And don't spend a lot of money to replace those that get lost. The thing to do is fix the fence." What was wrong, according to Benson, was that the government was spending $2 billion annually to support wheat at 90 percent of parity, and over $750 million annually to support corn at 90 percent of parity, when the average market prices of these commodities was 82 percent and 79 percent of parity, respectively. Over the years, he said, farmers had received better prices for their nonsupported crops than they had for their supported crops. Huge stocks of government-held commodities were jeopardizing farm prosperity and endangering the free-market system.[23]

The president's agricultural program in 1954 caused a great deal of controversy in both houses of Congress. While it appeared that those in favor of high, rigid price supports had the votes to block it, the administration had what Secretary Benson called "an ace in the hole."[24] Since the Defense Production Act was about to expire, if Congress failed to enact legislation the president could approve, then the Agricultural Act of 1949 with its provision for the flexible support of "basic" crops between 75 and 90 percent of parity would automatically go into effect. This was because the Defense Production Act had not repealed the Agricultural Act of 1949; it had only put off implementation of it. So, if Congress voted an extension of 90 percent supports, the president could veto it, and since Congress probably did not have the two-thirds majority necessary to override his veto, the administration would get the 75–90 percent flexible scale it had asked for.

At a cabinet meeting on May 21, 1954, Benson reviewed the status of the agriculture program in Congress and the president reiterated his support for it. When the question of a veto was brought up, Eisenhower indicated that if Congress passed a rigid, high-level price support program he would confer with Secretary Benson and in all likelihood veto the bill. The president also gave Benson permission to tell the press he would recommend such a veto if the situation warranted it. At a legislative leaders' meeting on June 7, Eisenhower passed this information along to Republican congressional leaders.[25]

The House acted on the administration's proposals first. On June 8, the House Agriculture Committee flatly rejected the administration's request for a system of flexible price supports. By a vote of 21–8 it recommended to the full House that existing supports be continued through 1955. A recommendation to make 90 percent supports permanent failed by the narrow margin of 15–14.[26] Only two days later, President Eisenhower took his appeal straight to American farmers in a television address. The administration's program "is for all farmers, regardless of their politics, and for all America," he said. "Many have told me, that it would not be good politics to attempt solution of the farm problem during an election year. . . . In this matter I am completely unmoved by arguments as to what constitutes good or winning politics. . . . I know what is right for America is politically right."[27]

Without the votes to kill the House Agriculture Committee's bill through amendments, the situation would have been very grave for the administration had it not been for its "ace in the hole," which forced Congress to take the threat of a veto seriously. Charles Halleck (R-IN) offered a compromise amendment, sponsored by Representative Robert Harrison (R-NE), to set price supports for the "basic" crops on a range of 82.5–90 percent of parity through 1955, after which the range would become 75–90 percent. This would put the range for 1955 exactly halfway between the 75–90 percent requested by the president, and the 90 percent favored by the House. House Speaker Joseph Martin (R-MA) then took the floor. "You and I know there is not going to be any legislation unless it is acceptable to the president," he said—a clear warning of the veto he knew would come if the Agriculture Committee's bill was sent to the White House. Speaker Martin then predicted that Eisenhower would accept the Harrison Amendment as a step in the right direction. His statement was persuasive, and the Harrison amendment was approved 228–170 (R 182–23).[28]

Martin's prediction that the president would accept a compromise proved correct. This begs the question of why the Eisenhower administration would be willing to accept a bill that called for an 82.5–90 percent scale when it could get 75–90 percent by vetoing anything short of that and forcing the implementation of the 1949 legislation. Benson later explained: "Winning this one battle by a veto could conceivably lose us the whole war." Implementing flexible support with over half of Congress in opposition could have seriously undermined the administration's influence in many areas besides agriculture. "We wanted and we *needed*," Benson explained, "the passage of a flexible support bill."[29] By agreeing to the 82.5 percent compromise, the administration would get less than was possible through a veto, but it would be an act of good faith that could, potentially, help the administration in future battles with Congress.

In the Senate the administration bill was guided by Senator George Aiken. Aiken separated the provision for spending $1 billion to remove surpluses from the market by donating them to needy countries from the rest of the bill. This aspect of the program was popular, and Aiken did not want the president to be forced to veto it along with an omnibus farm bill. It was later passed as Public Law (PL) 480 (see Chapter 6). After that, the debate proceeded in a manner similar to that in the House. The Senate Committee on Agriculture and Forestry proposed a bill that included price supports rigidly set at 90 percent of parity. Senator Aiken then offered an amendment that mirrored the bill passed in the House, establishing a flexible scale for support of "basic" crops between 82.5 and 90 percent of parity for 1955. This amendment passed by the narrow margin of 49 to 44 (R 39–8) on August 9, 1954.[30]

The final provisions of the Agricultural Act of 1954 represented a victory for the Eisenhower administration. Eisenhower and Benson had not received the 75–90 percent scale they were asking for, but they had succeeded in establishing the principle of flexible support. Furthermore, the 82.5–90 percent scale would be used only through 1955, after which the 75–90 percent scale would go into effect on all "basic" crops except tobacco, which would be kept at 90 percent. Prices for other commodities covered by the law would be supported between 60 and 90 percent of parity. In other provisions, the president's request that $2.5 billion worth of surplus goods currently held by the federal government be set aside for charitable purposes and left out of the parity calculations was also approved. In addition, all future price supports would be set using "modern" parity, with the safeguard that support would not drop by more than 5 percent in any one year. "Dual" parity was ended. Eisenhower signed the Agricultural Act of 1954 into law on August 28, 1954, stating that "at last our farmers are assured of greater freedom instead of the rapidly increasing regimentation and Federal domination they were sure to suffer under a continuation of the present system of rigid price supports."[31]

The Soil Bank

The Eisenhower administration's success with its agricultural program in 1954 was only a limited one. It did not solve the farm problem. The main problem in agriculture in the United States was the surplus. There was no real hope for improving farm income unless the surplus could be eliminated. The amount of agricultural commodities in government storage reached $4 billion in October 1954 and $6 billion by November 1955.[32] Throughout 1955 the surplus was the main concern of the Department of Agriculture. Secretary Benson considered four main alternatives for solving this problem. First, the surplus could be moved into the domestic market. This was already being done in a limited way by the provision of the Agriculture Act of 1954, which set aside $2.5 billion of the surplus to be used for charitable purposes. This, Benson believed, was the maximum extent to which this could be done since the surplus commodities could not be allowed to enter into direct price competition with crops currently being produced or prices would plummet. Second, the government could sell or give the surplus away overseas. This was being carried out to a limited extent through PL 480. There was also a limit to how much of the surplus could be diverted in this way without upsetting world markets, depressing world prices, and causing foreign governments to enact retaliatory measures. Third, the surplus could be destroyed. This had been done during the New Deal, and Benson thought the possibility of repeating it "unthinkable." The fourth alternative was to bring about a drastic reduction in production, while compensating farmers for their losses. To put it more simply, this alternative was to pay farmers not to farm. Benson also found this alternative very distasteful, but as surpluses continued to pile up he came to accept the possibility. "The only way we could justify it," Benson said, "was because the government itself was largely responsible for the whole mess." Benson set about trying to find a way to make this fourth alternative "as unobjectionable as possible."[33]

Benson presented his preliminary proposals for farm legislation for 1956 at a cabinet meeting on October 7, 1955. President Eisenhower was not present, having suffered a heart attack while vacationing in Denver, Colorado. Benson pointed out that it would take time for the Agriculture Act of 1954 to have any effect and that the farm situation was not likely to improve in 1956. His plans for dealing with the surplus were modest, reflecting his distaste for the programs his department had been forced to consider. The main points of his plan were an accelerated program of surplus disposal and an expansion of exports, an enlarged program of soil conservation and incentive payments to divert cropland into grass or trees, and programs to assist farmers in adjusting to market demands and making better use of the land.[34]

Meanwhile, on his hospital bed in Denver, Eisenhower had begun to think in much bigger terms. He had been talking to his brother Milton about the long-term future of America's farmland. The things that the president wanted to do in the areas of soil and water conservation would be expensive and time consuming, so he wanted to get started on them right away to ensure "a soil in our country that was permanent and lasting and could be turned over to coming generations as an enriched soil rather than a depleted soil."[35]

Each of the cabinet secretaries came, in turn, to Denver to meet with Eisenhower and discuss business related to their departments. When Benson's turn came on October 29, he presented his preliminary plan for legislation in 1956. Eisenhower approved of his plans but wanted Benson to think in bigger terms. Seizing upon Benson's program of soil conservation and incentive payments for farmers to divert cropland into other uses, Eisenhower proposed a half-billion dollar program that would take marginal land out of production by paying farmers to leave it idle. The plan, for which Eisenhower proposed the name Soil Bank, would not only conserve the soil as he had been contemplating but reduce the surplus and raise the price of agricultural commodities as Benson was attempting to do. Eisenhower would later add his desire to begin to buy back some of the farmland, now of marginal productive value, that had been given away under the Homestead Act of 1862.[36]

The idea of buying farmland was later dropped. Eisenhower could not convince his cabinet, particularly Humphrey and Benson, to buy back land that the government had given away nearly a hundred years earlier.[37] The Soil Bank, however, became the central focus of the Eisenhower administration's agriculture program for 1956. It consisted of two main parts. The first part was the Acreage Reserve, which was designed to reduce the production of the crops that were in greatest surplus: wheat, cotton, corn, and rice. Under the plan, a farmer who had, for instance, a one-hundred-acre allotment of wheat under the current program could voluntarily choose to plant only eighty acres. The other twenty acres would be placed in Acreage Reserve, and the farmer would agree not to grow any crops on it. For participating in the program the farmer would receive a certificate that could be exchanged for cash or an equivalent amount of wheat. This program was a short-term emergency program designed to last three to four years and greatly reduce the surplus by taking twenty to twenty-five million acres out of production.[38]

The second part of the Soil Bank was called the Conservation Reserve. Farmers would voluntarily agree to shift their farmland permanently out of cultivation by planting forage or trees or by creating ponds or reservoirs. The farmer would be paid a share of the cost of converting the land, plus an annual payment for the length of time necessary to establish the new use of the land. This was a long-term program designed to last up to fifteen years and to take twenty-five million acres permanently out of production.[39] Altogether, the Soil Bank had the potential to take an estimated fifty million acres of land out of production, one-eighth of the nation's farmland.

Eisenhower presented the plan to Congress on January 9, 1956. His message stated that, of all the problems that faced American agriculture, "mountainous surpluses overshadow everything else." These surpluses, he pointed out, consisted of commodities needed in volume during the war, but "wartime production incentives were too long continued," and the surplus commodities were now unmarketable. During the previous three years, there had been no lack of effort to get rid of surplus stocks, but the disposal efforts were not able to keep pace with the problem.[40] Reduction of the surplus would cause a simultaneous rise in prices, boosting farm income. Although the program would be expensive to administer, it was less expensive than the current price support program plus the costs of buying and storing the surplus (estimated to be about $1 million a day), making the plan cost effective as well. The Soil Bank had the added appeal of seeming to address the root causes of the farm problem, rather than merely treating the symptoms.[41]

Despite the Soil Bank's potential, Secretary Benson was less than excited about it. "In theory, the Soil Bank was just about the most attractive proposal for licking the surplus anybody had yet devised," Benson later wrote. "Still I could not get as enthusiastic about it as some of my staff. Maybe just the idea of paying farmers for not producing—even as a one-shot emergency measure—outraged my sensibilities. . . . However, when I thought of what the Soil Bank might do—if all went according to plan—certainly it deserved a chance."[42]

Meanwhile in Congress, Democrats and farm-state Republicans refused to let go of their desire to reestablish high, rigid price supports. On May 5, 1955, over the administration's vehement objections, the House had narrowly passed a bill to do just that (206–201, R 21–172).[43] The Senate, which had put off action on the House bill until 1956, was considering it simultaneously with the administration's Soil Bank proposal. On February 11, the Senate Committee on Agriculture and Forestry followed the House's lead and sent a bill to the floor that contained a return to rigid parity at 90 percent.[44] Senator George Aiken and Senator Clinton Anderson succeeded in adding amendments to the committee's bill that effectively eliminated the return to high, rigid price supports, but in conference committee the House insisted on restoring them as well as reinstating dual parity. The bill that emerged included these features and the president's Soil Bank proposal, despite the fact that they were contradictory. House Minority Leader Joseph Martin made one final attempt to kill the high support provisions of the bill on April 11, moving that it be sent back to committee and the 90 percent price supports and dual parity be removed. This motion was defeated 181–238 (R 167–27). The conference bill was then passed 237–181 (R 48–186).

Eisenhower would later call the legislation "a monstrosity of a farm bill, which while incorporating the recommended soil-bank plan, made the great error of going back to the 90 percent of parity price supports. . . . In effect it was less a piece of farm legislation than a private relief bill for politicians in that election year." He was baffled as to why "In my own party many of the so-called 'conservative' or 'right-wing' members coming from farm states voted for rigid, high price supports, usually considered a 'liberal' solution."[45] Eisenhower called the three Republicans on the Senate Agriculture Committee who had voted in favor of a return to 90 percent parity "three weaklings." Benson concurred: "Never had I known a legislative process to be so indicative of political expediency and so devoid of principle. . . . It was probably the worst piece of farm legislation ever approved by either House of Congress. Our program recommended by the President had been mutilated, distorted and emasculated until the proposals were hardly recognizable."[46]

All parties involved had already begun to consider the possibility of a veto. Democrats and farm state Republicans in Congress thought the chances that the president would veto a "give-away" farm bill in an election year were slim.[47] The White House staff agreed that a veto would be a politically risky move. Benson gave a report on the situation at the legislative leadership meeting on April 9, 1956, stating that if the bill, then still in conference, were passed, the Department of Agriculture would recommend a veto. Benson added that if the bill were vetoed with a strong message and the president followed it up with a television address to the American people, that a majority of farmers would support his actions.[48] White House Chief of Staff Sherman Adams echoed the concerns of the White House staff when he asked Benson, "Did you ever hear of a President vetoing a farm bill in an election year?" Benson responded, "I don't know, [but] this is not a farm bill. This is a political bill. The President can't afford to sign this. [There] isn't anything in it for farmers. It's nothing but a political bill to try and embarrass him."[49]

In addition to the White House staff, three Republican governors from farm states were also pressuring the president to support the bill: Leo Hoegh of Iowa, Fred Hall of Kansas, and Joe Foss of South Dakota. Benson refused to relent. On April 13 he went to Augusta, Georgia, where the president was vacationing in order to make his case. Benson had reason to be confident that the president would support him. He and Eisenhower saw eye to eye on the farm problem, and back in January when it had been suggested that Congress might pass both the administration's agriculture bill and a bill requiring high, rigid price supports, the president had asserted he would not go out of office with such price supports in place.[50] The secretary, however, was still apprehensive; he did not say so at the time, but he had been contemplating resignation if the bill were signed into law.[51]

In his memoirs, Benson wrote about his meeting with the president. "My staff is just about unanimous that I've got to go along with it," Benson later recalled Eisenhower saying. "Mr. President," he replied. "Do you remember not too long after you came into office, we had a discussion . . . in which we agreed that if a thing is right, it ought to be done and that if it is right it will also prove to be the best politics? This bill is *not* right. It's not right for *farmers*. It's not right for the *country*. The only right thing to do is veto it." According to Benson, Eisenhower reflected momentarily before nodding his head in assent, and then he said, "I know it, and that's why I'm going to veto it."[52]

On April 16, 1956, Eisenhower vetoed the bill on the grounds of its inclusion of high, rigid price supports and the use of dual parity. He stated that the major problem facing America's farmers was the surplus. The bill in question, he claimed, would encourage surplus production. Eisenhower also pointed out that the two portions of the bill to which he objected would work at cross purposes to the portion containing the Soil Bank, which was designed to help eliminate the surplus. It was, therefore, self-defeating.[53]

Later that evening Eisenhower made a radio and television address from the White House to the American people to explain his reasons for vetoing the farm bill. "I know you are depending on me to tell the truth as I see it," he said, "and the truth is this: I had no choice. I could not sign this bill into law because it was a bad bill. In the months ahead, it would hurt more farmers than it would help. In the long run it would hurt all farmers. It was a bad bill for the country. It was confusing—in some aspects self-defeating, and so awkward and clumsy as to make its administration difficult or impractical." Regarding the Soil Bank he added, "I was happy that the Administration's Soil Bank was still in it. But the disappointing thing was that other provisions of the bill would have rendered the Soil Bank almost useless. The fact is that we got a hodgepodge in which the bad provisions more than canceled out the good." The president ended his address by requesting that Congress quickly pass a bill containing the Soil Bank but leaving out the other offending provisions. In a cabinet meeting Secretary Benson noted that the Department of Agriculture had received very little mail on the veto and the mail it had received was favorable to the president.[54]

On April 18, the House attempted to override the president's veto. This maneuver fell far short of the two-thirds majority necessary in a vote of 211–202 (R 20–173). It was now late in the growing season, and legislators conceded it was time to move on if they wanted to pass a farm bill before the November elections. In relatively short order, they drafted a compromise that was adopted by both chambers. The bill incorporated the Soil Bank, including both the Acreage Reserve and the Conservation Reserve, and deleted most of the objectionable provisions that had caused the April 16 veto, including the return to 90 percent parity. Eisenhower signed the Agricultural Act of 1956 into law on May 28, 1956. The administration was forced to compromise on a few points. It agreed to a one-year freeze on the transition to "modern parity" for some crops, and minimum acreage levels for cotton and rice, both in heavy surplus. These concessions helped to win support among southern Democrats who had lost out on high, rigid price supports.[55]

The Political Fortunes of Secretary Benson

With two major pieces of legislation now on the books to deal with the surplus (PL 480 and the Soil Bank), Benson and the Department of Agriculture began to consider a problem likely to be the unwanted side effect of surplus disposal. The Agriculture Act of 1954 had established the principle of a sliding scale for price supports. When a particular crop was in surplus, the price support would be lowered to discourage its further acquisition by the government. When the supply was down, the price support, by law, would go up until it reached 90 percent. When price supports reached this artificially high level, they acted as an incentive for farmers to increase production of the crop for sale to the government, thus once again building up the surplus. Benson had foreseen this problem, but considering the difficulty the administration had experienced in 1954 and 1956, he felt lucky just to have established the principle of lower price supports. Now that the 1956 legislation was on the books and had begun to deplete the surplus, Benson hoped to implement a plan for weaning American agriculture from high price supports.[56]

Considering the controversy over farm policy in the past, Benson knew this would be a tough sell. On April 12, 1957, Benson presented his preliminary plan to the cabinet. He explained that the price support laws had a built-in mechanism for creating new surpluses as fast as the old ones were eliminated, and that acreage controls were not enough to counteract this tendency. Benson proposed new legislation that would gradually relax acreage controls and increase the discretion of the secretary in setting support levels. He thought of this as the beginning of a long-range program that would eventually put American agriculture back on a free-market system. Since PL 480 and the Soil Bank were proceeding faster than previously planned, Benson felt the time was right to broach this plan, especially since it would certainly mean another fight with Congress.[57] The president and the cabinet unanimously approved the plan.

Meanwhile, the agriculture situation began to improve. Benson reported to the cabinet in June 1957 that farm prices and income were up slightly from the previous year and that markets continued to expand. Much of the improvement, he said, was due to the success of PL 480 and the Soil Bank, particularly the Acreage Reserve program, which had taken twenty-one million acres out of production. The Conservation Reserve had removed another six and a half million acres. The Acreage Reserve was expensive, though, and Benson was anxious to cut back on production controls and make price supports more flexible.[58] Not everyone agreed that the Acreage Reserve program was a success. Democrats and farm-state Republicans claimed it was not effective in reducing production because only marginal lands had been taken out of cultivation. To make matters worse, in some areas, entire farms had been retired, depressing the economy in those regions. Furthermore, they claimed, paying farmers not to farm was causing resentment in the nonfarm community. These groups favored a return to high, rigid price supports.[59]

Eisenhower presented the administration's agriculture plan to Congress on January 16, 1958. The most important and most controversial aspects of the plan were Benson's proposals to ease acreage restrictions and give the secretary of Agriculture more flexibility in setting price supports. Other specific recommendations included expansion of the Conservation Reserve program and elimination of the Acreage Reserve program after the 1958 harvest; easing of the restrictions on the production of the "basic" crops; a lowering of the minimum level of price supports to 60 percent of parity; and elimination of the "escalator clause," the provision in the law requiring that price supports be raised as soon as the surplus of a crop was reduced.[60]

As one might have expected, Democrats and farm-state Republicans, who had always favored a return to high, rigid price supports, did not respond favorably to the proposal to lower the parity level further. Benson's approval ratings had gone up and down with farm prices over the years, but he had never been popular with those congressmen who favored high supports. For this group, the administration's recommendation in 1958 was the last straw.

In late February a group of twenty Republican congressmen held a secret meeting to discuss forcing Benson's resignation. On February 21, Arthur L. Miller (NE) and Walter Judd (MI) came to Benson's office on a matter of "great importance." Miller, claiming to represent the views of twenty midwestern Republican congressmen, said they feared that they could not be reelected in November if Benson continued on as secretary of Agriculture and pushed forward with the current farm program. Later that day Benson gave out a press release that stated that as a Republican and as a member of the cabinet in a Republican administration, he was naturally concerned about the political fortunes of Republican congressmen, but "concern for political fortunes of individuals could not transcend the very function of government, which is to protect and help its citizens."[61]

This defense did not deter Benson's opponents. The next day Congressman Miller followed up his visit to Benson's office with a letter to the secretary. Referring to the fact that Benson had once said that, as a loyal cabinet member, his resignation was always on the desk of the president, Miller wrote, "I would like to suggest, Sir, that after this Republican group . . . present[s] their views to the President that you then again offer your resignation. . . . There seems little doubt among this group of men that your policies and your staying on as Secretary of Agriculture will cause defeat of 25 to 30 members of Congress. It may prevent the election of others who ought to be helping to carry the views of the administration."[62]

Representative Miller and his coconspirators were mistaken if they believed that they could persuade the president to participate in their plan to force Benson's resignation. Eisenhower refused to meet with representatives of the "group of twenty." In the next Republican legislative leadership meeting, he said, "It is a sad commentary when men like Secretary Benson, who stands for integrity and principle, are asked to leave government because a few congressmen refuse to support a sound program and get themselves into political difficulty."[63]

While Benson's job was safe, the same could not be said of his legislative proposals. On March 7, the Senate Agriculture Committee reported out a bill permanently barring reductions in price supports or acreage allotments for any crops below the 1957 levels. Despite strong opposition from the administration, the measure passed 50–43 (R 20–26) on March 13. The House Agriculture Committee reported out a similar bill, putting a freeze on the reduction of price supports for 1958 and on acreage allotments for 1958–1959. The House passed its bill 210–172 (R 44–141). The Senate then adopted the House version of the "freeze bill," and it was sent to the president.[64]

As in 1956, the White House staff and the Republican legislative leadership urged the president to seek a compromise position that would preclude the necessity of a veto. Again, Eisenhower backed his secretary of Agriculture, putting principle above political expediency. This time, however, there were signs that the president might be softening, perhaps because there was very little support in the House for the administration's position. Eisenhower wrote to Benson that he should take note of the German aphorism, "Never lose the good in seeking too long for the best." He recalled that for five years they had been "working hard to get Federal programs affecting American Agriculture on a sounder basis. . . . But we should observe that never in any one year have we gotten exactly what we wanted. Even when we first got some flexibility in farm prices, we had to take it on a step-by-step basis." Eisenhower pointed out that the congressional leadership had shown some signs of flexibility and that, in future planning, the administration should avoid "advanced positions of inflexibility." He told Benson, "It is *not* good *Congressional* politics to fail to listen seriously to the recommendations of our own Congressional leaders."[65]

Despite these conciliatory statements and the continuing objections of his staff and congressional Republicans, Eisenhower, for the second time, vetoed a farm bill in an election year. His veto message was worded less strongly than in 1956, however: "I have given earnest consideration to the many representations made to me both for and against it. It is my judgment that to approve this resolution would be ill advised, from the standpoint both of the nation and our farm families as well." The reasons he gave for the veto, however, were familiar: The bill would pile up more farm products in government warehouses, it would restrict the growth of markets, and it would postpone the day when agriculture could be released from government controls.[66]

The administration's position in the stalemate improved in the months following the veto. Farm prices for the months of March, April, and May 1958 averaged 10 percent above those in 1957. If Benson had not yet realized that his approval ratings were directly linked to the price of farm commodities, he could not have failed to do so in the spring of 1958. A few months earlier, Republican congressional leaders had been asking for his job; now he was being called one of the leaders of the conservative wing of the party. The media began to mention his name as a possible candidate for elective office, possibly even the vice presidency. "What a difference a couple of dollars in the prices of hogs and cattle make," Benson quipped.[67]

Benson's newfound popularity and the higher prices of farm commodities did not solve the administration's problem of getting farm legislation through Congress, although its bargaining position did improve. In June the House Agriculture Committee reported out a farm bill that, like the bill Eisenhower vetoed in 1956, included some of the administration's proposals but also included many provisions that made it unacceptable to the president. Benson called it a "monstrosity." Many who had supported the "freeze bill" in the House voted against it, and it was defeated 171–214 (R 21–162) on June 26, 1958. On July 25 the Senate passed a bill that the administration was willing to work with, but the House was still not willing to concede defeat. If it could pass a bill on the floor under suspension of rules, it would have the upper hand in conference committee with the Senate. Under suspension of rules, debate is limited and no amendments are allowed from the floor, but a two-thirds majority is required for the bill to pass. If the bill does pass, it has the benefit of a large enough majority to override a presidential veto. This maneuver failed 210–186 (R 38–148) on August 6. Now the administration had the upper hand. Time was running short, and Congress could not afford to adjourn without farm legislation. Using the Senate bill as a model, the House finally passed a bill acceptable to both the Senate and the administration.[68]

Eisenhower signed the Agricultural Act of 1958 into law on August 28. The measure clearly represented a compromise, but once again, it favored the administration. The Conservation Reserve was continued, but with slightly less funding than the administration had asked for. Acreage allotments were eliminated on corn, but no action was taken on the administration's request to allow the secretary to ease acreage allotments on the other "basic" crops. In response to the administration's request to lower the minimum price support for "basic" crops to 60 percent of parity, the act granted a minimum level of 65 percent for corn, 70 percent for cotton and rice in 1961 and 65 percent beginning in 1962, and took no action on wheat, peanuts, or tobacco. The law would end the "escalator clause" for rice in 1959, and for cotton in 1961.[69]

After passing the farm bill, Congress quickly adjourned for one last round of campaigning before the November elections. It is difficult to say whether dissatisfaction with farm legislation contributed to the Republican Party's losses in 1958 as Congressman Miller had predicted it would. Considering the rise in farm prices in 1958, it is possible that many of the farm-state Republicans who lost their seats in 1958, like Miller himself, did so because they opposed the administration. In any event, the enlarged

Democratic majorities of 64–34 in the Senate and 283–153 in the House would prevent the Eisenhower administration from passing any further significant farm legislation.[70]

Trouble with the New Congress

The president's message to Congress on agriculture for 1959 did not concede defeat on its principles regarding agriculture, despite the most thorough Democratic victory since the Roosevelt landslide in 1936. Eisenhower's plan was the most ambitious yet in terms of returning agriculture to the free market. In it he abandoned the entire concept of price supports based on parity. Instead, supports for a commodity in any given year would be fixed at a percentage of its average market price during the previous three years. He called this the "three year moving average." He suggested a range of 75–90 percent of the three-year average, with the exact figure determined by the secretary. In this way, he believed, prices would be allowed to adjust slowly downward toward a truer market price based on supply and demand. The function of the support would be to prevent large price drops from year to year, rather than to sustain artificially high prices.[71]

The heavy Democratic majorities in both Houses ensured that the administration's farm program for 1959 would not be passed. In fact it got very little consideration. Instead Congress passed two bills that, once again, resulted in presidential vetoes. The first was a wheat bill that attempted to end the rise in support costs for the crop in biggest surplus without cutting too deeply into wheat farmers' incomes. It cut acreage allotments on wheat by 25 percent but raised the price support to 90 percent of parity. Eisenhower vetoed this bill arguing that it was a step backward; the new acreage restrictions would not compensate for the incentive to production created by the high price supports. The second bill he vetoed called for a freeze on the current acreage allotment and continuation of the 90 percent price support for tobacco. The administration had asked that they be lowered since the high price of U.S. tobacco was causing it to lose world markets to lower-cost foreign products.[72]

Without legislation to correct it, the wheat problem continued into 1960. Eisenhower's last message to Congress on agriculture stated that his preferred solution was that Congress eliminate production controls and adopt the three-year moving average. If Congress failed to do this, however, he was willing to consider a variety of different approaches to bring down the production of wheat as long as they did not stimulate more production through high price supports.[73] The Senate passed a wheat bill along the same lines as the previous year. The House failed to pass a bill at all, and the situation went unattended for another year. The president did sign a relatively uncontroversial tobacco bill that froze support at the 1959 dollars and cents level—not the parity level—for 1960, after which it would be adjusted upward in proportion to the rise in the cost of living above that for 1959.[74]

Conclusion

Agriculture was the one area of domestic policy where Eisenhower was in favor of overturning the policies of his predecessors. Nevertheless, he still found himself at odds with members of his own party. On this issue Eisenhower, although he was promoting the conservative policy of returning agriculture to the free market, was still opposed by conservative Republicans who, because they came from farm states, favored the more liberal policy of continuing price supports. These Republicans, when joined by southern Democrats, made a formidable obstacle to Eisenhower's policy proposals.

As in other areas he sought a "middle way." He accepted the system of high, rigid price supports inherited by his administration until its mandate ran out. In the meantime he proposed new legislation designed to make the system more flexible—hoping to gradually wean farmers and their representatives in Congress away from government supports. Another aspect of the "middle way" for agriculture was the implementation of the Soil Bank. By taking farmland out of production, the Soil Bank would address the root cause of American agriculture problems—overproduction. Like "reinsuring" health insurance companies and guaranteeing the bond issues of school building authorities, the Soil Bank was a way that the federal government could act as a catalyst for solving domestic problems without accepting permanent responsibility for them. In this case that meant facilitating the removal of one-eighth of America's farmland from production.

"So ended the legislative story on agriculture of these eight years," Benson summed up in his memoir. "In view of this history, I feel entirely justified in repeating what I said so often during the eight years as Secretary: *The farm problem is largely the refusal of Democratic Congresses from 1955 on to make long-needed changes.*" Benson complained that the opposition had sought to pin the blame on the administration, claiming that Congress had given Benson everything he had asked for but the program had not worked. "This is false," Benson added. "We never had anything like the full program we asked for. We got some of what we recommended—but even this, in many cases, came too late to be most effective. Where we had, or were given, the authority to make price supports realistic, the results were good."[75] What Benson failed to point out was that Republican Party conservatives had been just as responsible for holding up the administration's program as the Democrats.

Civil Rights, States' Rights, and Federal Responsibilities

As a public speaker, Eisenhower was usually at his best when he put aside his prepared notes and spoke extemporaneously. When talking to African Americans, however, this practice often resulted with him unwittingly offending his audience. This was the case on May 12, 1958, when he addressed the Negro Publishers' Association. Toward the end of his address, Eisenhower took off his glasses and began to ad-lib. In regard to desegregation, he told the four hundred members of the organization that, they must acknowledge, racial prejudice is deeply rooted in people's hearts and could only be changed through education. Referring to the audience as "you people," he told them they needed to "be patient." According to one observer, when Eisenhower spoke these words "the roof fell in." The audience responded to the speech with polite applause, but the press coverage of the address reflected the intense disapproval African Americans felt toward the president's plea for patience.[1]

Eisenhower's comments to the Negro Publishers' Association, coming as they did from his heart rather than from his notes, reflect the two fundamental beliefs that formed the basis of his policy on black civil rights. The first was that the role of the federal government in this field should be limited to those areas where it had direct jurisdiction. This enabled Eisenhower to make significant progress in the desegregation of the District of Columbia and the U.S. military, but it allowed the southern states to delay the extension of civil rights within their own jurisdictions. The second of these fundamental beliefs was that people's feelings on the subject of race could not be changed through legislation or executive action. Eisenhower believed that only the passage of time would end racial discord in America. This belief alienated many African Americans, not only because it played into the hands of southern segregationists attempting to delay compliance with Supreme Court decisions, but because, more than seventy-five years after the end of Reconstruction, most blacks felt they had waited long enough.[2]

Although Eisenhower had assured his friend General Chynoweth that his dedication to the "middle way" excluded "the field of moral values," his civil rights policy remained consistent with his belief that "anything that affects or is proposed for masses of humans is wrong if the position it seeks is at either end of possible argument."[3] Most would consider civil rights to be a moral values issue, but Eisenhower pursued the "middle way" here just as he did in other areas. In this case he sought a position between African Americans and liberals who wanted equal opportunities and immediate integration, on the one hand, and segregationists and conservatives who opposed any action by the federal government in what they considered a matter for state and local government, on the other.

Desegregating Areas of Federal Jurisdiction

In Eisenhower's first State of the Union address he promised to use "whatever authority exists in the Office of the President" to end segregation in the District of Columbia, the federal government, and the armed forces.[4] Implementation of this pledge was, initially, made more difficult by the ruling of a federal circuit court in *District of Columbia v. John R. Thompson Co.,* just two days after the inauguration. In this case, involving segregated restaurants in Washington, D.C., the circuit court ruled that the "lost laws"—laws prohibiting segregation, passed by District of Columbia legislative assemblies during Reconstruction—were invalid. In one of the first acts of the new administration, Attorney General Herbert Brownell filed a "friend of the court" brief with the U.S. Supreme Court on March 10 opposing the court of appeals ruling on the Thompson case. Brownell argued that the District of Columbia had the authority to enact antidiscrimination laws similar to those of the territories. On June 8, the Supreme Court upheld the 1872 law banning racial discrimination in public restaurants.[5]

The Supreme Court's decision in the Thompson case assisted Eisenhower in his desire to make the nation's capital a "showplace of peaceful civil rights progress."[6] Armed with this ruling, the administration began to persuade local business owners to desegregate. Eisenhower himself got involved in the process, asking his Hollywood studio executive friends to put pressure on Washington movie theater owners to desegregate their establishments. By the end of the year these activities had yielded a fair amount of success. Segregation had officially ended in the District of Columbia's hotels, theaters, and restaurants. These results, coming in only his first year in office, won Eisenhower the praise of local civil rights advocates, but they were only a small step toward eliminating the racial prejudice that permeated society in Washington, D.C.[7]

The case of E. Frederic Morrow, a black executive, is an interesting case study on the state of race relations in Washington in the 1950s. In August 1952, Morrow took a leave of absence from his public affairs position at the Columbia Broadcasting System (CBS) in New York to serve as a consultant for Eisenhower's presidential campaign. After the election, President-elect Eisenhower asked Sherman Adams to identify some qualified blacks to serve in the executive branch. Adams told Morrow he had been impressed with his work on the campaign and offered him a White House job. Morrow, who had never considered permanently leaving his job at CBS for a career in politics, was surprised. He agreed to take the position, but he made it clear he had no desire to be the president's advisor on minority affairs. On Adams's advice Morrow tendered his resignation at CBS.

When inauguration day arrived, two months after Morrow's resignation from CBS, he still had not received official confirmation of a White House position and his personal savings were dwindling quickly. Once the Eisenhower staff moved into the White House, Morrow had difficulty getting through to his former contacts. Three months after the inauguration, Bernard Shanley, special counsel to the president, returned Morrow's call to tell him that he was sorry but there was no position available for him at the White House. Morrow was later offered and took the position of advisor on business affairs in the Department of Commerce. For a black man in 1953 this was a position of great significance, but Morrow could not help but think of it as a consolation prize.

Two years later Morrow received a phone call from Sherman Adams, who was now White House chief of staff, telling him to report to his office "on the double." Morrow was finally given a position at the White House as administrative officer for special projects. He was the first black man to hold such a position. Morrow later found out that the delay regarding his White House position was due to a "high-ranking staff member" who had threatened to walk out and take his staff with him if Morrow was given a job. Petty jealousies continued to plague Morrow even after he was given his job. White House staff members are normally commissioned in a ceremony attended by the president shortly after they take office. Morrow did not receive his official commission until 1958, more than three years after he had started. Eisenhower, embarrassed by the delay, did not want to draw attention to the ceremony and did not attend.[8]

Morrow's difficulties did not end when he was finally given a position at the White House. Despite his status as a member of the president's staff, he had difficulty acquiring housing suitable to perform the social functions that accompanied his official position. In the course of his duties Morrow often had difficulty gaining access to the hotels, train cars, and churches, not to mention country clubs and golf courses, where he was asked to meet his colleagues. Hotel operators even refused to place his calls to the White House. At social functions some of his coworkers, the ones Morrow referred to as "socially insecure," would act as though they did not know him, and their unsuspecting wives and other strangers would hand him their coats and car keys.[9]

Morrow's experiences proved, to a certain extent, Eisenhower's contention that it would take more than legislation or executive action to end racial discrimination. Despite this, however, Morrow tried to convince Eisenhower that urging blacks to "be patient" was not the answer. He argued that if laws were made to allow blacks to use public facilities and have equal employment opportunities, they would give whites the chance to "discover for themselves whether all of them [blacks] are scoundrels, or whether some of them are decent, and they will form their own opinion, rather than form it through hearsay or through tradition."[10]

In addition to making Washington, D.C., a "showplace of peaceful civil rights progress," Eisenhower had also promised to use his executive authority to wipe out segregation in the armed forces. Anyone who had followed Eisenhower's military career might have doubted this promise. In 1948 he had testified before a congressional committee that he was opposed to desegregation in the military below the platoon level. In this hearing Eisenhower said, "If we attempt merely by passing a lot of laws to force someone to like someone else, we are just going to get into trouble."[11]

Despite Eisenhower's opinion, in July 1948 President Truman issued Executive Order 9981 calling for a progressive breakdown of segregation barriers in the military, to be completed by June 1954.[12] This order was responsible for considerable progress. By the late summer of 1953 the U.S. Army, which had the most black personnel, reported that only eight all-black units remained and that 95 percent of its black troops were in desegregated units. The U.S. Air Force and the U.S. Marines, with smaller numbers of black troops, were able to desegregate more quickly, finishing their programs by late 1952.[13]

Truman's desegregation of military units did not mean the end of racial discrimination in the military. Black servicemen still encountered difficulties in many areas of military life such as promotion and transfer, job assignment, medical care, housing, recreation, and education. Conditions were particularly bad at southern naval bases such as those in Norfolk, Virginia, and Charleston, South Carolina. After the conditions at these bases were publicized in March 1953, Navy Secretary Robert Anderson issued a directive pledging to dedicate the U.S. Navy to racial equality at all of its facilities. When conditions had not improved by June, Congressman Adam Clayton Powell (D-NY) wrote to the navy secretary listing the specific charges of racial segregation and charging Anderson himself with "insubordination" for dragging his feet on this issue.

In August 1953, Anderson issued a statement to all commanders of southern naval bases "requesting" them to "steadily and expeditiously" end all segregation. After hearing news reports quoting some of these commanders, including the commander at Norfolk, as saying that they would not proceed until ordered to do so, Anderson reissued the letters, "directing" rather than "requesting" them to desegregate their bases. Furthermore, he required them to issue reports every thirty days on their progress in this area. Once the order had been given, the desegregation of southern naval bases proceeded quickly. By the end of November, fifty-nine out of sixty naval bases were desegregated. Eisenhower was impressed that Anderson had handled the situation without drawing too much attention to it. He later rewarded the Texas Democrat by promoting him to assistant secretary of Defense.[14]

The desegregation of schools for the dependents of military personnel proved more difficult than the desegregation of other base facilities. This was because of the variety of different situations involved. Some schools were entirely under federal control while others were jointly administered by the federal government and local school boards. At a March 19, 1953, press conference, reporters questioned Eisenhower about the existence of segregated schools on military bases in the South. In response, the White House released a memorandum from Eisenhower to Secretary of Defense Charles Wilson directing him to look into the situation of jointly operated schools. The memorandum stated that, if the federal and local governments could not come to terms on the integration of these schools, then other arrangements would be considered. These would include the possibility of allocating the necessary funds for the federal government to take over complete control of these schools.[15]

On March 25 Eisenhower announced that, by the beginning of the fall 1953 term, all schools operated by the federal government would be opened on a completely integrated basis.[16] Despite the president's letter to Secretary Wilson, however, the administration was making little progress on the subject of jointly operated schools. Secretary Hobby of the Department of Health, Education, and Welfare, the department that administered the base schools, tried to explain the delay by pointing out to the president the many problems associated with integrating such schools. She recommended that the federal government delay action until the Supreme Court's ruling on school segregation, expected in early 1954.[17]

Once again, Representative Powell forced Eisenhower's hand. In a telegram to Eisenhower that he leaked to the press on June 3, 1953, Powell charged that Hobby (a Democrat, Texan, and former head of the Women's Army Corps) had "virtually countermanded" Eisenhower's stated policy regarding the integration of base schools. Attempting to defuse the situation, Eisenhower overcame his initial anger with Powell and made a conciliatory reply promising to "carry out every pledge I made with regard to segregation." Eisenhower also promised to make "inquiries of the officials to which you have referred." Powell released the president's letter along with his own reply, which referred to Eisenhower's note as a "Magna Carta for minorities and a Second Emancipation Proclamation."[18]

Despite Powell's hyperbole, it was another eight months before the administration issued a formal statement on jointly operated base schools. Its stated goal was to completely desegregate such schools by the beginning of the 1955–1956 school year. If the appropriate arrangements could not be made with local authorities, the federal government would take over the schools. The program was, for the most part, successful. In most cases, schools were integrated by local school boards. The schools on seven bases were taken over when local officials refused to desegregate them. Only Fort Meade, Maryland, and Pine Bluff Arsenal, Arkansas, remained segregated. Both of these bases had long-term leases with local school boards and, therefore, could not be taken over by the federal government.[19]

Brown v. The Board of Education of Topeka, Kansas

The controversy regarding the integration of schools on military bases was mild compared to what the Eisenhower administration would face when it came to the desegregation of public schools. Eisenhower's desire to keep the federal government out of public school desegregation was thwarted by the Supreme Court's ruling on *Brown v. The Board of Education of Topeka, Kansas*. The Court's May 17, 1954, decision on this case declared that "in the field of public education, the doctrine of 'separate but equal' has no place," thereby denying segregated schools protection under the Court's 1896 decision in *Plessy v. Ferguson*. One year later, on May 31, 1955, the Court ruled that the desegregation of public schools should proceed "with all deliberate speed." While the primary responsibility for desegregation lay with the local school boards, these decisions thrust Eisenhower into the heart of the most controversial issue of the decade. *Brown v. Board* had made desegregation the law of the land, and Eisenhower, sworn by his presidential oath to uphold that law, could not long refuse to play a role.[20]

Eisenhower wanted to keep the federal government out of the controversy surrounding the desegregation of public schools in the South. Many have used this fact to argue that Eisenhower disagreed with the Supreme Court's decision in *Brown v. Board* and, because of that, regretted his appointment of Chief Justice Earl Warren to the Court. Eisenhower is often cited as having declared that the appointment of Warren was "the biggest damn fool mistake I ever made." An important element of this argument is the belief that Warren had been promised a spot on the Supreme Court as part of a political payoff for pledging his delegates to Eisenhower during the 1952 Republican National Convention in Chicago, when both men were candidates for the Republican nomination.[21]

At the 1952 convention Warren, then governor of California, was running as a "favorite son" candidate, and all California delegates were pledged to him until he released them. In a close nomination, the delegates of a "favorite son," particularly one from a large state, could be used to throw the nomination to another candidate. After the first ballot, however,

Eisenhower was only nine votes away from securing the nomination, and Warren still made no move to throw his state's seventy votes to him. In fact there was no change in the California delegation until after Eisenhower had been nominated and a motion was made to make the nomination unanimous. This suggests that no deal was made between Eisenhower and Warren. Despite these facts, many contemporaries believed a deal had been made. Barry Goldwater, for instance, recalled: "It was Lodge and Brownell who made the deal with Earl Warren. In return for the California governor's support in Chicago, they promised him an appointment as Chief Justice of the Supreme Court. Ike kept that commitment. He was never happy about it." Goldwater must have realized that Brownell and Lodge could not have known the position of chief justice would be open during Eisenhower's term.[22]

Herbert Brownell, an instrumental member of Eisenhower's campaign team and his first attorney general, disputed there had been a convention deal between Eisenhower and Warren promising the California governor a spot on the Supreme Court. According to Brownell, an offer of the "first vacancy" was made to Warren in December 1952, six months after the convention.[23] Eisenhower also stated that "a few months prior" to Chief Justice Frederick M. Vinson's death on September 8, 1953, he told Warren he was "considering" appointing him to the Supreme Court and that he was "inclined" to do so if a vacancy occurred. When Vinson died, Eisenhower felt no obligation to appoint Warren, however, since no one had anticipated that the "first vacancy" would be the position of chief justice.[24] Eisenhower considered the possibility of promoting one of the associate justices but ruled the possibility out because all were either too old, in failing health, or too liberal. All of the justices had been appointed by Democrats; only Justice Harold Burton was a Republican. Eisenhower also considered a number of other possibilities, including Secretary of State John Foster Dulles who turned down the job, but in the end he came back to Warren.[25]

At the time of Warren's appointment the *Brown* case was already before the Supreme Court. Eisenhower was well aware that the chief justice he appointed to take Vinson's place would play an important role in a decision of great importance to American race relations. Eisenhower was also aware of Warren's reputation as a progressive in this area, with a history of supporting fair employment legislation for black citizens.[26] Eisenhower, in fact, admired Warren's nonpartisan California administration. Defending his choice to his more conservative brother Edgar, who called the appointment "a tragedy," Eisenhower wrote, "To my mind he [Warren] is a statesman. We have too few of these. . . . [He is] a man of national stature . . . of unimpeachable integrity, of middle-of-the-road views, and with a splendid record. . . . I am not trying to please anybody politically."[27]

The Senate was in recess in October 1953 when Eisenhower appointed Warren chief justice, but they took up his nomination when they returned in January 1954. With the help of Democrats and other conservative

Republicans, Senator William Langer (ND), chair of the Senate Committee on the Judiciary held up the nomination in committee for two months. This prompted Eisenhower to say that if "Republicans as a body should try to repudiate him [Warren], I shall leave the Republican Party and try to organize an intelligent group of independents, however small."[28]

As to whether Eisenhower ever regretted the appointment of Warren, it is difficult to say for sure. He certainly never publicly made the comment that appointing Warren was the "the biggest damn fool mistake I ever made." Brownell, Eisenhower's closest advisor on judicial matters, said that Eisenhower never made the comment to him either, and Brownell doubted he would have made it to others, stating that it did not reflect the president's views and would have been "uncharacteristic." Brownell did admit the possibility that Eisenhower may have made the remark in an "offhand" way, perhaps when dealing with someone who hoped that Eisenhower regretted the choice.[29]

Another indication that Eisenhower's opinion of Warren did not change after the Court's decision in the *Brown* case was his reaction to the possibility that Warren might run for president in 1956. In a news conference in January of that year, before Eisenhower had decided whether he would run for a second term, reporters inquired whether he thought Warren would make a good candidate. Eisenhower, who did not believe Warren had any desire to run, responded he did not think that the Supreme Court and politics should be mixed.[30] Later, after Press Secretary James Hagerty told the president that Warren had been annoyed by the remark, Eisenhower wrote in his diary that, if this meant that Warren was in fact considering a run for the presidency, "it would be a great relief," for he could then retire with the knowledge that Warren would continue his legacy.[31]

Although the Supreme Court's decision in the *Brown* case did not make Eisenhower regret his decision to appoint Warren, he was not in complete agreement with the Court on the question of implementing desegregation. In addition to his belief that legislative action could not change the minds of segregationists, there were political implications to consider. In 1952 Eisenhower had been the first Republican presidential candidate to make significant inroads into the "solid South," winning the electoral votes of four southern and three border states.[32] Most of those in the South had been "Eisenhower Democrats" who voted for him because of his personal popularity and status as a war hero, not because of his party affiliation. Eisenhower's political advisors believed that if he came out strongly in favor of the Supreme Court's ruling in *Brown v. Board* he may win some additional votes from blacks and liberals in the North who were in favor of desegregation. These converts, however, would not make up for the white southern votes they believed he would certainly lose in the event he took such a stand.[33]

The White House was deluged with letters from the South expressing concern and resentment over the *Brown v. Board* decision, many of which blamed Eisenhower personally. "I am one of the many young Democrats in the South who foolishly jumped the political fence," one letter began. "You said that you would represent us and give us a change. The recent biased Supreme Court decision on segregation in our public schools, demonstrates to us what kind of change you meant. . . . Earl Warren was appointed to the Supreme Court mainly because of his left-wing liberal viewpoints. He was acceptable to the enemies of the southern white man, and would support the pinkish left-wing theories of centralized government."[34]

Rather than writing off such sentiments as reactionary or obstructionist, Eisenhower became bothered that white southerners considered *Brown v. Board* a Republican, or worse, an Eisenhower administration decision. He was quick to point out that the *Brown* case was before the Court before he took office, and aside from appointing Warren, he had done nothing to affect the decision. To critics who blamed the *Brown v. Board* decision on Warren, Eisenhower replied that it made no sense to blame a unanimous decision on one justice, particularly one who had been on the Court such a short time.[35]

Eisenhower was also uncomfortable with the role Attorney General Herbert Brownell played in the case. In June 1953 the Supreme Court invited the attorney general to file an *amicus curae* ("friend of the court") brief stating his opinion on whether segregated public schools in the South were in violation of the Fourteenth Amendment. Brownell was of the opinion that segregation by race in public schools was unconstitutional, and he was willing to share this opinion with the Supreme Court. Eisenhower, unfamiliar with the Supreme Court's procedures and the history of constitutional law, was taken aback by this invitation and considered it a breech of the separation of powers. In a memo to Brownell, Eisenhower stated his opposition to the request: "The court cannot possibly abdicate; consequently it cannot delegate its responsibility and it would be futile for the Attorney General to attempt to sit as a court and reach a conclusion as to the true meaning of the Fourteenth Amendment."[36]

The president did not realize that it was common for the Supreme Court to request such *amicus curae* briefs. The Justice Department had filed many such briefs in the past. In fact the Truman administration had already filed one on *Brown v. Board,* taking a strong stand against the constitutionality of segregated public schools. Gradually, Eisenhower became aware of these facts and realized that such a brief would have to be filed, but he was still uncomfortable with the idea.

Governor James F. Byrnes of South Carolina wrote to the president to try to influence how the administration would respond to the Court's invitation. Eisenhower was already concerned about how the executive branch would enforce a Supreme Court ruling that segregated public schools were unconstitutional. Governor Byrnes predicted that such a ruling would result in the southern states virtually shutting down their public school systems and giving state funds to private schools for whites only. This made the president even more certain that the White House should stay out of the controversial issue as much as possible. In Eisenhower's response to Byrnes, he disassociated himself from the *amicus curae* brief that Brownell would file on behalf of the Justice Department. "It became clear to me that the questions asked of the Attorney General by the Supreme Court demanded answers that could be determined only by lawyers and historians," Eisenhower responded. "Consequently, I have been compelled to turn over to the Attorney General and his associates full responsibility in the matter. He and I agreed that his brief would reflect the conviction of the Department of Justice as to the *legal aspects* of the case. . . . It is clear that the Attorney General has to act according to his own conviction and understanding."[37]

The most controversial position Eisenhower took in the field of civil rights, perhaps the most controversial position he took in any field during his presidency, was his refusal to state approval of the *Brown* decision. His public response was limited to statements saying that the Court's decision was law and that he would abide by it. In his memoirs, Eisenhower later rationalized that, while he agreed with the Court's unanimous ruling, he refused to say whether he agreed with it out of principle. "I believed that if I should express, publicly, either approval or disapproval of a Supreme Court decision in one case, I would be obliged to do so in many, if not all cases," Eisenhower wrote. "Inevitably I would eventually be drawn into a public statement of disagreement with some decision creating a suspicion that my vigor or enforcement would, in such cases, be in doubt." Moreover, he said he believed that "To indulge in a practice of approving or criticizing Court decisions could tend to lower the dignity of government, and would in the long run, be hurtful."[38]

Eisenhower's failure to show support for the *Brown* decision should not be interpreted as outright disagreement with the Supreme Court's verdict. He was not a segregationist. He did, however, have a certain amount of empathy for white southern views. Most of Eisenhower's closest friends were southerners, and he had spent the majority of his life on segregated army posts. While he had little patience for those who talked of nullification or noncompliance with the Court's decision, he empathized with the average white southerner who was apprehensive about the effect the *Brown v. Board* decision would have in the South. He did not wish to criminalize people who had until now, by virtue of the 1896 *Plessy v. Ferguson* decision, been within the law. Because of this, Eisenhower hoped that the Court would adopt a stand of gradualism in implementing the *Brown v. Board* decision.

In the year between the Court's May 1954 decision and May 1955 when it announced how the verdict would be implemented, Eisenhower went on record as favoring a gradual implementation of school desegregation. In a presidential statement read to the delegates present at the Forty-fifth Annual Meeting of the National Association for the Advancement of Colored People (NAACP) in June 1954, Eisenhower said: "We must have patience without compromise of principle. We must have understanding without disregard for differences of opinion which actually exist. We must have continued social progress, calmly but persistently made."[39]

Eisenhower hoped that the Court would adopt such a stand as well. In a letter to his lifelong friend Swede Hazlett in October, he wrote, "The segregation issue will, I think, become acute or tend to die out according to the character of the procedure orders that the Court will probably issue this winter. My own guess is this—they will be very moderate and secure a maximum of initiative to local courts."[40]

Once again the Supreme Court invited the attorney general to file a brief stating his opinion regarding the decision it would make in 1955 regarding the implementation of desegregation. This time there is no record of Eisenhower considering such a request an abdication of the Court's powers. All indications are that he hoped the Court would adopt his view that the decision should be implemented gradually. At a press conference on November 23, 1954, the day before Brownell filed his brief, Eisenhower hinted at what it contained. In response to a question about his views on implementation, the president referred to "great practical problems" and "deep-seated emotions." He said he hoped that the Court would "take into consideration these great emotional strains" and "try to devise a way where, under some form of decentralized process, we can bring this about."[41]

The brief filed by Brownell the next day reflected Eisenhower's preference for a gradual, decentralized implementation of the Court's decision that would take into account circumstances unique to the local situations. The brief recommended that the federal court system serve as the overseer of the desegregation process. Local school boards should develop and implement programs under the supervision of the federal district court that served the affected school district. The brief recommended that these district courts should enforce the desegregation of schools as "circumstances permit."[42]

The administration had some cause to be pleased with the Supreme Court's May 1955 decision on implementation. The Court placed primary responsibility for developing desegregation plans with the local school boards. The district courts would have jurisdiction and were directed to take into account local factors when judging implementation plans. The school boards, however, were to make a "prompt and reasonable start" and proceed "with all deliberate speed." The burden of justifying delays was to be borne by the local authorities.[43]

Although the Supreme Court had adopted the decentralized, gradual approach to desegregation recommended by the administration through Brownell's brief, Eisenhower was still not entirely pleased with the outcome. In future years, when civil unrest in the Deep South forced a presidential response, Eisenhower would often blame the troubles on the Supreme Court. To his secretary, Ann Whitman, Eisenhower said, "The troubles brought about by the Supreme Court decision [*Brown v. Board*] are the most important problem facing the government, domestically, today." When Mrs. Whitman asked what alternative course the Court might have adopted, the president responded that "Perhaps they could have demanded that segregation be eliminated in graduate schools, later in colleges, later in high schools, as a means of overcoming the passionate and inbred atti-tudes" that had developed over generations.[44] To his friend Swede Hazlett, Eisenhower complained: "No single event has so disturbed the domestic scene in many years as did the Supreme Court's decision of 1954 in the school desegregation case." This decision and other subsequent ones, he said, "have interpreted the Constitution in such fashion as to put heavier responsibilities than before on the federal government in the matter of assuring to each citizen his guaranteed constitutional rights."[45] These comments, however, were made only in private and only to trusted friends and associates.

In public, Eisenhower still refused to give his outright support to the decision. He urged his cabinet members, when speaking on the issue, to stress the need for "calmness, sanity, and reason" in the hopes they might pacify the racial tension that had been growing in the South since the *Brown v. Board* verdict. He also expressed his disappointment in the fact that southern authorities were devoting their energy to acts of defiance rather than to developing plans to comply with the Court's decision.[46] Eisenhower also realized, in the wake of the decision, the importance of appointing federal judges who had not publicly opposed the ruling and would faithfully uphold it in their districts. Occasionally, southern senators would appeal directly to Eisenhower to change his appointments for posts in their states, even offering legislative support if he would nominate can-didates who were unsupportive of civil rights. According to the attorney general, Eisenhower never failed to support one of his nominees in such a situation. The president even appointed a northern Democrat, William J. Brennan, to the Supreme Court in 1956 to show that partisan politics was not the major consideration in his judicial appointments.[47]

The Civil Rights Act of 1957

In 1956 and 1957 the emphasis of the Eisenhower administration's civil rights program shifted away from desegregation and toward the passage of a new civil rights act that would, among other things, create mechanisms to enforce the right of southern blacks to vote. There were several reasons for this shift. First, the administration wished to shift emphasis away from the explosive issue of desegregated schools; second, Eisenhower believed that if blacks had the right to vote, they could more readily achieve their other civil rights without the federal government having to step in; and finally, with blacks beginning to play an important role in northern poli-tics, liberal Republicans and northern Democrats were anxious to tap into the southern black vote.

On January 5, 1956, in his State of the Union address, Eisenhower made his first proposal for civil rights legislation. He recommended that Congress create a bipartisan commission to look into why, in some areas, "allegations persist that Negro citizens are being deprived of their right to vote and are likewise being subjected to unwarranted economic pressures."[48] In light of the actual conditions faced by southern blacks in the 1950s, referring to civil rights violations as mere "allegations" was definitely the understatement of the evening. Asking for the creation of a bipartisan commission was only the least controversial of a number of proposals Brownell had been working on since the 1955 *Brown* decision.[49] When the cabinet considered Brownell's proposals for inclusion in the State of the Union address, members had been reluctant to include ones that would alienate the South. Instead they wanted to emphasize achievements and uncontroversial issues.[50]

Brownell presented his full civil rights program to Eisenhower and the cabinet in March. The first proposal was to create the bipartisan commission on civil rights that the president had mentioned in his State of the Union address. To this Brownell added three others. The second proposal was for the creation of a new Civil Rights Division in the Department of Justice, to be headed by an assistant attorney general. The third would give authority to the federal government to use civil procedures for the protection of civil rights. This was the most controversial component of Brownell's proposal. It would allow the attorney general to sue to redress all civil rights violations in cases where the Supreme Court had defined the civil right as one protected by the Constitution. This provision sought to implement the promise of equal protection under the law made by the Fourteenth Amendment. It would provide a mechanism for the Department of Justice to get involved in cases where it believed that local courts had not provided this protection. The last provision of the program would allow for broader statutes to protect the right of blacks to vote, including civil remedies for enforcement. Since most elections in the South were decided in the Democratic primaries, with the Democratic nominee running unopposed in the general election, this provision would need to cover primary elections as well.[51]

Secretary of Defense Charles Wilson and Secretary of Health, Education, and Welfare Marion Folsom favored sending only the first two provisions. If these proposals passed, the bipartisan congressional commission and the Civil Rights Division in the Justice Department could devote further study to the other proposals and make recommendations later. Anything more at this time, they believed, would only "add fuel to the fire." Secretary of Labor James Mitchell backed Brownell on all four proposals. Eisenhower did not state his opinion at the cabinet meeting but told Brownell that he would give him his decision later. In the later meeting, Eisenhower told the attorney general he would support all but the controversial third provision that would allow the attorney general to sue to redress civil rights violations. The president, however, did tell Brownell that he could submit all four proposals to Congress as the Department of Justice's plan. Brownell agreed to this and submitted the entire program to Congress on April 9, 1956. Later, during the 1956 campaign, Eisenhower came out in favor of all four proposals.[52]

Republican legislative leaders were torn over the bill. They liked the idea of exposing the regional split within the Democratic Party, but they feared that supporting Brownell's bill would hurt their chances of making further Republican gains in the South. They thought that the bill asked for too much. Eisenhower disagreed, believing the proposal was in keeping with his pursuit of the "middle way." He said he had been over the whole proposal very carefully and that he "couldn't imagine anything more moderate or less provocative." In fact, he argued, Congress was lucky to have such a moderate bill before it, since "radicals" on Brownell's staff had wanted to go a lot further. In response to criticism that had begun to appear in the southern press, Eisenhower complained that southerners "start to shout on seeing the words 'civil rights' without reading what was in the proposal." On the other hand, he continued, "The civil rights extremists never stop to consider that although you can send in troops, troops can't make anyone operate schools. Private schools can be set up, and Negroes would get no education at all."[53]

On May 21, 1956, the House Judiciary Committee reported a bill to carry out the administration's civil rights program. On July 13, before debate could begin on the House floor, eighty-three southern representatives, four of them Republicans, presented a "Civil Rights Manifesto," urging Congress to "join with us in the employment of every available legal and parliamentary weapon to defeat this sinister and iniquitous proposal." Many of the signatories had also signed an earlier "Declaration of Constitutional Principles," criticizing the Supreme Court's decisions in the *Brown v. Board* case. Despite the Manifesto, the bill was passed by the House 279–126 (R 168–24). Parliamentary maneuvering in the Senate Judiciary Committee, chaired by James O. Eastland (D-MS), prevented the bill from reaching the floor of the Senate before the Eighty-fourth Congress adjourned.[54]

In 1956 Eisenhower was reelected in a landslide, but he failed to carry either house of Congress. There was, however, some good news for the Republican Party. A *Congressional Quarterly* study of the election results showed that the African American vote had reached substantial proportions in northern industrial cities and that the northern black vote was shifting from the Democratic to the Republican Party. Ironically, Eisenhower was able to pick up additional northern black votes while continuing to gain ground with white southerners. The president had added the border states of Kentucky and West Virginia to his southern inroads, while losing only Missouri. Eisenhower explained this by saying, "The administration had steered a difficult course between extremist firebrands and extremist diehards. This was due to conviction, not politics."[55]

Civil rights was given a higher priority in the 1957 State of the Union address than in the previous year, but the message was simple. "Last year the Administration recommended to the Congress a four-point program to reinforce civil rights," Eisenhower said. "I urge that the Congress enact this legislation."[56] The *Congressional Quarterly* study showing a shift in the northern black vote had renewed interest in both parties for civil rights legislation, but the administration's bill continued to be plagued by southern intransigence.

Once again, the House led the way. The Judiciary Committee reported a bill that left the administration's civil rights program relatively intact. On June 18, 1957, this bill was passed by the full House without change, 286–126 (R 168–19). Eastland's Senate Judiciary Committee had still not sent a civil rights bill to the floor, however, and it seemed that the House bill was doomed to the same fate as the 1956 version of the bill—referral to Eastland's committee where it would never be heard from again. Hoping to avoid this, Senator Paul Douglas (D-IL) and Minority Leader William Knowland (R-CA) conspired to circumvent the Judiciary Committee by placing the House bill directly on the Senate calendar where it could be called up for consideration at any time by a majority vote. This move prompted a point of order by Senator Richard Russell (D-GA). The point of order was rejected 45–39 in the first crucial civil rights vote in the Senate in 1957. Among the thirty-nine who voted against the House bill being placed directly on the Senate calendar were five Republicans: Barry Goldwater (AZ), George Malone (NV), Karl Mundt (SD), John Williams (DE), and Milton Young (ND).[57]

On July 8, Senator Knowland moved that the Senate begin consideration of the House bill. After eight days of debate the motion was passed, and on July 16 the Senate finally took up the issue of civil rights.[58] Senate debate on the civil rights bill concentrated on two key points: section 3, the most controversial section of the proposed legislation; and the issue of whether those cited with criminal contempt of court under sections 3 and 4 of the proposed legislation would be entitled to a jury trial. Section 3 of the administration's bill empowered the attorney general to sue anyone who had violated a person's civil rights. If the suit was successful, then a federal court would issue an order against any such action. A person who violated such an order would be cited with civil or criminal contempt of court. This section, which had been virtually ignored in the House, was attacked by southerners in the Senate. They argued that its breadth would allow the federal government to intervene in all types of local affairs, forcing such things as the immediate integration of housing and schools. Furthermore, they added, the act would be enforceable by an 1866 statute allowing the president to use federal troops to enforce or prevent violation of civil rights legislation.[59]

On July 2, Senator Russell said that section 3 was so "cunningly contrived" that even the president did not understand it. Eisenhower did not help the administration's case, when in a news conference the next day, he admitted he was not clear on the implications of the section. When Eisenhower was asked if he was willing to have the section rewritten, he responded: "I would not want to answer this in detail . . . I was reading part of the bill this morning and . . . there were certain phrases I didn't completely understand." Emphasizing that he was not a lawyer, Eisenhower promised to consult with the attorney general "and see exactly what they do mean."[60]

Knowland and Hubert Humphrey (D-MN) tried to save section 3 by offering an amendment that repealed the 1866 statute giving the president power to use troops to enforce civil rights legislation. The amendment passed 90–0 on July 22, but opposition to the section remained. Two days later section 3 was eliminated from the bill by a vote of 52–38. Eighteen Republicans voted in favor of elimination, but this is not a good gauge of their stand on civil rights since many of them voted in favor of elimination out of fear that section 3 would sink any chance of passing a civil rights act. Eisenhower, who had never been enthusiastic about this provision of the bill, conceded the point. When the House began considering Senate changes to the bill, Eisenhower told a press conference that he would not insist on any portion of section 3 of the bill being restored.[61]

The other major stumbling block for the administration's bill was whether those who had been cited for criminal contempt for violating someone's civil rights would be entitled to a jury trial. A criminal contempt case is one in which a court sentences an individual to a specified term because that individual has breached public order by challenging the authority of that court. Normally criminal contempt is decided by a court without a jury, but Reconstruction Era civil rights acts had included the right to a trial by jury for those cited with criminal contempt. In a civil contempt case, a court attempts to enforce compliance by sentencing an individual to an unspecified term, which ends when the individual agrees to comply. Civil contempt cases are always decided by a court alone, without a jury. In 1957 the issue was first brought up by southern Democrats in the House who claimed that it would be a violation of a defendant's constitutional rights for a federal court to try them without a jury. Supporters of the administration's bill argued that there was no constitutional right to trial by jury in contempt of court cases. Implicit in this argument was the assumption that southern juries would not convict a white man for violating the civil rights of a black man. If this was true, then granting a jury trial in such cases would have the effect of nullifying the enforcement mechanism of the law.

Five attempts to attach a jury trial amendment to the legislation were defeated in the House. The danger for the administration was that in the Senate enough Republicans would join with southern Democrats to allow such an amendment to pass. Despite the fact that it was well known that such an amendment would cripple the bill, many Republicans and some northern Democrats found it hard to justify voting against something that sounded so fundamental as the right to trial by jury. In meetings with the president, Republican legislative leaders said that those who supported the jury trial amendment feared that the bill would make federal judges into "Gestapos" who could arbitrarily sentence civil rights violators to long prison terms. Eisenhower and the attorney general disputed this, reminding the congressional leaders that cases originating in the South would be tried in southern courts. The president remarked that it was "a mystery" to him how any Republicans could fail to support such "mild" proposals as the ones before them.[62]

On August 2 the Senate, by a vote of 51–42, passed an amendment that guaranteed a defendant's right to a jury trial in all criminal contempt cases, not just those arising out of the civil rights bill. Twelve Republicans voted in favor of the amendment. Eisenhower called the passage of the amendment "one of the most serious political defeats of the past four years."[63] He immediately issued a statement saying how "bitterly disappointing" the vote was and claimed that the amendment would "make largely ineffective the basic purpose of the bill—that of protecting promptly and effectively every American in his right to vote."[64]

On August 7, the Senate passed the amended bill, and two weeks of discussions on a compromise began between the House and Senate. House Republicans suggested that the right to a jury trial be limited to criminal contempt cases arising only out of the bill in question, not all criminal contempt cases. Furthermore, in civil rights cases, judges would have discretion over whether to call a jury, but if they imposed a penalty greater than ninety days in jail or a three-hundred-dollar fine the defendant would have the right to a new trial with a jury. Both houses agreed to the compromise, and on August 27 the House passed it. In the Senate, Strom Thurmond (D-SC) waged a one-man battle against the bill delaying a vote on it with a twenty-four-hour-and-eighteen-minute filibuster, a record for a single person. After Thurmond collapsed on the evening of August 29, the Senate passed the bill.[65]

The question that remained was whether the president should sign the bill. Several prominent black leaders had written him following the Senate's adoption of the jury trial amendment and urged him not to sign it. Ralph Bunche, distinguished scholar and recipient of the Nobel Peace Prize, wrote, "It would be better to have no bill than one as emasculated as that which has come out of the Senate." Baseball great Jackie Robinson sent a telegram: "Am opposed to civil rights bill in its present form. . . . disagree that half loaf is better than none. Have waited this long for bill with meaning—can wait a little longer." A. Philip Randolph, president of the Brotherhood of Sleeping Car Porters, agreed, telling Eisenhower the present bill was "worse than no bill at all."[66]

The Republican legislative leaders urged Eisenhower to sign the bill. Most were in favor of getting some kind of civil rights bill signed into law in the current session. Senate Minority Leader William Knowland asserted that this was the best the Eighty-fifth Congress could do since there was no chance of eliminating the jury trial amendment. He favored signing the bill, getting the new assistant attorney general and the Civil Rights Commission, and building from there.[67] Martin Luther King Jr., then emerging as a prominent leader in the civil rights movement, also thought that Eisenhower should sign the bill. In a letter to Vice President Nixon, King said, "The present bill is far better than no bill at all. . . . I feel that civil rights legislation is urgent now, and the present limited bill will go a long way to insure it. So it is my hope that the President will not veto the bill."[68] Despite Eisenhower's desire to "prevent the pseudo liberals from getting away with their sudden alliance with the southerners on a sham bill," he decided to sign it. On September 9 the Civil Rights Act of 1957 became law.[69]

The sense of victory had been spoiled somewhat by the attachment of the jury trial amendment, but the Civil Rights Act of 1957 was still the first civil rights legislation since Reconstruction, and Attorney General Herbert Brownell thought that its passage offered a fitting end for his tenure in government. Circumstances quickly changed, however, forcing a postponement of Brownell's retirement plans. Just five days after the Senate passed the Civil Rights Act, Governor Orval Faubus of Arkansas began using the National Guard to prevent black students from enrolling at Little Rock Central High School. Eisenhower's worst fears regarding the *Brown v. Board* decision had been realized. He now had to contemplate the use of troops to force a state governor to comply with a federal court order in a school desegregation case. "Well, of course you can't leave now," the president told Brownell. "It would look as though you and I disagreed on the course of action at Little Rock."[70]

Little Rock

In May 1955 the U.S. Federal Court for the Eastern District of Arkansas accepted a desegregation plan submitted by the Board of Education of Little Rock. The plan called for the complete integration of all of Little Rock's public schools by 1963. The Arkansas NAACP challenged the board's plan, charging that it took too long to achieve its goal. The result of this challenge was an announcement by the board that it would, in compliance with the court's orders, initiate its plan with the desegregation of Central High School in the fall of 1957. This announcement greatly divided the Little Rock community. On the opening day of the fall term, Governor Orval Faubus, claiming that it was necessary to maintain the peace, called out the National Guard to prevent blacks from entering the school.[71] Governor Faubus, by stepping in to prevent the Little Rock Board of Education from complying with a federal court order, had caused the federal-state confrontation over school desegregation that Eisenhower had sought to avoid since the Supreme Court's 1954 decision.

In response to Faubus's defiance of a court order, Federal District Judge Ronald N. Davies requested that the Justice Department begin collecting information concerning those individuals, including Faubus, who were preventing the desegregation of Central High School. This ended Eisenhower's hope that the crisis could be defused without the direct involvement of the executive branch. In response to a telegram in which the Arkansas governor had pleaded with the president for understanding and cooperation, Eisenhower responded that he intended to support and defend the Constitution by all legal means at his command. Eisenhower added that he expected Faubus to cooperate fully with the Justice Department's investigation.[72]

Despite Eisenhower's terse reply to Faubus's telegram, he was still seeking a way to defuse the situation before a direct confrontation became necessary. Congressman Brooks Hays (D-AR) intervened on behalf of Faubus and asked White House Chief of Staff Sherman Adams about the possibility of a meeting between Faubus and the president. Adams was convinced that Faubus realized he had made a mistake and was looking for a way out of the situation. He told the president that he thought such a meeting was a good idea, adding his belief that Faubus was not really a segregationist since his son went to an integrated college, but that he just thought that desegregation should proceed more slowly. Brownell was against such a meeting, taking the hard line that Faubus had violated a federal court order and should be forced to comply. Eisenhower rejected this argument, saying it failed to take into consideration the situation in the South. The Justice Department, he said, should make clear it only wanted to ensure that the National Guard was not being used to prevent a court order from being carried out: "By no means does the Federal government want to interfere with the governor's responsibilities." Adams's argument for a meeting appealed to Eisenhower's philosophy of gradualism and moderation, and he agreed to meet with Faubus if the governor would request a meeting and state in his request that he would be "guided by federal court orders."[73]

On September 11, Governor Faubus submitted such a request, and Adams set up a September 14 meeting between Faubus and Eisenhower.[74] The meeting was held in the president's office at the Naval Station in Newport, Rhode Island, where the president was on a working vacation. The two men were alone. Faubus went to great lengths to tell Eisenhower he was a law-abiding citizen and he recognized that federal law is supreme to state law. Eisenhower sensed that Faubus wanted to resolve the situation. He later recalled suggesting to the governor that he "Go home and not necessarily withdraw his National Guard troops, but just change their orders. . . . Tell the Guard to continue to preserve order but to allow the Negro children to attend Central High School." Eisenhower also made clear that it would not be beneficial to have "a trial of strength between the President and a Governor," because "There could only be one outcome—that is, the State would lose." He added that he "did not want to see any governor humiliated." When Faubus left, Eisenhower was under the impression that the governor had agreed he would change the National Guard's orders immediately upon returning home.[75]

Faubus returned home and, after consulting with his political advisors, decided not to change the National Guard's orders. When Eisenhower heard of this, he was furious. He telephoned Brownell in Washington and said, "You were right, Faubus broke his word." The president, however, was reluctant to use military force to make Faubus comply with the court's orders out of fear that he would shut down the public school system and that other southern states would follow suit. Brownell began to fear they would have no other choice and told the president he would begin conferring with the secretary of the army in case such a move was necessary.[76]

On September 20, Faubus failed to appear in federal court as he had been ordered, prompting Judge Davies to issue an order forbidding Faubus or the Arkansas National Guard from interfering with his previous order to integrate Central High School. That evening Faubus withdrew the National Guard, suggesting the possibility that the crisis might end without the direct confrontation Eisenhower hoped to avoid. Eisenhower's statement the next day reflected his relief that the situation seemed to be coming to an end. He asked the people of Little Rock to "preserve and respect the law—whether or not they personally agree with it," and to "vigorously oppose any violence by extremists."[77]

Eisenhower's hope that the crisis would end now that Faubus was not using the National Guard to defy the courts was not realized. Faubus's prediction of imminent violence, which he had used as justification for calling out the National Guard, had become a self-fulfilling prophesy. Encouraged by Faubus's defiance of the courts, groups such as the White Citizens Councils had whipped segregationists into a frenzy. On the morning of September 23, a mob of several thousand converged on Central High to protest the admission of black students, and local law enforcement was having difficulty controlling them.[78] The next day the situation worsened. Woodrow Wilson Mann, the mayor of Little Rock, sent Eisenhower a telegram at 9:06 a.m. Central Time: "The immediate need for federal troops is urgent. The mob is much larger in numbers at 8 a.m. than at any time yesterday. . . . Situation is out of control and police cannot disperse the mob."[79]

The telegram from Mayor Mann prompted a swift response from Eisenhower. It was now clear that there was no way to avoid the use of federal troops. Tentative plans to use National Guardsmen from other parts of the state were abandoned in favor of using regular army troops. Eisenhower federalized all the Arkansas National Guard, and by the end of the day one thousand paratroopers from the 101st Airborne Division, many of them Korean War veterans, arrived from Fort Campbell, Kentucky. In another important step, Eisenhower decided to leave Newport and return to Washington. Eisenhower had, up to this point, resisted returning to Washington for two reasons. First, he thought, "To rush back to Washington every time an incident of serious character arose would be a confession that a change of scenery is truly a 'vacation' for the President and is not merely a change of his working locale." Second, he did "not want to exaggerate the significance of the admittedly serious situation in Arkansas. I do not want to give a picture of a Cabinet in constant session, of fretting and worrying about the actions of a misguided governor who, in my opinion, has been motivated entirely by what he believes to be political advantage in a particular locality."[80]

The stated purpose for Eisenhower's return to Washington was to deliver a national television and radio address to the American people to explain the federal government's response to the recent events in Little Rock.

Eisenhower explained that a "mob" in Little Rock, "under the leadership of demagogic extremists," had deliberately prevented the carrying out of federal court orders to admit black children to Central High School. Local authorities, he said, had been unable to control the mob. The president explained, "Whenever normal agencies prove inadequate to the task and it becomes necessary for the Executive Branch of the Federal Government to use its powers and authority to uphold Federal Courts, the President's responsibility is inescapable." In accordance with that responsibility, he had ordered the use of federal troops. These troops, he said, "are not being used to relieve local and state authorities of their primary duty to preserve the peace and order of the community. Nor are the troops there for the purpose of taking over the responsibility of the School Board and the other responsible local officials in running Central High School." The troops were only there "for the purpose of preventing interference with the orders of the Court."[81]

Eisenhower's moderate, gradualist stance on integration, and his failure to give public support to the *Brown v. Board* decision may have encouraged segregationists to defy the Supreme Court's decision. On this occasion, when such defiance resulted in a direct confrontation between federal and state authority, Eisenhower still chose not to give support to the actual decision but merely to say that it should be obeyed because it was the law. "It is important that the reasons for my action be understood by all our citizens," Eisenhower said. "As you know, the Supreme Court of the United States has decided that separate public educational facilities for the races are inherently unequal and therefore compulsory school segregation laws are unconstitutional. Our personal opinions about the decision have no bearing on the matter of enforcement; the responsibility and authority of the Supreme Court to interpret the Constitution are very clear."[82]

The president made every effort to direct blame away from the people of Little Rock, pointing out that many of the agitators had been brought in from outside the community. Although Governor Faubus was not mentioned by name, the implication was clear that the president considered him to be one of the "misguided extremists." In a telegram to Senator Richard Russell (D-GA) released four days later, Eisenhower's opinion of Faubus's role became more explicit: "Had the police powers of the State of Arkansas been utilized not to frustrate the orders of the Court but to support them, the ensuing violence and open disrespect for the law and the Federal Judiciary would never have occurred," Eisenhower wrote. "As a matter of fact, had the integration of Central High School been permitted to take place without the intervention of the National Guard, there is little doubt that the process would have gone along quite smoothly and quietly as it had in other Arkansas communities."[83]

Contrary to Eisenhower's earlier statement that any direct confrontation between federal and state power would inevitably result in a federal victory, the situation in Little Rock remained a standoff. Black children were admitted to Central High School, but only because federal troops remained on the premises to keep the peace. A group of four southern governors attempted to intervene on Faubus's behalf, but the Arkansas governor's duplicity ensured a continuation of the crisis. Eisenhower refused to remove federal troops until Faubus agreed he would not obstruct court orders and would maintain order in Little Rock so that those orders could be carried out. Faubus agreed that he personally would not obstruct court orders, but he refused to offer assurances that he would not allow others to do so.[84]

On October 14, one-half of the army troops were withdrawn and four-fifths of the National Guard were defederalized. On November 27, the last of the 101st Airborne left Little Rock and the remaining federalized National Guard took over control of the school area. These National Guardsmen would remain until school let out in May 1958.[85] This was not the end of the standoff. In September 1958 Governor Faubus, using powers given to him by the Arkansas state legislature, closed all the public high schools in Little Rock. In June 1959 the federal court ordered that the schools reopen for the fall 1959 term. When school began, local law enforcement authorities were successful in dispersing a small crowd and three black students enrolled without further incident.[86]

The Civil Rights Act of 1960

The Little Rock crisis greatly affected the Eisenhower administration's legislative proposals in the field of civil rights during his last two years in office. The new attorney general, William P. Rogers, sought to avoid a repeat of the mob violence in Little Rock by proposing an "anti-mob" bill that would make it a federal crime to interfere with a federal court desegregation order. Rogers also sought to prevent the destruction of desegregated schools by making it a federal crime to cross state lines to avoid prosecution for the bombing or burning of a public school. In the fall of 1958, the state of Virginia followed Faubus's lead by closing its public schools. Arthur Flemming, secretary of Health, Education, and Welfare, wanted legislation to deal with school districts that avoided desegregation by closing their public schools. He also wanted a bill providing for emergency schooling for dependents of U.S. military personnel in such cases. Flemming also proposed financial aid to help school districts that were attempting to convert from segregated to integrated schools.[87]

Eisenhower himself remained reluctant to support legislation that would draw the federal government further into the process of desegregating schools. He preferred instead to strengthen the Civil Rights Act of 1957 with legislation that would make it easier for blacks to register and vote, such as requiring the maintenance of voting records that could be inspected by the Department of Justice. This corresponded with Eisenhower's belief that, if the right to vote was ensured, then the administration would have done its duty and all other civil rights would follow as a matter of course. All of these proposals were incorporated into the administration's

1959 civil rights legislative package submitted to Congress on February 5.[88]

Opinion on civil rights legislation in the Eighty-sixth Congress was split three ways. Southerners continued to oppose civil rights legislation of any kind. They were joined by a few conservative Republicans who opposed it on the grounds of limiting federal power. The majority of Republicans and many northern Democrats were in favor of moderate, "middle way" legislation such as that proposed by the president. They took this position either because they believed in the moderate approach or because they feared that going too far would result in no legislation at all. Finally, there was a group of some northern Democrats and a few liberal Republicans who favored stronger civil rights legislation. If the administration was going to overcome the opposition to its "middle way" program from those who wanted stronger legislation and those who wanted none at all, the "moderate majority" of Republicans and northern Democrats would have to reach an agreement.

Uncooperative committees in both houses prevented civil rights bills from reaching the floor during the 1959 session, but in 1960 moderates took control of the proposed legislation. Senate Majority Leader Lyndon Johnson (D-TX), Senate Minority Leader Everett Dirkson (R-IL), House Speaker Sam Rayburn (D-TX), and House Minority Leader Charles Halleck (R-IN) fended off attacks from both sides and secured passage of the Civil Rights Act of 1960. The act incorporated both of Secretary Rogers's proposals, making it a federal crime both to cross a state line to avoid prosecution for the bombing or burning of a public school and to interfere with a federal court desegregation order. It also incorporated Secretary of Health, Education, and Welfare Arthur Flemming's proposal providing for emergency schooling for dependents of U.S. military personnel in areas where public schools had been closed to avoid desegregation. The act rejected his proposal for financial aid to help school districts that were attempting to convert from segregated to integrated schools. It also strengthened the voting rights aspects of the 1957 act by requiring the maintenance of voting records that could be inspected by the Department of Justice and allowing for the appointment of court-supervised referees in areas where a "pattern or practice" of depriving blacks the right to vote had been established. Finally the act extended the life of the Civil Rights Commission, due to expire, for another two years.[89]

Conclusion

Eisenhower believed that the role of the federal government in the field of civil rights should be limited to those areas where it had direct jurisdiction. This enabled him to make significant progress in the desegregation of the District of Columbia, the federal government, and the U.S. military, but it allowed the southern states to delay the extension of civil rights within their own jurisdictions. He also believed that only the passage of time would end racial discord in America—that people's feelings on the subject of race could not be changed solely through legislation or executive order. This played into the hands of southern segregationists who used the delay to avoid compliance with Supreme Court decisions.

Eisenhower claimed that his dedication to the "middle way" excluded "the field of moral values." While it seems that this exclusion should have applied to civil rights, in this field Eisenhower nonetheless pursued a "middle way" between many African Americans and liberals who wanted immediate integration and segregationists and other conservatives who opposed any action by the federal government. In doing so, Eisenhower failed to provide the country with the leadership it needed in the field of civil rights in the crucial years following the Supreme Court's ruling in *Brown v. Board.* With the Democratic Party deeply divided between its northern liberal wing and its southern segregationist wing, strong leadership in the field of civil rights by a Republican president during this period may have succeeded in recapturing for the "party of Lincoln" some of the black vote it had lost during the New Deal. Instead Eisenhower's policies solidified the Democrats' hold on the African American vote to the point where future generations of Republicans would forsake it altogether, implementing instead a "southern strategy" designed to win the votes of white southerners.

Republican Internationalism

President Eisenhower's conservative critics often referred to his domestic programs as "creeping socialism," because they involved the federal government in areas they believed were the responsibility of state and local governments, or individuals. Eisenhower countered that, by addressing societal problems without significantly extending the responsibilities of the federal government, his programs actually stemmed the encroachment of socialism. In doing so, they represented a "middle way" between socialism on the left, and laissez-faire on the right.

In the field of foreign economic policy, Eisenhower's philosophy was similar. At the beginning of his administration, Eisenhower emphasized trade rather than foreign aid. Liberalizing American trade policy would allow friendly nations to export more of their products to the United States. The resulting influx of American currency would not only make it easier for these nations to purchase American products but would also make them more capable of defending themselves against Soviet aggression. This would, in turn, allow Eisenhower to significantly reduce foreign aid and defense expenditures. As Eisenhower became more concerned about the vulnerability of the "Third World" nations, he began to emphasize both trade and aid. Since these nations were not economically developed enough to engage in extensive trade with the United States, foreign aid would be necessary to provide them with the military, economic, and technical assistance they needed to resist Soviet influence. Since, by this time, the Western European nations were capable of taking care of themselves, aid to the developing world would not represent a drastic increase in overall foreign aid.

Just as Eisenhower's domestic programs were intended to stem the encroachment of socialism without significantly increasing the responsibilities of the federal government, his foreign economic policies were intended to prevent the spread of communism without increasing the burden of U.S. foreign aid and defense spending. Once again, Eisenhower sought a "middle way," this time between the high level of foreign aid projected by the Truman administration and the increased level of defense spending that would be necessary if foreign aid were completely eliminated. In pursuing these policies, Eisenhower's support came primarily from Democrats. In his own party, he faced a persistent strain of isolationism and protectionism. Most congressional Republicans, while supporting defense spending and urging the president to be tough on communism, failed to recognize the security benefits of liberalized trade and foreign aid.

Before Eisenhower could begin his pursuit of these policies, he would have to fight a preliminary battle with Senate Republicans who sought to limit the president's powers in the field of foreign policy. As in other areas, members of Eisenhower's own party made it difficult for him to pursue the "middle way."

Trouble with McCarthy

Eisenhower's honeymoon with the conservative members of Congress did not last long in the field of foreign policy. On February 5, 1953, less than two weeks after his inauguration, he submitted the name of Charles E. "Chip" Bohlen to serve as ambassador to the Soviet Union. Senator Joseph R. McCarthy (R-WI), who had already become agitated over other Eisenhower nominations, resolved to prevent the confirmation of Bohlen because he had been present at the Yalta conference in 1945, although only as an interpreter. During confirmation hearings Bohlen refused to repudiate the Yalta agreements. Although the Senate Foreign Relations Committee had unanimously approved Bohlen's nomination, McCarthy, along with Senators Pat McCarran (D-NV) and George Malone (R-NV), led a fight against him on the Senate floor. "We find that his entire history is one of complete, wholehearted, 100 percent cooperation with the Acheson-Hiss-Truman regime," McCarthy said, referring to Dean Acheson, the former secretary of State; Alger Hiss, the subject of a 1948 House Un-American Activities Committee (HUAC) investigation led by Richard Nixon, then a House member; and the former president.[1]

Eisenhower sent Vice President Nixon to talk to Senator McCarthy. Nixon had already begun to serve as intermediary between the president and the conservatives in Congress. Eisenhower's moderate views and his desire to remain above the political fray, not to mention his inexperience in the world of politics, made such an intermediary necessary; and Nixon's credentials with conservatives made him an excellent choice. While Nixon was successful in preventing McCarthy from holding up the president's earlier nominations, he was unable to prevent a floor fight over Bohlen. Eisenhower stayed loyal to his nominee, and Bohlen was ultimately confirmed, but Eisenhower was disturbed that eleven of the thirteen senators who voted against Bohlen's confirmation were Republicans: John Bricker (OH), Styles Bridges (NH), Everett Dirksen (IL), Henry Dworshack (ID), Barry Goldwater (AZ), Bourke Hickenlooper (IA), Karl Mundt (SD), Andrew Schoppel (KS), Herman Welker (ID), Malone, and McCarthy. Eisenhower commented, "there were only two or three that surprised me by their vote; the others are the most stubborn and essentially small-minded examples of the extreme isolationist group in the party. I was surprised by the vote of Bricker and Goldwater. These two seemed to me a little bit more intelligent than the others."[2]

The Bohlen nomination would not be the last time McCarthy caused problems for Eisenhower. Despite McCarthy's reckless tactics, however, Eisenhower refused to denounce him publicly. There were several reasons for this decision. One was political. Not only was McCarthy a fellow Republican, but Eisenhower shared in the popular belief that McCarthy controlled seven or eight votes in the Senate. Among these were believed to be Bridges, Dirksen, William Knowland (R-CA), and William Jenner (R-IN). As committee chairs, these men were leaders in the Senate with whom Eisenhower would have to work. Others supported McCarthy as well, including Barry Goldwater who had called McCarthy "the one man in the United States Senate endeavoring to focus congressional attention on the foreign policy decisions of the Truman administration."[3]

The second reason Eisenhower refused to denounce McCarthy was his belief that the best way to neutralize him was to ignore him. "I really believe that nothing will be so effective in combating his particular kind of troublemaking as to ignore him. This he cannot stand." Eisenhower maintained that McCarthy fed off his own popularity. "Nothing would probably please him more than to get the publicity that would be generated by public repudiation by the President. . . . My friends on the Hill tell me that of course, among other things, he wants to increase his appeal as an after-dinner speaker and so raise the fees that he charges." For this reason Eisenhower was angry at the attention given McCarthy in the national news media: "I was rather resentful of the fact that the very [news] agencies who had made McCarthy were the ones most offended by his practices and methods, and were loudest in their demands that I be the one to cut him down to size."[4]

The last reason was of a more personal nature. Eisenhower did not want to lower himself and the presidency to the level of a public feud with McCarthy. "I just won't get into a pissing contest with that skunk," he told his brother Milton. Eisenhower was aware of the rift in the Republican Party between himself and the conservative old guard, but he was not willing to give the rival faction equal billing by engaging it in public debate. In the early days of the administration, Nixon recalled, "Most Republicans in the House and Senate were then still strongly pro-McCarthy and wanted Eisenhower to embrace him, while the predominantly liberal White House staff members opposed McCarthy and wanted Eisenhower to repudiate him," but the president "was reluctant to plunge into a bitter personal and partisan wrangle, aware that if he repudiated McCarthy or tried to discipline him, the Republican Party would split right down the middle in Congress and in the country." Nixon was forced to "broker their feud." He soon learned that "the go-between is seldom popular with either side."[5]

The Bricker Amendment

Linking Bohlen to Yalta was not merely an excuse for conservatives to oppose his nomination. Yalta was the site of a February 1945 meeting between Franklin Roosevelt, Winston Churchill, and Joseph Stalin. Many Republicans blamed the Soviet Union's postwar domination of Eastern Europe on the agreements made at Yalta. Denouncing the Yalta agreements was a major objective for Republicans, one they had pledged themselves to in the 1952 platform: "The Government of the United States, under Republican leadership, will repudiate all commitments contained in secret understandings such as those of Yalta which aid Communist enslavements." Eisenhower wanted to meet this platform pledge and denounce the way the Soviets had used Yalta, but without giving up the right to enter into such agreements. In his first State of the Union message Eisenhower said he would "ask the Congress at a later date to join in an appropriate resolution making clear that this government recognizes no kind of commitment contained in secret understandings of the past with foreign governments which permit this kind of enslavement."[6]

When Eisenhower submitted his resolution to Congress, however, conservatives were greatly disappointed. The resolution would "declare to the world that the United States had never acquiesced in the subjugation of free people."[7] Eisenhower refused to do what "extremists" asked him to do: repudiate in their entirety the Yalta agreements. He believed this action would endanger the United States' rights in Vienna and Berlin, affirmed at Yalta, and "rake over the ashes of the dead past." Besides not wanting to jeopardize the basis for U.S. occupation of its portions of Berlin and Vienna, Eisenhower was protecting the presidency from congressional encroachment in an area where he believed executive control to be essential. Eisenhower was let off the hook by an unexpected event. On March 5, 1953, Joseph Stalin died. His death made a resolution seem unnecessary, and hope for a better situation with a new Soviet leader made it seem inopportune. Stalin's death "silenced the wrangling of the Congressmen," he later said.[8]

While they consented to let the issue of denouncing Yalta drop after the death of Joseph Stalin, conservative senators were more reluctant to let go of their desire to prevent the president from entering into similar agreements. On January 7, 1953, Senator John Bricker (R-OH) introduced a Senate resolution proposing an amendment to the Constitution that would curtail the president's authority to enter into executive agreements and also limit the effect of treaties and executive agreements on U.S. law.[9] The resolution had the cosponsorship of sixty-two other senators including forty-four of the forty-seven Republicans in the upper house. The amendment had three main sections:

> Section One: A provision of a treaty which conflicts with this Constitution shall not be of any force or effect.
> Section Two: A treaty shall become effective as internal law in the United States only through legislation which would be valid in the absence of treaty.
> Section Three: Congress shall have power to regulate all Executive and other agreements with any foreign power or international organization. All such agreements shall be subject to the limitations imposed on treaties by this article.[10]

The amendment was supported by two groups. The first was led by the amendment's sponsor, John Bricker. This group was concerned about the potential effects of treaties on constitutional law. When a treaty is ratified by the U.S. Senate it becomes, based on article 6, the "supreme law of the land." This is the case even if provisions of the treaty are contrary to the Constitution. For example, a treaty could put the U.S. military under the command of an international organization, regardless of the fact that article 2 makes the president of the United States commander in chief of the armed forces. Section 1 of the proposed amendment would prevent this. Eisenhower dismissed the danger of such an eventuality, saying section 1 was "like adding an addition to the Constitution that said you couldn't violate the Constitution, how silly."[11] Bricker was also concerned about a treaty having the effect of domestic legislation where none currently existed. For example, a United Nations treaty on human rights with a provision prohibiting race from being used as a qualification for employment, if ratified by the Senate in 1954, would have made this practice illegal ten years before Congress passed the Civil Rights Act of 1964. It was this possibility that was addressed by section 2, the most controversial section of the Bricker amendment. This section came to be referred to as the "which" clause, because of its statement that a treaty would only become effective as internal law "through legislation *which* would be valid in the absence of treaty." Critics of the amendment pointed out that the Senate was unlikely to ratify a treaty that took away rights granted by the Constitution or had the effect of domestic law.

The other group that supported the proposed amendment was more politically motivated. This group, because of their lingering hatred of Franklin D. Roosevelt, sought to blame the Soviet Union's postwar actions in Eastern Europe on his alleged usurpation of executive power at Yalta and the other wartime conferences. Seeking to prevent such transgressions in the future, they wanted to limit the power of the president to make executive agreements. This was the purpose of section 3 of the proposed amendment, which would have made all such agreements subject to the limitations placed on treaties by sections 1 and 2. Such limitations would not have affected Yalta, however, since nothing agreed to at Yalta, or any of the other allied war conferences, contradicted the Constitution or had the impact of domestic legislation. Furthermore, agreements made by the president at these wartime conferences would have fallen under the president's powers as commander in chief.[12]

Due to overwhelming support in the Senate, the Bricker amendment would almost certainly have passed if not for Eisenhower's personal objections. Secretary of State John Foster Dulles warned Eisenhower that the amendment "would seriously limit executive authority and make impossible effective conduct of foreign affairs."[13] Dulles explained that the weak treaty-making powers granted to the national government under the Articles of Confederation had been one of the most urgent reasons for calling the Constitutional Convention. He pointed out that some of the proposals contained in the Bricker amendment were made at the convention and rejected. For instance, New York Governor Robert Morris had made a motion that no treaty should be binding "which is not ratified as a law." This motion was voted down eight to one. Dulles also pointed out that the Supreme Court had never had a reason to declare that a treaty was unconstitutional, nor had one been made that could be used as an example of an abuse of treaty-making powers. He warned that the Bricker amendment "would create a no-man's land in foreign affairs. . . . The primary objective of the framers of our constitution would be defeated."[14]

Dulles's unqualified objection to the Bricker amendment was important to the president, not only because he was Eisenhower's closest and most trusted advisor on such matters but because a speech that Dulles had made in April 1952 contributed to the tide of support in favor of the amendment. At a meeting of the American Bar Association Dulles said that the U.S. Constitution made treaties supreme to ordinary laws. "Congressional laws are invalid if they do not conform to the Constitution," he said, but "Treaty law can override the Constitution." He went on to explain that treaties can take powers away from the Congress and give them to the president; take powers from the state and give them to the federal government or to some international body; and even take away rights given to the people by the Bill of Rights. The founders deliberately gave this extraordinary power to the federal government, he said, to give it "untrammeled authority" to deal with international problems.[15] In the course of opposing the Bricker amendment, Dulles would testify that he had not accurately stated his views when he said "treaty law can override the Constitution."

In opposing the Bricker amendment Eisenhower had the support of the majority of his cabinet, the most important being his attorney general, Herbert Brownell, and Dulles. This support, however, did not extend to some members of Eisenhower's own family. Edgar Eisenhower had political views that were more conservative than the president's. In Edgar's correspondence with Dwight he sounded more like a disapproving older brother than an admiring relative. On one occasion, in regard to the Bricker amendment, Edgar wrote, "Nobody is trying to curtail the legitimate powers of the executive, but because the lawyers of this country know of some of the screwy proposals that have already been made by the U.N. we sincerely desire to protect the citizens of this country against some unwise treaty." The president refuted each of Edgar's reasons for supporting the Bricker amendment and then concluded, "It seems to me that it is useless [for us] to pursue further the subject of the Bricker amendment."[16]

The president of the United States has no official role in the process of amending the Constitution. Eisenhower believed, however, that as president and head of his political party it was appropriate and necessary for him to participate in the debate according to his beliefs. He concurred with Dulles that such an amendment would cripple the president's ability to conduct the nation's foreign affairs, and also that limiting the president's role in this field and increasing the role of Congress, and therefore the states, would be a step back toward isolationism, since so many disparate voices would result in a lack of any coherent, coordinated policy. In Eisenhower's opinion, the Bricker amendment, under its guise of protecting people's rights, was just another expression of reluctance to assume responsibilities that could not be avoided. Eisenhower's Chief of Staff and former New Hampshire Governor Sherman Adams concurred, explaining that "the big question was whether or not the United States was willing to accept the leadership of world democracy that had inevitably been thrust upon it after World War II."[17]

At a February 25, 1953, cabinet meeting, Eisenhower began to organize the anti–Bricker amendment forces. Each cabinet member was instructed to study the implications of the amendment for their department and to report back, so as to coordinate information and opposition.[18] Thus the cabinet room became the informal headquarters for opposition to the amendment as the president and his key advisors made plans for how best to kill or render it harmless without tearing apart the Republican Party.

Vice President Nixon thought that the amendment's supporters could be convinced they had already accomplished their goal simply by drawing attention to the issue. Dulles, however, predicted a "head-on collision" between the administration and the amendment's supporters. One by one, the president and members of the cabinet were dispatched to discuss the matter with Bricker. Eisenhower, Nixon, Dulles, Brownell, Secretary of Commerce Sinclair Weeks, and Secretary of the Treasury George Humphrey all discussed the matter with him and attempted to get him to accept the establishment of a commission or other alternatives to the amendment. Eisenhower and Dulles concluded on the basis of their talks with Bricker that the senator would not insist on the specific content of his amendment, but that he greatly desired to enact one that would carry his name "as his one hope of achieving at least a faint immortality in American history." Dulles warned that such an amendment was "impossible," even if revised, since even a harmless amendment would set a dangerous precedent.[19]

Throughout the spring of 1953 the Senate held hearings on the Bricker amendment. While Eisenhower publicly maintained his stance that the amendment was unnecessary, he told cabinet members who were called to testify that they should present their own views. The cabinet secretaries, however, presented a solid front in opposition to the amendment, with Dulles and Brownell leading the way. Eisenhower's brother was not so loyal. In a move that could have been made only to embarrass the president, the Senate called Edgar Eisenhower to testify in favor of the amendment. Edgar patronizingly told Bricker, "I don't think my brother ever fully comprehended what this [the Bricker amendment] was about," and said he thought the president had been influenced by the "liberals" in the cabinet.[20]

Eisenhower did not want to compromise on this issue, while public opinion in favor of the amendment and the number of congressmen who had publicly supported it made the search for a compromise an inevitable part of the process. If a compromise could be found that was acceptable to both sides, meaning one that appeared to address the issue but did not actually change the way foreign policy was conducted, it would "save face" for the senators who had staked their reputations on the amendment and make the issue go away. Vice President Nixon and Attorney General Brownell favored this solution, believing that outright defeat of the amendment would not silence public opinion and would result in a "serious split in the Republican Party." When Brownell expressed concern over whether Bricker would be willing to compromise, the president became angry and expressed amazement over "the complete readiness of the Republican Party to tear us apart."[21]

On July 22, 1953, a compromise presented itself when Senator William Knowland submitted a substitute amendment. The Knowland amendment stated, "A provision of a treaty or other international agreement which conflicts with the Constitution shall not be of any force or effect." Furthermore, "When the Senate so provides in its consent to ratification, a treaty shall become effective as internal law in the United States only through the enactment of appropriate legislation by the Congress." The Knowland amendment thus eliminated the "which" clause. If the Senate wanted to require legislation to make a treaty effective as internal law, it would have to say so as a condition of ratification, otherwise no legislation would be necessary. In the original wording, after a treaty was ratified, Congress would be required to act to make the treaty effective as domestic law.[22]

Eisenhower sent a message to Congress on the same day that Knowland's amendment was introduced, giving it his "unqualified support." The Knowland amendment, the president stated, confirmed that presidential power could not be used contrary to the Constitution but did not hamper the president's ability to conduct foreign affairs. These were the two elements that Eisenhower and his advisors believed would lead to a workable compromise.[23] This, however, was not the case. Senator Bricker said he refused to give up any part of the "which" clause. The lines of difference were now clear, Eisenhower said. "It was no longer possible for the supporters of Bricker to say that their purpose was merely to clarify the meaning of the Constitution. Their aim was to change it radically. There was nothing else to do but get ready for a fight to the end."[24]

When Congress reconvened in 1954, it resumed consideration of the Bricker amendment. On January 27, Senator Walter George (D-GA) offered a substitute for the Bricker amendment that replaced section 2 and section 3 with a provision that stated, "An international agreement other than a treaty shall become effective as internal law in the United States only by an Act of Congress."[25] This would give Congress some say in international executive agreements without significantly changing treaty law. The administration opposed this substitute, arguing that it would infringe on the president's role as commander in chief and his power to recognize foreign governments. Instead, the administration supported a substitute offered by Senator Homer Ferguson (R-MI), which deleted sections 2 and 3 of the Bricker amendment entirely. This proposal was reported out of the Senate Judiciary Committee and approved by the Senate on February 17 by a vote of 44 to 43 (R 38–4, D 6–39). When Senator George's amendment was reported out of the committee on February 26, however, the Senate voted 61–30 (R 30–16, D 31–13, I 0–1) to substitute the George amendment for the Ferguson amendment. The fact that this substitution was approved by a two-thirds majority, the margin necessary to send a proposed constitutional amendment to the states, made the administration's case look very bad. To make matters worse, Senate Majority Leader Knowland, who had been working to find a compromise acceptable to the president, announced that he would vote in favor of the amendment.

All, however, had not been lost. When the final vote on the amendment was held later that day, four senators who had voted in favor of the substitution, one Republican and three Democrats, switched sides and voted against the amendment, more than making up for Knowland and two others, both Republicans, who switched sides in the other direction. The proposed amendment was rejected by one vote 60 to 31 (R 32–14, D 28–16, I 0–1).[26] Eisenhower had won in a close battle but declared, "If it's true that when you die the things that bothered you most are engraved on your skull, I am sure I'll have the mud and dirt of France during the invasion and the name of Senator Bricker."[27]

Reciprocal Trade Agreements

Many of the same conservatives who wanted to limit the president's power to make treaties also wanted to eliminate Eisenhower's authority to negotiate reciprocal trade agreements. In 1950 the United States exported more than 25 percent of all its agricultural products and more than 10 percent of all its manufactured goods. Eisenhower realized that for the United States to continue selling its products abroad on such a scale, the nations that purchased American goods had to have American dollars.[28] There were two ways this could be accomplished. The United States could provide foreign aid to the countries in question, or it could liberalize its trading policies to allow foreign countries to sell more of their own products in the United States.

In the early years of his administration Eisenhower preferred trade to aid.[29] Trade would allow the budget-conscious Eisenhower to cut back on foreign aid without endangering economic prosperity. To maintain a high level of foreign trade, Eisenhower would first have to convince Congress, particularly Republicans, to extend the Reciprocal Trade Agreements Act of 1934. This would be no easy task. The last time the Republicans controlled Congress they had passed the Hawley-Smoot Tariff Act of 1930, raising tariffs to their highest level in history. The Hawley-Smoot tariff, combined with the Great Depression, had a stifling effect on world trade. By 1932 duties on covered imports were 59 percent of their value, dropping their entry into the United States to $1.3 billion, the lowest level since 1909; retaliatory measures limited U.S. exports to $1.6 billion, the lowest level since 1905.[30]

In an attempt to assist economic recovery at home by expanding U.S. exports, President Franklin D. Roosevelt asked the Seventy-third Congress, controlled by Democrats, to delegate some of its power to regulate commerce by authorizing the president to negotiate reciprocal trade agreements with other nations. The result of this request was the Reciprocal Trade Agreements Act of 1934 (RTAA), which passed despite the nearly unanimous opposition of the minority Republicans. The RTAA allowed the president to cut U.S. tariffs by as much as 50 percent in return for equivalent concessions from other nations. The RTAA was extended six times but was due to expire on June 12, 1953.[31]

Eisenhower's belief in free trade should not have been a surprise to congressional Republicans. A committed internationalist, Eisenhower's campaign speeches had supported free trade. At a speech in New York City he stated that "While maintaining tariff policies that operate in the interest of agriculture and industry, we should seek opportunities to increase imports of commodities, goods and services which will improve our own economy and help make our allies self-supporting." At another in Springfield, Massachusetts, he said, "Wise leadership will promote the proper kind of trade abroad so that we can get the . . . things we don't have (tungsten, uranium, manganese, tin, cobalt, platinum, etc.) and in turn it will take our surpluses."[32] Despite the prevalence of protectionism within the party, Eisenhower was able to secure the nomination and win the presidency on a platform that favored the expansion of world trade.[33] Because of opposition within his party, however, he was forced to move more slowly on this issue. In his first State of the Union message on February 2, 1953, he recommended that "Congress take the Reciprocal Trade Agreements Act under immediate study and extend it by appropriate legislation."[34] Eisenhower's secretary of Commerce, Sinclair Weeks, warned Eisenhower that a Republican-controlled panel called to study RTAA would recommend its elimination, but Eisenhower disagreed, insisting that "reasonably intelligent men in possession of all the facts . . . will come to general agreement in support of extension."[35]

In Eisenhower's words, the administration "never proposed to blow a Joshua's trumpet which would bring all tariff walls crashing down." In fact, his requests were quite modest. He abandoned his hope that the RTAA would be extended for two years and amended to allow him more latitude in negotiating trade agreements. Instead, on April 7, 1953, he asked Congress merely to renew the act as it was currently worded for one year. This one-year extension was intended as an "interim measure . . . pending completion of a thorough and comprehensive re-examination of the economic foreign policy of the United States."[36]

Despite this pared-down request, opponents of the RTAA backed a more restrictive bill introduced by Congressman Richard Simpson (R-PA). The Simpson bill would raise tariffs, set new import quotas, expand the Tariff Commission from six to seven members to "rescue it from the blight of domination by executive powers," and require the president to follow the commission's "peril point" and "escape clause" recommendations. The "peril point" and "escape clause" were provisions of the 1951 RTAA. The "peril point" on a product, recommended by the commission, was the minimum tariff rate necessary to protect domestic producers against imports of similar products. The president was allowed to offer rates below the "peril point" but was required to tell Congress why. The "escape clause" required the Tariff Commission to investigate any allegation of "serious injury" to domestic producers caused by the tariff rate and, if necessary, recommend modifications. As with the "peril point," the commission's recommendations were not binding. The Simpson bill would require the president to follow the Tariff Commission's recommendations in both cases.[37]

While protectionists in Congress were arguing in support of the Simpson bill, an actual "escape clause" case came to the president for a decision. The volume of imports and the number of American workers affected in the United States were inconsequential in this particular case (involving briar pipes), but the timing of the case for establishing future policy gave it a drama that far exceeded its actual importance. There was no question that briar pipes met the conditions for escape-clause action, and the Tariff Commission recommended an increase in their tariff rate, but a refusal by the president to raise the rate would be symbolic of his stance in favor of freer trade. On the other hand, with the existing law justifying a rate increase and a protectionist Congress debating the extension of the RTAA, a failure to follow the Tariff Commission's recommendation might result in passage of the Simpson bill or a failure to extend the RTAA altogether.[38] Eisenhower decided to stand his ground on this case and refused to follow the Tariff Commission's recommendation on briar pipes.

The debate continued throughout the spring and summer, becoming quite heated. At one point, House Majority Leader Charles Halleck (R-IN) reported that Secretary of State Dulles had told a congressional hearing there was no need to extend the RTAA because the administration was not going to make any more reciprocal agreements. When Eisenhower heard of the false report he said, "If that's so, we'll get a new Secretary of State!"[39] A frustrated Eisenhower confided in his diary that he was "impressed by the short-sightedness bordering on tragic stupidity of many who fancy themselves to be the greatest believers in and support-ers of capitalism (or a free competitive economy), but who blindly sup-port measures and conditions that cannot fail in the long run to destroy any free economic system."[40]

Eisenhower's supporters eventually won out, but support from Republicans was underwhelming. In the House, two RTAA extension bills were reported out of committee. The first, HR 5495, extended the RTAA for one year and included only one of the restrictions proposed by Representative Simpson, the expansion of the Tariff Commission. The sec-ond, HR 5894, also extended the RTAA for one year but included all of the Simpson restrictions.[41]

The bill HR 5495 came before the House on June 15. Frank Smith (D-MS) moved to recommit the bill with instructions to strike the provision for expanding the Tariff Commission. The vote on this motion was a clear indication of the lack of support for Eisenhower's position among House Republicans. Despite the administration's request that the RTAA extension not be encumbered by restrictions, two hundred Republicans voted against Smith's motion, which failed (R 6–200, D 178–15, I 1–0). The bill then passed 363–34. On July 2 the Senate passed HR 5495, but only after elimi-nating the provision for an expanded Tariff Commission and replacing it with the requirement that if the commission deadlocked in a three-to-three tie, both recommendations be sent to the president. The Senate version was accepted in conference, and on August 8 Eisenhower signed HR 5495, the Trade Agreements Extension Act of 1953, into law.[42]

On July 23, while final action on HR 6595 was still pending, the House voted 242–161 to kill HR 5894, with its full complement of Simpson restric-tions. Republicans were evenly divided (104–105) on this vote, showing once again a strong predilection for protectionism.[43]

In addition to extending the RTAA for one year, the Trade Agreements Extension Act established a seventeen-member Commission on Foreign Economic Policy, which included five senators, five representatives, and seven presidential appointees. The commission was headed by Clarence Randall, chairman of the board of Inland Steel, and was to study the field of foreign trade and make recommendations regarding the future of RTAA after its current extension ended on June 12, 1954.[44] The Randall Commission included both advocates of liberalized trade policy and pro-tectionists. The Eisenhower appointees were primarily free-trade advocates, including Randall himself, while the congressional appointees were prima-rily protectionists. Three of them—Senator Eugene Millikin (R-CO), Representative Daniel Reed (R-NY), and Simpson—were among the most zealous protectionists in the Congress.[45]

The final report of the Randall Commission, released in January 1954, supported the administration's preference for trade over foreign aid.[46] The report made two primary recommendations. First, it asked that most types of foreign aid be terminated. This included both economic aid and emergency relief aid that had become a major part of U.S. foreign economic policy since the end of World War II. Technical assistance should continue, but not increase dramatically. Foreign economic development should be assisted, the report said, primarily through private investment. Such private investment should be encouraged through tax and antitrust relief for U.S. companies doing business abroad. On the subject of trade, the commission report recommended that the RTAA be renewed for not less than three years. In a concession to protectionists, however, it recommended retaining the "peril point" and "escape clause" provisions.[47] These concessions were not enough to satisfy the protectionist members of the commission. Senator Millikin and Representatives Reed and Simpson each published dissenting reports attached to the main report.

On March 30, Eisenhower announced to Congress his foreign economic program for 1954. Based heavily on the recommendations of the Randall Commission Report, the program asked for a three-year extension of the RTAA. "Our aim must not be to fill the dollar gap, but rather to help close it," Eisenhower said. "Our best interest dictates that the dollar gap be closed by raising the level of trade and investment."[48] The Republican Party was badly split on the matter of another RTAA extension, however, and with the midterm elections quickly approaching, it was unlikely that Eisenhower would convince protectionist congressmen to back his proposals. This was particularly true since any tariff legislation would have to pass through the Ways and Means Committee, chaired by Daniel Reed.

Eisenhower threatened to withdraw support for Republican congressmen who refused to vote for extension of the RTAA in 1954. According to Press Secretary James Hagerty, Eisenhower saw "no reason getting anyone elected who is trying to double-cross us." If someone was willing to change their vote, he would "look upon him as a prodigal son and kill the fatted calf." If not, he said, "I have need for my own beef."[49] In the end, however, Eisenhower compromised. In a May 20 letter to Charles H. Percy of Bell and Howell Company, Eisenhower stated he would be satisfied with a one-year extension of the RTAA if Congress would agree to full hearings on his proposals in 1955. Anxious to settle a controversial matter in an election year, Congress complied and again gave the RTAA a one-year extension.[50]

In his 1955 State of the Union message and in a special message on foreign economic policy, Eisenhower reminded Congress of its pledge by renewing his request for a three-year extension of the RTAA and authority to reduce tariffs by 5 percent in each of the three years.[51] The Congress that

Eisenhower faced in January 1955 was significantly different from the one he had faced the previous summer. The Republican Party had lost control of both houses of Congress. The House of Representatives now consisted of 232 Democrats and 203 Republicans. In the Senate, the majority was slimmer at forty-eight Democrats, forty-seven Republicans, and one Independent. Democrats now chaired all the committees and held all the leadership positions. On the subject of trade, this new arrangement was beneficial to the president.

On February 14, after three weeks of hearings, the House Ways and Means Committee reported out an RTAA bill favorable to the administration. It provided for a three-year RTAA extension and authority to reduce tariffs by 5 percent a year, but it made no changes in the existing "peril point" or "escape clause" provisions. House Republicans proved as reluctant as ever to back the president. Many wanted to amend the bill to make Tariff Commission recommendations "final and conclusive," but in a crucial vote the House approved a request to bar floor amendments by a vote of 193–192 (R 65–104). Republicans who wanted to amend the bill then moved to send it back to committee. This motion was defeated 199–206 (R 119–66). On February 18, the House passed the Ways and Means Committee's version of the bill 295 to 110 (R 109–75).

While the administration's bill managed a close victory in the House of Representatives, it was not so lucky in the Senate. On April 28, 1955, the Senate Finance Committee reported a bill that contained several restrictions. The Senate version of the bill amended the "peril point" provision to permit the Tariff Commission to recommend action if any segment of an industry, rather than the industry as a whole, would be damaged by imports, and it amended the "escape clause" provision to provide relief if imports "contributed substantially toward causing or threatening serious injury" to a domestic industry. The Senate bill also required the Tariff Commission to make its recommendations public at the same time they were submitted to the president.[52]

On May 4, the Senate passed the Finance Committee's bill by a vote of 75–13, after rejecting attempts to amend it on the floor. The conference report, agreed to by both houses, included the restrictive provisions added by the Senate. Eisenhower, despite the addition of the restrictions, found the bill "satisfactory" and "an important milestone in the development of our country's foreign economic policy."[53] The legislation, by extending the RTAA for three years, freed Eisenhower from the yearly wrangle with Congress. By allowing the president to lower tariffs by 5 percent annually, the first tariff-cutting authority to be added since 1945, it also gave the United States the flexibility to enter into the General Agreement on Tariffs and Trade (GATT) negotiations then taking place. Eisenhower had received a better deal with fewer Republicans in Congress.

Mutual Security

During World War II, the United States began distributing massive amounts of foreign aid. The "Lend-Lease" program provided $40 billion of assistance to the Allies between 1941 and 1945. During the war, the United States made further financial commitments, playing the lead role in the creation of the International Monetary Fund (IMF) and the International Bank for Reconstruction and Development (World Bank) at Bretton Woods in 1944, and the United Nations (UN) in 1945. It was clear that the United States did not intend to return to the isolationism that had defined its prewar foreign relations; it would stay on an internationalist course. A key aspect of this internationalism was the continued distribution of foreign aid. The motive behind this aid was not so much selfless altruism but, rather, protection of the long-term economic and national security interests of the United States. Promoters of foreign aid argued that economically troubled nations were more vulnerable to communism and that American assistance would help them to resist. Once these nations were on the road to economic recovery, they could then become markets for American trade and investment.

Foreign aid was distributed through a number of programs during the Truman years. These included $400 million in bilateral aid to Greece and Turkey following the pronouncement of the Truman Doctrine in 1947; the European Recovery Program, or Marshall Plan, which provided nearly $13 billion in economic aid to the nations of Western Europe between 1948 and 1951; and the Mutual Defense Assistance Act, which provided more than $2 billion in military aid, primarily to North Atlantic Treaty Organization (NATO) allies in 1949 and 1950. In "point four" of his 1949 inaugural address, Truman asked for $45 million to start a program that would provide technical assistance and capital investment in underdeveloped regions of the world. Congress did not allocate funds that year, but in 1950 the Point Four Program got off to a modest ($27 million) start. Beginning in 1951, the Truman administration combined all of its foreign aid requests and submitted a single mutual security program to Congress. By using the term "mutual security" and combining military aid for Western Europe together with economic aid for the developing world, Truman was hoping to get a reluctant Congress to cooperate. Congress cut $1 billion off Truman's $8.5 billion request, but by passing the Mutual Security Act of 1951, they established the framework for a decade of foreign aid debates.

During Eisenhower's first term, his emphasis was on trade rather than aid, but his administration nevertheless continued the legacy of foreign aid. Eisenhower accepted that it was in the "enlightened self-interest" of the United States to provide military and economic assistance to its allies and the developing regions of the world.[54] As early as 1948, in his World War II memoir, Eisenhower recognized that "Wherever popular discontent is found or group oppression or mass poverty or the hunger of children, there communism may stage an offensive that arms cannot counter. Discontent can be fanned into revolution, and revolution into social chaos." The way to avoid this discontent, he believed, was to promote healthy economies.[55] Eisenhower and Harold Stassen, his chief foreign aid advisor, hoped that eventually trade and private investment would eliminate the need for foreign aid, but in the case of the underdeveloped nations, the standard of living would have to be improved and the economies stabilized before such techniques would be successful.[56]

Eisenhower did believe that the amount of aid being given could be drastically reduced from what the Truman administration had projected. A smaller sum of money, he believed, "if competently used, will be more effective than vastly larger sums incompetently spent for vague and endless purposes." Such an approach would have the added benefit of helping Eisenhower to balance the budget, which he hoped to do within four years. The amount requested by Eisenhower for mutual security in 1953 was $5.5 billion, more than $2 billion less than Truman had projected for 1953.[57]

Despite these deep cuts in Truman's projections, congressional opponents of foreign aid, particularly Republicans, still thought the figures were too high. At a time when there was tremendous pressure to cut government spending and reduce taxes, foreign aid seemed a colossal waste of money to many Republicans. Foreign aid was also an easy target since there was no domestic constituency that benefited directly from it. Furthermore, since the benefits of foreign aid are long-term and the war being fought was a "cold war," it was difficult to show that the aid program was paying off. These factors led to characterization of foreign aid as a "give-away" program. One congressman declared that it was time to "bring to an abrupt end this utterly useless and ineffective attempt to buy support and friendship from other nations."[58] In response to their demands for further cuts, Eisenhower reminded Congress that he had already carefully reviewed past mutual security figures and dramatically reduced them. What he had requested was what was needed. The amount was "large because that is the size of the threat before us."[59]

Despite Eisenhower's pleas, however, by the time the bill completed its appropriations phase, Congress had cut the amount down to slightly more than $4.5 billion, nearly $1 billion less than the administration had requested, and $2.4 billion less than Congress had given Truman in 1952. Of the $4.5 billion appropriated by the Mutual Security Act of 1953, over $4 billion was used for military purposes, while less than $500 million was used for economic and technical assistance. The military orientation of the program was further underscored by the increased amounts channeled to the major "hot spots": Korea, where U.S. military action had just ended; Formosa (Taiwan), whose conflict with mainland China was escalating; and Indochina (Vietnam), where the seven-year French-Indochina war was coming to a conclusion unsatisfactory to the United States.[60]

The 1953 battle over mutual security appropriations was only the first of eight annual battles that Eisenhower would have with Congress over foreign aid. The 1954 battle was nearly a carbon copy of the one waged the previous year. Eisenhower submitted a request for $3.5 billion, an amount significantly pared down from the previous year. Congress, most notably its Republican members, then proceeded to cut it further, this time to $2.8 billion. The military orientation of the program remained, with over $2.5 billion going for military purposes and only $300 million for economic and technical assistance.[61] Supplementing the economic assistance aspects of the mutual security program, however, was the Agricultural Trade Development and Assistance Act of 1954 (PL 480). PL 480 authorized the sale of $700 million worth of surplus farm commodities to friendly nations, and the gift of $300 million worth of surplus farm commodities for famine or relief purposes over a three-year period. This action, which Eisenhower had requested the previous year, had the added benefit of depleting agricultural surpluses, thus raising domestic farm prices. It also helped to develop new markets for American products abroad.[62]

"Third World" Development Aid

Ironically, it was in 1955, the year that Eisenhower won a three-year extension of the RTAA, that his foreign economic policy shifted from emphasizing trade to emphasizing both trade and aid. This shift was caused by a growing concern about the vulnerability of the underdeveloped nations of Asia, Africa, and Latin America. Many of these Third World nations had recently won, or were struggling to win, their independence. Some, such as Korea and Vietnam, had recently been involved in armed conflict with communist forces. Most were politically and economically unstable. Because of their instability and lack of administrative and technical skill, foreign investment in these nations was low and, therefore, capital was scarce. Since the economies of the Third World were not developed enough to engage in extensive trade with the United States, foreign aid was necessary to prevent the spread of communism there. This necessitated a shift in U.S. foreign economic policy. It would, henceforth, emphasize both trade and aid. Unfortunately for Eisenhower, the majority of Republicans in Congress opposed both.[63]

Concern about the spread of communism to the developing world was not new. Systematic aid to developing nations had begun with President Truman's Point Four Program. In November 1950, Truman instructed the International Development Advisory Board (IDAB), chaired by Nelson Rockefeller, to study U.S. economic policy toward the underdeveloped world and recommend the size and type of programs that should be undertaken there. The March 1951 report of the IDAB had concluded that strengthening the economies of the developing world should be considered a vital part of American defense. It identified two major problems that imperiled peace in the developing world: "The threat of military aggression and subversion and the threat of hunger, poverty, disease and illiteracy." From these regions came more than half of all U.S. imports, including 73 percent of the critical raw materials without which industry could not operate. "Soviet strategy, is seeking to chop off country after country in order to isolate us," the report warned. "Inside the Kremlin today sit a group of men with the map of the world spread out before them and who study the economics of the free nations with one thought in mind—how to foment trouble, how to sabotage production, how to chew away the ties of economic interdependence which bind the free peoples." Since the Soviets would search out the most vulnerable areas to weaken them, the report recommended that the United States search out those same areas and bolster them.[64]

That Eisenhower had, by 1955, adopted these views himself is reflected in his statements on foreign economic policy that year. These statements place a greater emphasis on the importance of the underdeveloped nations of the Third World. Eisenhower's special message on foreign economic policy stated that the nation's self-interest and leadership role could be fulfilled only by promoting a program that would stimulate economic growth in the free world. He went on to say that this was true, in part, because economic growth in underdeveloped areas was necessary to alleviate the political and economic instability that made these areas vulnerable to communist penetration and subversion. Economic development in these areas would further serve American interests because it would create a market for American goods, "therefore assuring our own economic growth and a rising standard of living among our own people."[65] The new emphasis is even more apparent in Eisenhower's message to Congress on the mutual security program.[66] The economies of Latin America, Africa, and the "vast arc of free Asia," were not developed enough for the United States to engage them in extensive trade, Eisenhower said. If their vast population was to be saved from communism, so that the potential of their markets could be tapped at a later time, aid would be necessary.

As in the previous year, Eisenhower requested approximately $3.5 billion for his mutual security program in 1955. For the first time, however, this figure did not include any economic aid for the original Marshall Plan countries of Western Europe, which Eisenhower said were now capable of taking care of themselves. This freed up substantial funds for the developing world. As in past years, Congress cut the figure drastically in the appropriations phase, this time to $2.7 billion. Despite these cuts, the new emphasis on the developing world can still be seen in the ratio of military aid to economic aid. The Mutual Security Act of 1955 allocates approximately $2 billion for military purposes and $700 million for economic aid.[67] Congress also increased the authorization for the sale of surplus agricultural commodities under PL 480 from $700 million to $1.5 billion.[68]

The emphasis on the developing world continued in 1956. Eisenhower requested nearly $4.9 billion in mutual security funds for fiscal year 1957, an increase of over $1 billion from the previous year. The principal reason for this increase was a new fund he proposed for the Middle East and Africa, and a heavier emphasis on programs in Asia. In order to put the United States in a position to act promptly to help governments in the Middle East and Africa with economic and social problems, Eisenhower requested $100 million for the creation of a special fund for nonmilitary mutual security programs for these regions. Eisenhower also requested an equal amount for the Fund for Asian Economic Development that had been authorized the previous year. These programs, he said, would "advance the cause of free-world security and economic strength."[69] The yearly battle over mutual security appropriations and the unpredictability of the outcome made it difficult for the recipients of American aid to plan long-term projects important to their development. This shortcoming in American policy became especially hazardous at this time since the Soviet Union was entering into the foreign aid picture.[70] For these reasons Eisenhower also requested authority to make commitments up to ten years in length to assist underdeveloped countries with long-term projects.[71]

The administration's program was not well received by Congress. It appropriated $3.8 billion, a figure $1 billion higher than the previous year, but still $1.1 billion less than the president had requested. The act apportioned $3.2 billion for military and defense support and $650 million for economic and development aid. The request for authority to make long-term commitments was denied, even though it called for only $100 million annually, with the funds appropriated each year. The act did not create a special fund for the Middle East and Africa, and it eliminated the Asian Economic Development Fund. Senate Minority Leader William Knowland also introduced an amendment barring military aid to Yugoslavia, which passed 50–42 (R 26–19). The administration favored aid to Yugoslavia as a way of exploiting that nation's break with the Soviet Union.

Several factors may have contributed to Congress's lack of enthusiasm for the president's foreign aid package in 1956. Senator Styles Bridges, chairman of the Republican Policy Committee, had echoed Knowland's concern about granting aid to neutral countries such as Yugoslavia and India. His warning that such aid would reward neutralism, sending a bad message to America's allies, may have influenced some of his colleagues.[72] The Senate Foreign Relations Committee chair Walter George (D-GA) offered another possibility. The Soviet "switch from a military emphasis to an economic emphasis in its attack on freedom has had a tendency to induce us to lower our guard." This was precisely the opposite effect Eisenhower hoped Soviet entry into the field would have on foreign aid appropriations. The most likely explanation for Congress's attitude, however, is that the lack of enthusiasm was political. Making cuts in an unpopular program in an election year would play well at home. Congress did increase the authorization for the sale of surplus agricultural commodities under PL 480 from $1.5 billion to $3 billion and the authorization for the donation of commodities for foreign relief from $300 million to $500 million.[73]

Supporters and opponents of foreign aid were beginning to feel that a major reevaluation of the mutual security program was necessary in order to refine its goals and methods. Congress refused to establish a joint commission consisting of congressional members and presidential appointees, so the Senate Foreign Relations Committee, the House Foreign Affairs Committee, and the president each set up their own independent commissions to conduct comprehensive studies of U.S. foreign aid.

The president's commission consisted of private citizens and was chaired by Benjamin Fairless, retired president of United States Steel. Other members of the committee included John L. Lewis, president of the United Mine Workers; General Walter Bedell Smith, former head of the Central Intelligence Agency; Whitelaw Reid, chairman of the *New York Herald Tribune;* Colgate W. Darden Jr., president of the University of Virginia; Richard R. Deupress, chairman of the board of Proctor and Gamble; and Jesse W. Tapp, chairman of the board of Bank of America. The commission was directed to study and make recommendations on the "purposes, scope, development, operation and effect" of all foreign assistance programs in relation to the national interests of the United States.[74]

The commission confirmed many of the fundamental principles upon which U.S. foreign aid policy had been based. Among these were the belief that economic development is as important to the collective security of the free world as military preparedness. Foreign aid was only one aspect of a broader foreign economic policy that was necessary to achieve this economic development, the commission stated. Other aspects should include liberalization of trade policy, including gradual reduction of tariffs, and government encouragement of private investment. The commission also gave its support to some requests that Eisenhower had made, but which Congress had denied. These included greater discretionary power for the president in the disbursement of both military and economic aid appropriations, and the ability to ensure aid over a period of time in order to promote long-term projects.

The commission also recommended several changes in the way the American aid program was administered. "Assistance in grant form," it recommended, "should be given only in those exceptional cases where it is clearly in the national interest to do so and where the recipient countries are judged to be unable to repay." All other aid should be given as loans, repayable in convertible currency. The commission also recommended that there be a separation between economic and military contributions. Military assistance should be submitted to Congress as part of the Defense Department budget. Economic assistance requests should be submitted separately and administered by the State Department. The Fairless Commission concluded that "a collective security program will be essential for some years to come," and "the United States must resolve to stay the course, and must abandon the false hope that collective security costs are temporary."[75]

Eisenhower incorporated the recommendations of the Fairless Commission into his 1957 message to Congress on mutual security. In this message he recommended four specific changes in the existing programs. First was that defense assistance programs be separated from programs for economic development. The second change was that defense assistance should be recognized as an "integral part of our own world-wide defense efforts." Accordingly, defense assistance appropriations should be included as part of the regular budget of the Department of Defense. This new method would help to convince Congress and the public that mutual security was a vital part of American defense and not just a "give-away" program. The third change recommended by the president was that economic development assistance should be provided primarily through loans, given on a continuing basis, and closely related to technical assistance. This would be accomplished through the creation of a Development Loan Fund (DLF) to finance specific projects and programs "which give promise of contributing to sound development." This fund would be used for economic development of long-term benefit to the borrowing country. Finally, the president recommended that projects not eligible for DLF money be considered on a case-by-case basis. This provision could be used to meet emergency short-term needs of a more discretionary nature. The total request for 1957 was approximately $3.9 billion.[76]

Eisenhower was concerned that the average American did not understand the mutual security program. In a letter to Treasury Secretary George Humphrey, he wrote that he believed enough had been said to allow "any man of intelligence" to understand the need for mutual security. "If these people, admittedly well-educated and generally informed . . . are so confused," he went on, then "the taxicab driver, the farmer, the miner, the carpenter, the barber, and all their wives, must be in a state of utter bewilderment."[77] It was in this rather condescending frame of mind that Eisenhower decided to make a national radio and television address in anticipation of the annual battle with Congress over mutual security.

The purpose of this address was to explain the "most misunderstood of any of the Federal Government's activities" and persuade the American people to share his view that, dollar for dollar, mutual security did more than any other program to secure the safety of the United States. He wanted to dispel the belief that the mutual security program consisted of "bundling up millions of green American dollars and shipping them to the far corners of the earth in a futile attempt to buy friends." In fact, he said, three-fourths of mutual security funds were spent in the United States and thus created jobs at home. The three main purposes of mutual security, he said, were to help friendly nations maintain armed forces for their own defense and the defense of the United States; to meet emergencies and special needs that affect the interests of the United States; and to help less advanced countries grow "in the strength that can sustain freedom as their way of life." Ending these programs, he explained, would vastly increase the threat of war in the long term, and greatly increase necessary defense expenditures in the short term. To terminate the mutual security program, he said, would be reckless and could mean "the loss of peace[,] . . . the loss of freedom," or "the loss of both."[78]

Eisenhower's appeal to the American people did little to win over reluctant members of Congress. His primary obstacle continued to be members of his own party. Senator Styles Bridges, ranking Republican on the Senate Appropriations Committee, made a speech labeling mutual security advocates "do-gooders." Eisenhower responded that "nothing could be further from the truth." He told Bridges that he understood it was a very popular thing to talk about saving a dollar, but that he would rather see Congress cut a billion dollars off defense than make deeper cuts into mutual security. He admonished Bridges, saying that his party should trust him a little more and not make speeches that misrepresented his policy.[79]

Bridges explained that he did not want to damage the program, but he thought cuts should go deeper, particularly in the case of neutral countries such as Yugoslavia, India, and Indonesia. Eisenhower disagreed, explaining that some countries probably should be neutral. India, with its eighteen-hundred-mile border with China, was one of those countries. With India neutral the United States was under no obligation to defend it, and if China were to attack, world opinion would be outraged at the violation of a neutral country. A great deal of money was necessary, however, just "to make it reasonably safe for them to even exist." In the case of Yugoslavia, Tito had been the only Eastern Bloc leader to risk a break with the Soviet Union. Helping him to maintain it might show others that it was possible.[80]

Eisenhower was quickly losing patience with Republican congressmen who characterized the mutual security program as a "giveaway" or an attempt to "buy friends." As in other situations he let it be known that these men need not call on him at election time. When Congressman Alvin M. Bently (R-MI)—who, according to the president, was "completely indifferent to any consideration of national good or party loyalty"— proposed additional cuts after the program had already been cut heavily in committee, Eisenhower exploded. He later recalled, "I told a staff assistant who brought me this information that I hoped the Congressman would never seek political support from me. If he did so, the answer would be far from satisfactory to him."[81]

Eisenhower was not pleased with the success of his mutual security proposals in 1957. In past years, the authorization phase of the process had gone fairly well, with the Senate Foreign Relations Committee and the House Foreign Affairs Committee recommending a relatively small reduction in the amount requested by the president. It was later, in the appropriations phase, that bigger cuts were made. In 1957 the difficulties began sooner. The Senate Foreign Relations Committee cut the president's request by $300 million. The House Foreign Affairs Committee reported out a bill that reduced the president's request by $600 million, which the full House then proceeded to cut by an additional $125 million. The House also accepted an amendment that set up the DLF for only one year, rejecting the request for long-term lending authority. Seventy-eight Republicans voted to eliminate the DLF entirely. The deep cuts approved by the House prompted the president to voice his concern over the matter and his hope that the Senate version would be accepted in conference. The final authorization, agreed to in conference, reduced the president's request by $500 million and established the DLF on a two-year basis.[82]

The appropriations phase did not go much better. In the House, the Appropriations Committee slashed an additional $900 million off the bill despite the president's threat to call a special session of Congress if mutual security appropriations did not meet what he considered minimum needs. Eisenhower fared better in the Senate, where Majority Leader Lyndon Johnson was able to restore over $500 million, but in conference the two houses agreed to split the difference, approving a figure of just under $2.8 billion, $1.1 billion less than the amount Eisenhower had requested in May. Although the president signed the authorization measure, he was greatly disappointed in the outcome.[83]

The Effect of *Sputnik*

The launching of *Sputnik*, the first man-made earth satellite, by the Soviet Union on October 4, 1957, marked the beginning of a new chapter in the history of the Cold War. While the satellite itself was relatively insignificant, it represented a great psychological victory for the Soviets. Public perception around the world was that the Soviet Union was winning the Cold War. Indeed, the launching of *Sputnik* put the United States behind in the race to win the "hearts and minds" of the Third World, the very region the United States had been trying to protect with mutual security funds.

Without mentioning *Sputnik* by name, Eisenhower referred to the escalation in the Cold War in his 1958 State of the Union message. "What makes the Soviet threat unique in history is its all-inclusiveness," Eisenhower said. "Every human activity is pressed into service as a weapon of expansion. Trade, economic development, military power, arts, science, education, the whole world of ideas—all are harnessed to this same chariot of expansion. The Soviets are, in short, waging total cold war." The only way to answer this threat, he said, was to dedicate "every asset" of the nation to "building the conditions in which security and peace can grow.[84] Just as the launching of *Sputnik* helped to win passage for the National Defense Education Act, it also eased the way for passage of mutual security appropriations and renewal of RTAA, each of which encountered less resistance than in past years.

Contributing to the relative ease of passage for mutual security was the fact that Eisenhower asked for roughly the same amount as he had the previous year, $3.9 billion, apportioned similarly between military aid and economic programs. He had also dropped the controversial request that he be given authority to grant funding for long-term projects several years in advance.[85] Gearing up for what he feared would be another difficult battle with Congress, Eisenhower delivered a speech at a dinner of the National Conference on the Foreign Aspects of National Security. "We are talking about a program that has been proving its worth in practice for over ten years," he told the assembled audience. "And yet, every time another year comes around, the Mutual Security Program is compelled to engage in a life-and-death struggle for its very existence." The reason, he said, was that the opposition did not base its attack on facts but on "slogans, prejudices, penny-wise economy, and above all, an out right refusal to look at the world of 1958 as it really is." What the "ostrich-like opponents" of mutual security were saying, according to the president, was "Billions for armament, but not one cent for peace!"[86]

Although Eisenhower was "deeply distressed" at the meager amount appropriated by the House Appropriations Committee, which at $3.1 billion was $800 million less than he had requested, he could not have been too disappointed with the final outcome. The Senate appropriation was $3.5 billion. In conference committee the difference was split with the final appropriation being $3.3 billion, nearly $500 million higher than the previous year. The only major disappointment was that the $625 million that had been authorized in 1957 for the DLF was reduced to only $400 million.[87]

Eisenhower also received close to what he asked for in his request for renewal of the RTAA. He gave two primary reasons why the RTAA should be renewed for an additional five years. The first was a rationale he had been using in support of mutual security since 1955: an increase in foreign economic activity by the Soviets. "The Soviet Union," he said, "is engaged in an intensive effort, through combined programs of trade and aid, to divide the countries of the free world, to detach them one by one and swing them into the orbit of communist influence." The second reason was the creation of the European Economic Community, which would have a common tariff. Eisenhower said that the five-year period would be necessary to negotiate with the European powers before their new policies went into effect in 1962.[88]

Congress, for the most part, complied with Eisenhower's request. It extended RTAA for four years and authorized the president to reduce tariffs by a total of 20 percent. Not all members of the president's party were eager to grant the extension under these terms. Protectionists backed a substitute measure sponsored by Representative Richard Simpson that would have given only a two-year extension with no new authority to cut tariffs and a provision that required the president to get permission from Congress to reject Tariff Commission recommendations in "escape clause" cases. When the Simpson substitute was rejected, Daniel Reed made an unsuccessful motion to kill the bill that was backed by eighty-five House Republicans. Both Simpson and Reed refused to sign the conference report giving final approval to RTAA extension. In the Senate, Republicans voted 26–21 in favor of a failed amendment that would have allowed a majority vote of both houses to override the president's rejection of Tariff Commission recommendations.[89]

The battle over mutual security in 1959 was similar to that of the previous year. Eisenhower again requested $3.9 billion, and Congress again agreed to only $3.3 billion. Despite these cuts, however, Congress approved several other major foreign aid measures. The Bretton Woods Agreement was amended to increase the U.S. contribution to the IMF by 50 percent and to the World Bank by 100 percent. PL 480 was also extended for another two years with an increase in authorization for sale of surplus commodities from $6.25 billion to $9.25 billion and an increase in authorization for the donation of surplus commodities from $800 million to $1.4 billion.[90]

Cold War tensions soared in 1960 when a "summit" meeting between Eisenhower, Soviet premier Nikita Krushchev, British prime minister Harold Macmillan, and French president Charles de Gaulle was cancelled after the Soviet Union shot down an American U-2 reconnaissance plane 1,220 miles inside Soviet territory on May 1, 1960. The tension contributed to Eisenhower's request for an increase in mutual security funds in 1960 to $4.2 billion. He added a request for an addition $100 million after the UN Security Council decided to send troops to the newly independent Congo. Although Eisenhower stated he was "deeply disturbed" by Congress cutting the figure to $3.7 billion in appropriations, the figure was substantially higher than the previous year and the amount cut from his request was significantly smaller.[91]

Conclusion

Shortly after taking office, Eisenhower fended off two challenges to his presidential authority. Republican Senator Joseph McCarthy, whose crusade against communism trumped his party loyalty, sought to prevent confirmation of Charles Bohlen, the president's nominee for ambassador to the Soviet Union. Eisenhower wanted to avoid a direct confrontation with McCarthy, and he was finally able to secure Bohlen's confirmation, but not without a distracting battle on the Senate floor. The more serious challenge was a proposal to amend the Constitution made by another Republican senator, John Bricker. The Bricker amendment would have limited the president's power to negotiate treaties and executive agreements. Support for the Bricker amendment in Congress was strong enough that the proposal almost certainly would have been sent to the states had it not been for Eisenhower's own vigorous opposition. Eisenhower complained that "All of our constructive work . . . has been overshadowed by the headline value of . . . the Bricker amendment debates. These have come to mean 'Republicanism' to far too many people."[92] Even after the sensation over the Bricker amendment died down, Republicans continued to obstruct his attempt to find a "middle way."

In the field of foreign economic policy, Eisenhower initially emphasized the liberalization of trade policy. Extending the Reciprocal Trade Agreements Act made it easier for the United States to sell the surplus products of its agricultural and industrial sectors while at the same time bolstering the economies of its allies and making them more capable of defending themselves against Soviet aggression. This allowed the United States to cut back on foreign aid. As the nations of Western Europe grew stronger, Eisenhower began to fear the spread of Soviet influence in the Third World. Since these nations were not developed enough to engage in extensive trade with the United States, foreign aid was necessary. Foreign aid, distributed through the mutual security program, would provide the nations of the developing world with the military, economic, and technical assistance they needed to modernize and resist Soviet influence. Eisenhower's foreign economic policies were intended to strengthen America's allies and the developing world, helping them to resist the spread of communism and lightening the burdens of foreign aid and defense spending. His pursuit of this "middle way"—between the high level of foreign aid projected by the Truman administration and the increased level of defense spending that would be necessary if foreign aid were completely eliminated—was obstructed by a persistent strain of isolationism and protectionism within his own party. Congressional Republicans failed to recognize the security benefits of liberalized trade and foreign aid. Once again, members of Eisenhower's own party made it difficult for him to pursue the "middle way."

The Politics of
Modern Republicanism

Eisenhower never made a public pronouncement that he would not run for reelection, but he had always hoped that by 1956 several acceptable candidates would surface, allowing him to step aside without fear for his legacy. As he contemplated whether to retire at the end of his first term, however, Eisenhower began to fear that the conservative wing would capture the party in his absence. "If they think they can nominate a right-wing, Old Guard Republican for the presidency, they've got another thought coming," he told Press Secretary James Hagerty. "I'll go up and down this country, campaigning against them. I'll fight them right down the line."[1]

Eisenhower believed that the political thinking of the party's right wing was completely out of step with the times. "I believe this so emphatically," he wrote in his diary, "that I think that far from appeasing or reasoning with the dyed-in-the-wool reactionary fringe, we should completely ignore it and when necessary, repudiate it. . . . they are the most ignorant people now living in the United States."[2] After a disappointing "mid-term" election in 1954, Eisenhower said that, aside from keeping the world at peace, he had just one purpose for the next two years: "to build up a strong, progressive Republican Party in this country. . . . If the right wing wants a fight, they're going to get it. If they want to leave the Republican Party and form a third party, that's their business, but before I end up, either this Republican Party will reflect progressivism or I won't be with them anymore."[3]

In private conversations, Eisenhower even mentioned the possibility of leaving the Republican Party. "If the right wing really recaptures the Republican Party," he told his friend Gabriel Hauge, "there simply isn't going to be any Republican influence in this country within a matter of a few brief years."[4] After one legislative defeat, he discussed with White

House Chief of Staff Sherman Adams whether he belonged in the Republican Party. He thought that perhaps the time had come for a new party that would accept a leadership role in world affairs, a liberal stand on social welfare policy, and a conservative stand on economic matters.[5] After a talk with the president on this subject Bill Robinson wrote in his diary that Eisenhower had said that if the "die-hard" Republicans fought his program too hard, he would have to organize a third party. Later, according to Robinson, Eisenhower smiled and admitted that this was an impractical alternative, but that he was not willing to give it up entirely.[6]

Many of Eisenhower's friends and advisors urged him, in his attempt to revitalize the party, to use the term "Eisenhower Republicanism," but he was against it. He agreed that personalizing the effort would be the easiest and perhaps the most successful way to reform the party, but he feared that if the effort revolved around him then in the event of his disability or death the movement would collapse. "The idea," he thought, "was far bigger than any one individual."[7] He wanted to broaden the party's appeal, not personalize it. Although he would later take up the term "modern Republican," the president resisted the use of any descriptive adjectives to define his wing of the party. His opinion on this issue is apparent in a letter to his brother Edgar, who had referred to himself as the only "real Republican" in the family. "I am a little amused about this word 'real' that in your clipping modifies the word 'Republican,'" the president wrote. "I assume that Lincoln was a *real* Republican—in fact, I think we should have to assume that every president, being elected leader of the party, is a *real* Republican. Therefore, the president's branch of the party requires, for its description, no adjective whatsoever." Rather, he believed, "The splinter groups, which oppose the leader, would be the ones requiring the descriptive adjectives."[8]

Eisenhower was convinced that the only way for the Republican Party to remain a vital force in American politics was for it to take a liberal approach to its domestic problems. "This party of ours," he explained to Paul Hoffman "will not appeal to the American people unless [they] believe that we have a truly liberal program." He was convinced that "Unless Republicans make themselves the militant champions of the Middle Way, they are sunk."[9] He had little sympathy for the reelection bids of conservative congressmen who did not agree. He could not understand why they failed to see that "The best way they can get re-elected is by supporting the liberal program we have submitted to them."[10] Eisenhower even expressed indifference as to whether conservatives were reelected to Congress, asking why he should bother campaigning for conservative Republicans when he was just as satisfied to have the Democrats in control.[11]

Eisenhower ultimately failed in his attempt to change the direction of the Republican Party. His failure was due primarily to his belief that the change he desired could be achieved on the strength of his policies alone. Eisenhower shared a trait common among those who are used to having their way—he believed that if people disagreed with him it was because they did not understand his position. If, after he had explained his position, they still disagreed with him, it meant they were stupid. Eisenhower believed so strongly in the "middle way" that he could not understand why others did not. For eight years he battled conservative opposition to his programs in Congress, which rarely gave him the opportunity to show what they might do. Without a body of successful domestic legislation behind it, the "middle way" could never achieve the status of the New Deal and, in doing so, change the direction of the party. The change that Eisenhower desired would, therefore, have to be achieved in some other way. He would have to use his enormous personal popularity to actively promote candidates who would perpetuate his legacy. This he failed to do. The consequences for the "middle way" were devastating.

Richard Nixon and the 1956 Campaign

The disappointing results of the 1954 election went a long way toward convincing Eisenhower to run for reelection in 1956. The Republicans lost eighteen seats in the House, one seat and control of the Senate, and nine governors. He believed that the poor performance of Republicans was due to their failure to accept the "middle way." "If you look at the whole gamut of Republicans nominated," he told journalist Merriman Smith, "you know you have people there that [although] they have character and principle, they are certainly stupid."[12] Eisenhower considered many possible candidates as alternatives to his serving a second term. He brought up the names of Herbert Brownell, Sherman Adams, Robert Anderson (a Democrat), Earl Warren, Henry Cabot Lodge, and even Tom Dewey as possible alternatives. The trouble was that, although he believed these men would do an admirable job as chief executive, he knew that none of them could get the nomination.[13]

Eisenhower took many factors into consideration before finally deciding to run for another term. Not least among them was the possibility that, if he decided not to, it was possible a conservative, most likely Senator William Knowland (R-CA), would get the nomination. This was something he wanted to avoid at all costs. Eisenhower had decided to run in 1952 primarily because he did not believe that the policies Taft and his wing of the party promoted were good for the United States. With the highly principled Taft now gone, he was even more distrustful of the conservative wing of the party. Eisenhower was proud, but not satisfied, with the achievements of his first term in office. He did not like the thought of the "middle way" being abandoned and his policy team being disbursed by a conservative, or for that matter, a Democratic administration. On February 29, after getting the go-ahead from his doctors, he announced to the press that he would run for another term.[14]

One name that Eisenhower did not mention when considering desirable successors was that of his vice president, Richard Nixon. Eisenhower's selection of Nixon as a running mate had been primarily a political one.

Being from California, Nixon offered geographic balance to Eisenhower's base of support on the East Coast. Nixon was also a seasoned politician, unlike Eisenhower who had no political experience whatsoever. Most important, however, were Nixon's ties to party conservatives. While Nixon agreed with most of Eisenhower's "middle way" policies, his role in the investigation of Alger Hiss while a member of the House had established his anticommunist credentials and won him the respect of the conservative wing of the party. He had been the perfect person to unite the Taft wing and the Eisenhower wing of the party after the convention. Nixon was one of a number of young Republicans that Eisenhower hoped would be ready to step in and take over when he retired, but at this point Eisenhower did not think Nixon had matured enough to accept that role.

Eisenhower's belief that Nixon had not sufficiently matured to take on the presidency was based, in part, on the fact that Nixon was intimately involved in day-to-day partisan political bickering. The irony is that this is precisely the role Eisenhower asked him to play. The president desired personally to stay above the political fray, but at the same time he did not want Democratic mud slinging to go unanswered. Nixon was the man Eisenhower called on to respond even while criticizing him for being too partisan. During the 1956 campaign, responding to Eisenhower's advice, Nixon tried to temper his rhetoric. Eisenhower took note of this, but when events called for a tough response he again turned to his vice president. "Everybody is now noting that you are talking the new high level," he told Nixon. "However, I think today you ought to take notice of some of these attacks that have been made on the administration and on me. . . . I want them called on it." Eisenhower went on to suggest specific things he thought Nixon should say. In a follow-up conversation, Herbert Brownell told Nixon, "I don't think we could win with a so-called 'high level' campaign. It has to be fair but you have to take the opposition on. It has to be hard-hitting."[15] Eisenhower would even, on occasion, compliment the vice president for his skill at playing political hardball, but he never seemed to remember this encouragement when it came to discussions of Nixon's political maturity.[16]

His desire for Nixon to mature made Eisenhower susceptible to the suggestion made by Sherman Adams and other political advisors that he "dump" Nixon from the ticket in 1956. Quoting poll results, they argued that Nixon would cost Eisenhower three or four points in a race with Adlai Stevenson. Eisenhower was not really concerned about losing the presidential race, but he took these figures as an indication that Nixon was not getting the experience he needed to eventually make a run for the presidency on his own. On the day after Christmas 1955, Eisenhower invited Nixon to his office to discuss the future. He cited the poll results to Nixon and then suggested that perhaps the vice president's best interests were not being served by remaining vice president. He pointed out that no incumbent vice president had been elected president since Martin Van Buren in 1836.

Eisenhower expected several of his cabinet secretaries to resign at the end of his first term. He suggested that the best thing for Nixon might be to withdraw from the vice-presidential race and join the cabinet. That way Nixon could gain high-profile executive experience rather than continue on in a position that most people considered unimportant.[17]

Nixon replied: "If you believe that your own candidacy and your administration would be better served with me off the ticket, you tell me what you want me to do and I'll do it. I want to do what is best for you." Eisenhower refused, "No, I think we've got to do what's best for you." He told Nixon that he should "make a searching survey of the probable advantages and disadvantages" to himself and the party before giving an answer.[18] Eisenhower added one additional factor for Nixon to take into consideration. In view of the president's recent heart attack, he told Nixon that if he believed Eisenhower would not last five years, then perhaps he should stay on.[19] Adding further ambiguity, Eisenhower closed his meeting with Nixon by telling him that if he wanted the vice presidency, as far as he was concerned, it was his.[20]

Most indications are that Eisenhower was sincere in his belief that it would be better for Nixon and the party if he left the vice presidency and took a cabinet position. He gave great weight to a letter from his friend George Whitney, which suggested that it would be "fairer to Nixon, and better for the future of the country, that he spend the next four years in some position where publicly he can demonstrate how good he is in his own right, rather than stay on in a position which, though it carries many important duties, . . . has the outward appearance to the public of a secondary job."[21] Eisenhower also hoped that by 1960 there would be a number of acceptable Republicans ready to run for president. So far Nixon seemed like the only one. "I am happy to have him as a personal friend, I am happy to have him as an associate, and I am happy to have him in government," Eisenhower said. "That still doesn't make him Vice President. . . . He is going to be the 'comer' four years from now. I want a bevy of young fellows to be available four years from now. Nixon can't always be understudy to the star."[22]

Nixon did not agree that getting off the ticket would be the best thing for him in the long run. While he admitted there was some truth to what Eisenhower had said about his chances of being elected president while holding the office of vice president, he knew that no matter what cabinet position he took, the press would interpret it as a demotion, thus hurting his political standing. He also disagreed that this course would be best for the party. Nixon was the president's only link to the party's right wing, who would be incensed if Nixon were "dumped" from the ticket. While Eisenhower may have believed that he did not need to court conservatives' support since they had nowhere else to go, Nixon believed that Eisenhower did need their money, their enthusiasm, and their organization to win. Because of Eisenhower's aloofness from political matters, Nixon was also his key link to the party machinery. The vice president believed that Eisenhower's chances of carrying the party to victory with him would be significantly hurt if he stepped aside.[23]

Eisenhower did not seem concerned with offending the right wing or with carrying other Republicans on his coattails. In fact, in a conversation with Len Hall, the Republican National Committee chairman, he discussed the possibility of running with a Democrat. Using the example of Abraham Lincoln's selection of Democrat Andrew Johnson as a running mate, the two men discussed the possibility of nominating Frank Lausche, the Democratic governor of Ohio. Being from a northern state, Lausche would not stir up the segregation issue like the southern Democrats who supported Eisenhower. Lausche was also a Catholic and Eisenhower liked the idea of beating the Democrats to the nomination of a Catholic to the vice presidency.[24] Nominating Lausche would be a step toward realigning the party on a "middle way" platform.

In response to a question about Nixon's place on the ticket at a March 7 press conference, Eisenhower told reporters that he had asked Nixon to "chart out his own course." When the reporters pressed the president on whether he personally wanted Nixon to stay on, he told them that other candidates would be "equally acceptable" to him. The press latched onto the "chart his own course" phrase and, while everyone had their own interpretation of what it meant, Nixon believed the consensus was that it suggested "varying degrees of indifference" toward him. After listening to Eisenhower's press conference, Nixon drafted an announcement that he would not be a candidate in 1956. He mentioned the draft to a Senate staff member who told Len Hall and White House aide General Jerry Persons. Within a few hours the two of them were in Nixon's office urging him to destroy the draft, saying that if he made such an announcement "the Republican Party would be split in two." Nixon, referring to the press conference, said he could "only assume" it was the president's way of saying he would "prefer someone else." They assured him this was not true. "You can't apply the kind of politically sophisticated standards to him [Eisenhower] that you do to anybody else," they reminded him. Nixon agreed to hold off on the announcement for a few weeks.[25] This exchange is especially interesting since Hall had been present when Eisenhower was discussing the possibility of Lausche as a running mate.

On March 13, the first primary for the 1956 presidential election was held in New Hampshire. Eisenhower, the only declared Republican candidate, received 56,464 votes; but the big story of the New Hampshire primary was that over 23,000 voters wrote in Nixon's name on their ballots. This overwhelming show of support for Nixon caused Eisenhower to soften his statements about Nixon and the vice presidency. Stopping just short of an outright endorsement, Eisenhower told reporters he would "be happy" to be on the ticket with Nixon.[26]

Eisenhower refused, however, to back away from his decision to put the matter in Nixon's hands. When reporters asked him on April 25 whether Nixon had "charted his own course" yet, he replied that the vice president had not reported back to him. Nixon had hoped that Eisenhower would simply drop the matter and endorse him for the number two spot on the ticket, but it was now clear this would not happen. The president's response convinced Nixon to act. The next morning he made an appointment to see the president. He told Eisenhower he would be "honored to continue as Vice President." He said the only reason he had waited so long in saying so was that he did not want to do anything to make it look like he was trying to force his way onto the ticket if Eisenhower did not want him. Eisenhower called Hagerty and told him the news, asking him to take Nixon out immediately and announce the decision to the press. "You can tell them that I'm delighted by the news," he added.[27]

Unfortunately for the vice president, this was not the end of the "dump Nixon" movement. On July 20, Harold Stassen, the president's cabinet-level advisor on disarmament, or "secretary of peace," as he was called, came to Eisenhower with the results of a poll he had commissioned privately. The poll showed that Nixon would lose more votes for Eisenhower than any of a number of other possible running mates. Stassen suggested that Eisenhower abandon Nixon in favor of Massachusetts Governor Christian Herter.[28] While Eisenhower claimed to be "astonished" by Stassen's attitude, he told him that, as an American citizen, he was free to follow his own judgment on such matters.[29]

This remark may have unwittingly encouraged Stassen. While Eisenhower was on a trip to Panama, Stassen publicly announced his opposition to the Nixon candidacy and his support for Governor Herter. In the president's absence, Hagerty responded that, although Stassen was free to follow his own judgment on the matter, he obviously could not undertake independent political activity while a member of the president's cabinet. When Eisenhower returned, he granted Stassen a leave of absence until after the convention.[30] By this time Stassen's statements had been widely publicized, prompting responses from many Nixon supporters. Most prominent among them was an endorsement by 180 of 203 House Republicans. Despite the lack of any support base for his position, Stassen persisted with his plan until the convention. When Stassen tried to make an appointment to see the president during the convention to discuss the matter again, however, Len Hall and Sherman Adams told him he could only see the president if he agreed to second the nomination of Nixon and limited his conversation with Eisenhower to informing him of this agreement. Stassen got the point; he dropped his opposition to Nixon and agreed to second his nomination.[31]

Unity was the theme of Eisenhower's acceptance speech at the Republican Convention in San Francisco. He reminded the delegates that when the party was founded it was a party of inclusion, not exclusion. "As far back as 1856," he told them, the party established "a record of bringing together, as its largest element, the working people and small farmers, as well as the small businessmen. It attracted minority groups, scholars, and writers, not to mention reformers of all kinds, Free-Soilers, Independent Democrats, Conscience Whigs, Barnburners, 'Soft Hunkers,' teetotalers, vegetarians, and transcendentalists!" One hundred years later, he asked that the Republican Party again become the rallying point for "Americans of all callings, ages, races, and incomes. . . . We want them all! Republicans, independents, discerning Democrats—come on in and help!"[32] Eisenhower's campaign was consistent with his rhetoric. He told his political advisors that he did not want to speak to just Republican groups or make strictly political speeches. He told those making speeches on his behalf to avoid exaggerated statements that would condemn the entire membership of the Democratic Party, reminding them that it was his goal to win over discerning Democrats.[33]

Although Eisenhower beat Adlai Stevenson in a landslide, the 1956 election was a partial failure for the Republican Party. The makeup of the Senate remained the same, but the Republicans lost two seats in the House and two governorships. It marked the first time since 1848 that the party winning the presidency failed to win either the House or the Senate. Eisenhower blamed the poor showing on conservative Republicans who had failed to adopt the "middle way." "You know why this is happening, Dick?" he asked Nixon while they were watching the election returns. "It's all those damned mossbacks and hard-shell conservatives we've got in the party. I think that what we need is a new party."[34]

Modern Republicanism

At 1:50 a.m., after Stevenson had conceded, Eisenhower went to his election headquarters at the Sheraton Park Hotel in Washington, D.C., to accept his victory. After thanking his supporters he said, "I think that modern Republicanism has now proved itself. And America has approved of modern Republicanism."[35] "Modern Republicanism" was a phrase that Eisenhower had used often during the campaign. To him it was "A political philosophy that recognizes clearly the responsibility of the Federal Government to take the lead in making certain that the productivity of our great economic machine is distributed so that no one will suffer disaster, [or] privation through no fault of his own."[36] The press had picked up the phrase and used it more generally to define the Eisenhower wing of the party.

Those who were already believers in the "middle way" applauded Eisenhower's words. Harold Stassen, whose dislike for the conservative wing prompted his ill-fated attempt to "dump Nixon," thought that Eisenhower should continue promoting "modern Republicanism." "The loss of both Houses of Congress at a time when the President wins decisively reflects an even greater party weakness than the loss of Congress on any other occasion," Stassen wrote in a letter to Sherman Adams shortly after the election. "It is clear that a significant and decisive portion of the American voters do not believe that the Republican Party represents the same policies as those of the President. Under these circumstances it seems to me to be very important that the President carry out an active Party leadership."[37]

Nixon, on the other hand, thought it a mistake to bring up such a controversial party issue as "modern Republicanism" on election night. He feared that the party regulars would interpret the remarks "either as a boast that Eisenhower had won the victory by himself, or as a threat that those within the party who did not share his views would gradually be replaced by those who did."[38] Nixon proved correct in his fear. Conservative congressmen agreed with Stassen that the president's views were different from those of the party, but they did not see this as a good thing. Senator Bricker (R-OH) spoke for many when, in response to Eisenhower's talk of "modern Republicanism," he said, "Much that sails under the banner of Republicanism today is certainly not Republicanism as we know it in Ohio."[39]

Barry Goldwater (R-AZ) concurred. In a Senate speech on April 8, 1957, he made what many called his "break" with the Eisenhower administration. Referring to the "tax and tax, spend and spend," philosophy of the New Deal and Fair Deal, he said, "In the Republican Party, there are also vociferous exponents of this incredible philosophy. It may be, in fact, that they are the 'Modern Republicans' about whom there has been so much discussion in recent months. Certainly, the faulty premises of 'Modern Republicanism' do not refute this big budget concept." The Eisenhower administration, he continued, had bowed to "the siren song of socialism" and was now merely "parroting the antics" of its Democratic predecessors.[40] Goldwater later claimed that it had not been easy for him to make an open break with the president. On the day after his speech he wrote Eisenhower, "Believe me Sir, that was the most difficult task I ever assigned to myself and I debated this seriously for nearly a week, but I finally came to the conclusion that I could not in justice to my conscience and to the promises I made to the people, leave what was in my heart and mind unsaid."[41]

The attacks on "modern Republicanism" by Goldwater and others angered Eisenhower. He had been "forced down the throats" of conservatives in 1952, he reminded Sherman Adams, and "some will never forget it." Any expression that he, or a member of his staff, used would be "picked up and criticized" by conservatives.[42] In retaliation, he decided that in future elections he would not help those who had publicly turned against him.[43]

Eisenhower may have been angered by Goldwater's speech, but he was more concerned with forging unity in the middle of the political spectrum than with recapturing the renegade right wing. He thought that the southern Democrats were politically much closer to the Republicans than they were to the northern Democrats. He suggested calling Harry Byrd (VA), Willis Robertson (VA), Spessard Holland (FL), Strom Thurmond (SC), John Stennis (MS), and Lyndon Johnson (TX) and saying, "Are we going to hang on to an antiquated loyalty to two parties who have reversed their positions since the time of Jefferson? The Republicans are the States' Rights party, and the Democrats are the party of centralized government. Let's take a look at this thing and see what we can do for the country in the two years ahead of us. If we do have to stress party differences, let us do it on relatively small matters."[44]

As the 1958 elections drew near, Nixon began to worry about the effect another hard-hitting political campaign would have on his chances of being elected president in 1960. Nixon's principal duties in the Eisenhower administration were to act as the president's link to party conservatives, and to defend the administration against partisan political attacks. With prominent conservatives openly criticizing the president, these two roles were in conflict. If Nixon wanted to maintain his friendly relations with the conservative wing of the party, he could not afford to act as Eisenhower's political point man during the 1958 campaign. On the other hand, the campaign would offer him the opportunity to maintain his close ties with party regulars throughout the country as he prepared to run for president in 1960.

Nixon would have to consider several other factors before deciding whether to participate in the 1958 campaign. In November 1957, Eisenhower had suffered a stroke and, although he was recovering quickly, he was not expected to play a significant role in the campaign. If neither the president nor the vice president participated, it could mean significant losses for the party. Nixon also had his own popularity to consider. In the spring of 1958, Nixon had made an official visit to South America. While in Venezuela, the vice president's motorcade was attacked by an angry mob that seemed determined to drag Nixon from his car. This brush with death had elevated Nixon's popularity at home to an all-time high. Meanwhile, owing to a downturn in the economy and a scandal surrounding the resignation of Sherman Adams, Eisenhower's approval rating was below 50 percent for the first time. A heated midterm election could only damage Nixon's popularity.

Those with Nixon's long-term interests in mind advised him to sit out the campaign. Tom Dewey warned, "I know that all those party wheelhorses will tell you stories that will pluck your heartstrings, but you're toying with your chance to be president. Don't do it Dick. You've already done enough, and 1960 is what counts now." But Nixon gave in to the party "wheelhorses," traveling throughout the country campaigning for Republicans, "because it had to be done, and because there wasn't anybody else to do it."[45]

Nixon's worst fears were realized. The Republican Party took a massive beating and lost thirteen seats in the Senate and forty-seven seats in the House. The Democratic majorities now stood at 62–34 in the Senate and 282–153 in the House. The Republican defeat extended to the state level as well. Out of twenty-one gubernatorial contests, the Republicans won only eight, a net loss of seven. One high-profile loss was that of William Knowland, who had resigned his Senate seat to run for governor of California on a "right-to-work" platform. The Democrats won control of thirty-four out of forty-eight statehouses. Overall it was the most thorough Democratic victory since 1936.[46]

Among the few bright spots for the Republican Party in the 1958 campaign were Nelson Rockefeller and Barry Goldwater. Nelson Rockefeller, former undersecretary of Health, Education, and Welfare, was elected governor of New York, defeating Democratic incumbent Averell Harriman by more than a half-million votes. On the other end of the Republican spectrum, Barry Goldwater was reelected to the Senate. In a year that had seen the defeat of such prominent conservative incumbents as John Bricker (OH), William Jenner (IN), and George Malone (NV), Goldwater's victory was truly significant. While Nixon had become irrevocably identified with the Republican's worst defeat in over twenty years, Rockefeller and Goldwater, his two major rivals for the presidency, had emerged victorious. Perhaps Dewey was right, Nixon later surmised, "I should have sat it out."[47]

Nixon, Rockefeller, and the 1960 Campaign

For Nixon to capture the Republican presidential nomination in 1960, he would need to win the support of both wings of the party. This would be a difficult task. Eisenhower's pursuit of the "middle way" had deepened party divisions. Serving as Eisenhower's link to party conservatives had allowed Nixon to maintain close ties with the "Old Guard." These conservatives, however, were now unsure of where Nixon stood on the major issues. During his eight years as vice president, he had been a loyal supporter of the president's policies. If he repudiated the president's policies during the campaign, it would make him appear a hypocrite and he would lose the votes of "Modern Republicans." It would also jeopardize any chance he may have had of winning the support of independents and "Eisenhower Democrats" in the general election. As the campaign got under way, the *Wall Street Journal* took note of Nixon's political ambiguity. "Mr. Nixon represents the 'Old Guard,'" the *Journal* editorialized. "Yet Mr. Nixon is in fact no darling of the conservatives in the Republican Party," who considered him "far too liberal on such matters as foreign aid, international involvement and welfare legislation." Sometimes, it said, "The accusation is that Mr. Nixon has no political convictions whatever.[48]

Under the circumstances, Nelson Rockefeller's decision to enter the 1960 presidential race was the best thing that could have happened to Nixon. With no prominent conservative challenger, the right wing had little choice but to support Nixon over the far more liberal Rockefeller. Furthermore, when Rockefeller began to criticize Eisenhower on defense spending, it made Nixon supporters out of the president's defenders, leaving the New York governor with only a small group of supporters on the party's left.

Rockefeller had resigned from the Eisenhower administration in December 1955, frustrated with the role of "team player." He was convinced that "You can't have a voice in your party unless you've proved that you know how to get votes."[49] Party leaders in New York had tried to dissuade him from running for governor in 1958. Thomas Dewey told him that no one with the name Rockefeller could be elected as a Republican in New York. Most voters there already considered the Republican Party the party of the rich, and Rockefeller would only further that notion. Dewey suggested that if he really wanted to get involved in New York politics, he would have to prove his dedication by starting at the bottom and working his way up. Dewey suggested an appointed position in New York City. Others suggested he run for U.S. Senate. Rockefeller rejected both suggestions; he thought he was better suited for executive work and he wanted to make the calls himself, not support other people's proposals.[50]

Rockefeller's advisor Pat Weaver had another solution. "Nelson, there's one thing you should face right away," Weaver told him. "You should do exactly what all the other guys in your position have always done, [U.S. Senator Herbert] Lehman, Franklin Roosevelt, Harriman. You should turn your back on your people, become a Democrat, and embrace the masses." Rockefeller told him to forget it. The way he saw it, "If I became a Democrat, I'd always be in the position of holding the party back, whereas if I stayed a Republican, I'd be pushing the party forward."[51]

Rockefeller ignored the advice of Dewey and others and won a convincing victory in the New York gubernatorial contest, making him an immediate contender for the Republican presidential nomination. Rockefeller's presidential ambitions were made clear by the 1958 publication of the *Rockefeller Panel Reports,* a collection of bold statements on foreign, military, economic, social, education, and political reform policy written by an all-star cast of political, academic, and business figures.[52] Going far beyond the responsibilities of a governor, the reports gave Rockefeller a national political identity. He was, according to *U.S. News and World Report,* "a hawk on military matters, an enlightened progressive on social programs, [and] an ardent foe of the budget-balancing propensities of the current administration."[53]

Rockefeller, however, was not sure that 1960 was the right time for him to run for president. There was no doubt in his mind that he wanted the office. Only the presidency would offer him a platform large enough for the goals he hoped to accomplish in the United States and the world. But there was still the problem of Nixon. Despite his ambiguity within the party, and his association with the devastating losses of 1958, Nixon still had the respect and appreciation of the party leaders throughout the nation who remembered the work he had put in for them since 1952, even when he was fighting in a lost cause.

Rockefeller, on the other hand, was little known outside Washington and the northeastern United States. In the recent past, Republican candidates from the so-called Eastern Establishment—Wendell Wilkie, Thomas

Dewey, even Eisenhower—had waged successful campaigns against the party regulars, but in each of these cases they had the support of the eastern business community. Despite the fact that the Rockefeller name was almost synonymous with eastern business, he was unlikely to win their support because of his liberal tendencies. William Shannon, political correspondent for the *New York Post,* explained the difficulty: "The GOP is a party of business. Conservative businessmen would not permit their party to become for very long the vehicle of liberal programs. . . . Rockefeller may have Franklin Roosevelt's personal charm, but FDR constructed the New Deal on a social and political base that Rockefeller as leader of the businessmen's party will not have."[54] This is not to say that Rockefeller would need the financial support of the eastern business community—he could easily pay for the campaign himself—but if the business interests decided to support Nixon, there was no way Rockefeller could win the nomination.[55]

In the final months of 1959, Rockefeller went on an extensive cross-country speaking tour to gauge public opinion before deciding whether he would run for president. Despite a positive response, national media coverage, and polls that showed he would make a strong challenger to Vice President Nixon, on the day after Christmas 1959, Rockefeller made a "definite and final" announcement he would not run for president and he would not accept the nomination for vice president. He gave as his reason: "The great majority of those who will control the Republican convention stand opposed to any contest for the nomination." Any attempt to win it, therefore, would make it impossible for him to fulfill his obligations to New York.[56]

Rockefeller's announcement seemed to assure Nixon an uncontested nomination, giving the Republican Party a significant head start over the Democrats as they began a heated primary struggle. Although Eisenhower had initially hoped for a wide field of candidates, recent party strife made him praise Rockefeller for his "wise decision," allowing for the "avoidance of divisive and costly struggles in the party." Eisenhower had now resigned himself to the fact that Nixon would get the nomination and considered him the best qualified of anyone who was capable of doing so.[57]

Nixon and Eisenhower had not heard the last from Nelson Rockefeller, however. During April and May of 1959 the governor began making speeches critical of the Eisenhower administration. On June 8, Rockefeller had breakfast with the president at the White House. Eisenhower had heard some of Rockefeller's speeches and was interested in what the governor's motives were. Rockefeller did not state his political intentions but told Eisenhower he did not feel that Nixon had made his positions clear on "certain issues." After breakfast, Rockefeller issued a statement to the press saying he was "deeply convinced and deeply concerned that those now assuming control of the Republican Party have failed to make clear where this party is heading and where it proposes to lead the nation." The statement also presented Rockefeller's position on nine major issues facing the nation and demanded that Nixon do the same before the Republican con-vention.[58] One recommendation in particular angered Eisenhower. This was Rockefeller's opinion, which he had not mentioned at breakfast, that defense spending be increased by $3.5 billion. This proposal was in response to the Democratic claim that recent Soviet production had opened a "missile gap" between it and the United States, a charge Eisenhower knew to be false. Eisenhower suspected that Rockefeller had been listening to "half-baked advisors" and did not appreciate being drawn into the dispute, but he defended Rockefeller's right as a prominent Republican to state his opinions and suggested that the governor be allowed to make a major speech at the convention.[59]

The day after he released his statement, Rockefeller attempted to call Eisenhower. He told Ann Whitman, the president's secretary, that he want-ed Eisenhower's judgment on whether he should become a candidate for the nomination. When Eisenhower returned his call two days later he expressed displeasure over Rockefeller's comments regarding the defense budget. Regarding a presidential candidacy, Eisenhower told Rockefeller that he thought it would be a mistake to enter the race after officially with-drawing. He warned Rockefeller that people would call him "off again, on again, gone again, Finnegan."[60] The next day, June 11, Rockefeller announced that his previous withdrawal still stood, but that he would run if drafted by the convention. Over the next several weeks he released a series of statements with specific recommendations on foreign policy, national defense, disarmament, economic growth, government reorganiza-tion, civil rights, medical care for the aged, and education. The media inter-preted the papers as an attack on the Eisenhower administration.

Rockefeller's statements gave birth to a national "draft Rockefeller" movement with headquarters in twenty-one states, but Rockefeller likely realized that there was not time to put together the kind of grassroots cam-paign that would result in a convention draft.[61] Joseph Persico, a Rockefeller aide, thought that Rockefeller's indecisiveness was due to his lack of political savvy. "In 1960, Rockefeller found it hard to accept that a presidential candidate . . . would be chosen on the strength of who had attended the most Lincoln day dinners," he said. "How could this minutiae matter when measured against a grand new vision and fresh answers to the nation's problems? How could a bright new political star fail to triumph over party wheelhorses?"[62] Rockefeller himself put it more simply, "I hate the thought of Dick Nixon being President of the U.S."[63]

Since the nomination was probably out of the question, it seems likely that what Rockefeller really hoped to do was influence the platform. The early drafts of the 1960 Republican platform had not satisfied him. He thought they lacked the urgency he had tried to convey in his own policy statements. Rockefeller's supporters, still hoping to win the nomination for the governor, were eager to fight these differences out on the floor of the convention. Nixon, on the other hand, wanted to avoid dissent at the convention and asked for a meeting with Rockefeller. Rockefeller agreed, but on his own terms. The meeting would be held, in secret, at Rockefeller's apartment. After its conclusion it would be announced in a press release written by Rockefeller and explained as having taken place at Nixon's request. The statement issued would not be a summary, but rather deal with substantive issues. Nixon agreed.[64]

Nixon and Rockefeller met at Rockefeller's Fifth Avenue apartment in New York City on July 22, 1960. Nixon began the meeting by asking Rockefeller to be his running mate. Nixon was convinced that the Democratic ticket would be John F. Kennedy and Lyndon B. Johnson. This would be "an uneasy and joyless marriage of convenience," but it would also offer the kind of balance that would ensure a party unified for the general election. Nixon thought that the perfect Republican counterpart to a Kennedy-Johnson ticket would be a Nixon-Rockefeller ticket. Rockefeller stuck to his earlier promise and declined. "I was not altogether sorry," Nixon later wrote, "because Rockefeller's independent temperament would have made him a much more difficult running mate for me to deal with than Johnson would be for Kennedy."[65]

The two men then got down to the business of the platform. Rockefeller had a list of policy positions he wanted included in the Republican platform if he were to come out in support of it. Several of the domestic policy positions called for a continuation of the basic principles that had guided the Eisenhower administration. Among these were further reorganization to make the executive branch run more efficiently; elimination of the agricultural surplus through the expansion of markets and removal of inefficient farmland from production; and amending the Taft-Hartley Act to preserve the rights of labor while protecting the health and security of the American economy. Nixon agreed to all of these points. While these positions differed little from policies pursued by Eisenhower, the fact that Rockefeller thought they needed to be explicitly stated implied that the president had not carried them out effectively. This would anger the president.

Three other domestic policy positions went significantly beyond what the Eisenhower administration had advocated: a contributory system to provide health insurance for the aged; "prompt and substantial" grant aid for the construction of schools, primarily on the basis of financial need; and a federal civil rights program designed to eliminate segregation and discrimination in voting, housing, schools, jobs, and public accommodations. Nixon's misgivings about the details of some of these positions, particularly the health insurance plan, led to more vague wording than Rockefeller had hoped for, but in the end Nixon agreed to all of them.[66]

Where the two men came into more serious conflict was in their discussion of foreign policy and national defense. As in domestic policy, Rockefeller had a list of policy positions that he wanted included in the Republican Party platform. The first two were relatively uncontroversial statements declaring the necessity for the United States to maintain and expand its role as a regional and global leader in the struggle against communism. The rest, however, recommended that the United States upgrade its level of military preparedness, implying that the Eisenhower administration had slighted its duties in this area. The last point stated that "The United States can afford and must provide the increased expenditures to implement fully this necessary program for strengthening our defense posture. There must be no price ceiling on America's security." This was an obvious reference to Rockefeller's demands that the defense budget be increased by $3.5 billion, from $1.5 billion to $5 billion. Eisenhower had strongly denied the need for such an increase.[67]

Nixon balked at these points, which he knew would anger Eisenhower. Rockefeller later recalled reaching the last point at around 2:30 in the morning: "I was trying to get into the platform a recommendation for increased expenditures . . . Dick gagged. . . . He was tired. And for twenty minutes he didn't say anything. Just sat there. Watching him, I began to realize that what he was doing . . . was thinking. He agreed pretty much, I think, with the position that I was proposing, but he was trying to think what President Eisenhower's reaction would be, and he didn't want to go against the president." Rockefeller claims that, after realizing what Nixon was up against, he agreed to soften the language a bit to make it less critical of the president and more oriented toward the future. "He was in a very strange situation," Rockefeller said. "He wanted to win on his own, without President Eisenhower. . . . But he didn't want the President to come out against him on something, so he didn't want to offend him. . . . He needed to go either one way or the other."[68]

Eisenhower understood Nixon's dilemma as well. The president admitted that "To promise and pledge *new* effort, *new* programs, and *new* ideas without appearing to criticize the current party and administration—that is indeed an exercise in tightrope walking." Although he may have understood Nixon's situation, Eisenhower found the Nixon-Rockefeller statement unacceptable. When they had completed their negotiations, Rockefeller and Nixon called Charles Percy, chairman of the Republican Platform Committee, and read him the declaration. When Percy gave the text to the platform committee, Bob Merriam, Eisenhower's representative on the committee, called Jim Hagerty who passed the news along to the president. Eisenhower was especially displeased with the final statement on defense. He considered it "Somewhat astonishing, coming as it did from two people who had long been in administration councils and who had never voiced any doubt—at least in my presence—of the adequacy of America's defenses." Hagerty returned Merriam's call to tell him that the wording was unacceptable, but Rockefeller had already made the text public.[69]

The press interpreted the "Compact of Fifth Avenue" as a Nixon "surrender" to Rockefeller. Outspoken conservatives agreed. Barry Goldwater called the statement "An American Munich." Goldwater considered

Rockefeller to be the "spokesman for an ideological grouping within the party" that he called "me-tooers." These were Republicans who, Goldwater said, embraced the objectives of the New Deal and Fair Deal.[70]

When Nixon phoned Eisenhower to discuss the statement and the fallout it had created, Eisenhower told him that he had been receiving reports of opposition among the members of the platform committee, which had nearly completed its work by the time of the Nixon-Rockefeller meeting. They were upset, he said, because Rockefeller had put out the statement unilaterally and they did not want to appear to be giving in to him. Others, he said, had urged him to support Barry Goldwater for the nomination. Eisenhower told Nixon that he wanted to support the party, but he said, it would be difficult for him to be "enthusiastic about a platform which did not reflect a respect for the record of the Republican administration, and a purpose of building on this record."[71]

Nixon told Eisenhower he was trying "to find some ground on which Nelson can be with us and not against us."[72] After his discussion with the president, however, he decided it was also important that Eisenhower be with him. He agreed to change the wording of the offensive passage to read: "The United States can and must provide whatever is necessary to insure its own security . . . to provide any necessary increased expenditures to meet new situations. . . . To provide more would be wasteful. To provide less would be catastrophic." This passage was acceptable to Nixon, Eisenhower, and Rockefeller.[73] Despite the controversy, Nixon was pleased with the agreement. The Democrats' charges of a missile gap had become impossible to ignore. Incorporating a plank on increased defense spending into the platform gave Nixon the freedom to address the issue without looking as though he was repudiating the policies of Eisenhower. The other issues addressed in the agreement would satisfy Rockefeller's supporters without losing Nixon the backing of conservatives, who had nowhere else to turn.

In his address to the Republican Convention on July 26, Eisenhower downplayed the divisions within the party. "Within this Convention," he said, "I hear that there is some dispute among the delegates concerning the platform. Now there is nothing wrong in this. It is good! . . . There is room for healthy argument within our party." During this and other addresses at the convention, Eisenhower seemed more concerned with protecting his own legacy than with helping to build a new one. He discussed his own accomplishments and reminded the delegates and the platform committee that he was the president and he would not have his policies repudiated while he was still in office. He also encouraged them to stay firmly on the course he had set. "Every Republican," he told the delegates, "every independent, every discerning Democrat should be appealed to on the basis that we are truly a middle-of-the-road party."[74]

Nixon easily won the presidential nomination and selected Henry Cabot Lodge as his running mate. Nixon was concerned that Lodge's views on domestic policy were too liberal, but he was still eager to avoid a floor fight with the Rockefeller supporters, and he knew that Lodge had wide support. He also asked Rockefeller to introduce him to the convention for his acceptance speech.[75] Knowing that his concessions to the party's liberal wing would upset conservatives (Barry Goldwater had called the selection of Lodge a "disastrous blunder"), he also invited Goldwater to address the delegates.[76] In Goldwater's speech to the convention he urged conservatives to support Nixon, but he had long-term, rather than immediate, goals in mind. He said that the Republican platform, while flawed, was a better alternative than the "blueprint for socialism presented by the Democrats." He warned conservative voters to participate in the campaign, saying they could best achieve their goals through the party. "Republicans have not been losing elections because of more Democratic votes," he told them, "we have been losing elections because conservatives often fail to vote. . . . Let's grow up, conservatives. . . . If we want to take this party back— and I think we can some day—let's get to work."[77]

The 1960 Presidential Election

What is remarkable about the 1960 general election is not that Nixon lost, but that he managed to make the election as close as it was. Democratic candidate John F. Kennedy won just 49.7 percent of the vote to Nixon's 49.6 percent, a margin of only 112,801 votes. Even the popular vote count, however, does not adequately indicate Kennedy's slim margin of victory. At a glance, the electoral college vote does not appear to be as close as the popular vote. Kennedy won twenty-three states with a total of 303 electoral votes, Nixon won twenty-six states with a total of 219 electoral votes. A switch of only 11,874 votes in the five closest states, however, would have swung the electoral count and, therefore, the election in Nixon's favor. Republicans also made a net gain of twenty-one seats in the House, two seats in the Senate, and two governorships.[78]

Nixon had carried five out of eight geographic regions of the United States, failing to win only Kennedy's home base of New England, the Mid-Atlantic, and the South. Civil rights was more of an issue in 1960 than it had been in 1952 and 1956 when Eisenhower made significant inroads into the South. Nixon's support for civil rights had prevented him from picking up southern Democrats. The number of votes he had picked up among northern blacks for this stand, however, were not enough to make up the difference. One explanation for this may be Nixon's failure to take decisive action after the arrest of Dr. Martin Luther King Jr. in Atlanta, Georgia, in 1960. John Kennedy, at the urging of his brother, Robert, had interceded and facilitated King's release, which endeared him to black voters nationwide.

Goldwater blamed Nixon's loss on his failure to give the voters a clear-cut choice. Voters, he claimed, had been presented with another "me-too" candidate, just as they had been in 1940, 1944, and 1948.[79] "We cannot win as a dimestore copy of the opposition's platform," Goldwater said after the election. "We must be different."[80] Goldwater had already begun to think about the 1964 campaign: "I want to figure in 1964, not necessarily as the top candidate. But I don't want Rockefeller in that spot."[81]

Despite Kennedy's slim margin of victory, the 1960 campaign eroded Nixon's credibility as a national figure. His image was further damaged by his unsuccessful run for governor of California in 1962. Although he was now associated with two devastating losses, Nixon remained the only major figure with ties to both wings of the party and, therefore, remained a possible compromise candidate for the future. Two men, however, had emerged relatively unscathed by the Republican defeat. Nelson Rockefeller had firmly established himself as the leader of the party's liberal wing, while Barry Goldwater had gained firm control of the right.

Conclusion

In his presidential memoir, Eisenhower wrote that he was disappointed he had failed to revitalize the party and make it popular enough to continue on successfully without him. "One of the goals I set for myself when I agreed to run for the Presidency," he recalled, "was to unify, and strengthen the Republican Party." He admitted to only "slight" success in achieving this goal. "Certainly I did not succeed in the hope of so increasing the party's appeal to the American electorate as to assure a few more years, after 1960, of Republican government." He wondered whether he had done the party a disservice by running for a second term, thinking that if he had not, Nixon or another Republican candidate might have been elected before the party had further declined, thus increasing the chances of a victory in 1960. In any event, he said "My principal political disappointment was the defeat of Dick Nixon in 1960."[82]

Eisenhower's reminiscences came five years after he left the White House. By then, given the party's further decline, he may have had such regrets. His actions as president, however, were not those of someone trying to unify his party. If party unity had been his goal, Eisenhower could have used his personal popularity indiscriminately to carry Republicans to victory, perhaps avoiding six years of divided government. His frequent refusals to campaign for conservatives who had opposed his policies demonstrate that he was not willing to do this. Despite his occasional threats, however, he was also unwilling to leave the Republican Party. His real goal was to change the party's direction. Unable to do so on the strength of his policies, he would have to actively promote Republican candidates who would perpetuate his legacy and inspire unity among those who shared his belief in the "middle way." This he failed to do. The long-term consequences for the "middle way" were devastating. Nixon's defeat in 1960 was only the beginning.

7

An Echo
or a Choice?

On the morning of September 3, 1963, Richard Nixon, who had moved to New York City after his loss in the 1962 California gubernatorial contest, received a call from his upstairs neighbor who was, coincidentally, Nelson Rockefeller. Rockefeller invited Nixon up for cocktails that afternoon. After some small talk, the New York governor got down to business. "I'm going to go for the nomination," he told the former vice president. "I have nothing to lose. I would worry if Barry [Goldwater] won, because he's just too shallow. He only went to college for one year. He doesn't have a good staff, and he has a very superficial approach to problems. I will take on the task of stopping Barry. If I don't he's going to get it by default." Rockefeller went on to consider the other possibilities for a "stop Goldwater" candidate: Governor George Romney of Michigan, who Rockefeller thought was weak on foreign affairs and too much of an independent for the party regulars; and Governor William Scranton of Pennsylvania, who had said he would only run if he were drafted, an eventuality Rockefeller thought unlikely. Then Rockefeller turned to the possibility of a Nixon candidacy. "Dick, you can't run actively," he said. "You *could,* but it would be a big mistake, and you don't make that kind of mistake. What we both have to recognize is that you and I are the only ones qualified on both foreign and national issues to serve as President. Despite some differences, we have generally agreed on basic principles." Rockefeller then got to the reason he had called the meeting. "What I want to suggest," he said, "is that if you will support me now, if there is a deadlock at the convention, I will support you."[1]

Although Nixon made no commitment, preferring to keep his options open, this exchange is significant for what it says about the campaign for the 1964 Republican nomination. Conservative forces were united behind

Goldwater as the one man who could break the hold that liberal and moderate candidates had had on presidential nominations since 1936. The only thing that liberal and moderate Republicans were united on was that they needed to "stop" Goldwater. Their lack of a consensus on an alternative candidate cost them the nomination.

Barry Goldwater on the "Middle Way"

Barry Goldwater, although he rarely criticized Eisenhower publicly, represented the antithesis of the "middle way." Over the years Goldwater's support for Eisenhower had declined. During the 1955–1956 congressional session, Goldwater voted with the administration 66 percent of the time, already well below the average Republican senator's score of 72 percent. During Eisenhower's second term, Goldwater's support for the president dropped significantly. His votes for legislation favored by the administration dropped to 57 percent in 1957–1958, and to 52 percent in 1959–1960.[2] After Eisenhower left office, Goldwater's support for legislation favored by the Republican leadership dropped even further. Assistant Senate Republican Minority Leader Thomas Kutchel (CA) compiled a list of the twenty-five legislative initiatives undertaken by the U.S. Senate between 1961 and 1964 that had been specifically favored by the 1960 Republican National Platform. Minority Leader Everett Dirksen (IL) had supported eighteen of these, chairman of the Republican Policy Committee Bourke Hickenlooper had supported seventeen, chairman of the Republican Conference Leverett Saltonstall had supported twenty, and Kutchel had supported all twenty-five. All but two of these had been favored by a majority of Senate Republicans. Goldwater had voted against all twenty-five.[3]

Many of the issues that Goldwater was most outspoken about were ones on which he was in direct disagreement with the policies of Eisenhower's "middle way." Several of these issues were in the field of social welfare policy. During Eisenhower's first term, HEW, under the direction of Secretary Hobby and Undersecretary Rockefeller, studied various proposals to overhaul Social Security. One such proposal was voluntary participation, which was rejected on the grounds that it would bankrupt the system. During the 1964 campaign, Goldwater resuscitated the issue of overhauling Social Security. "This is the only position I have on it," he told the *New York Times Magazine;* "If a man wants it, fine. If he doesn't want it, he can provide his own."[4]

Goldwater was also "opposed to every form of federal aid to education."[5] He consistently voted against school construction bills such as those introduced by the Eisenhower administration in 1955 and 1956, and bills to promote higher education, such as the successful National Defense Education Act of 1958. Goldwater believed that, since federal aid given to the states for education had been collected from them through federal taxes, aid to education was "an act of naked compulsion—a decision by the federal government to force the people of the States to spend more money than they chose to spend for this purpose voluntarily." Moreover, he believed that federal interference in this field was unconstitutional, unnecessary, and would lead to federal control of the educational process.[6]

Goldwater also differed from the "middle way" on the subject of labor. During his first term, Eisenhower had supported amendments to the Taft-Hartley Act on the grounds that it contained several provisions that were unfair to unions. Among these changes was a proposal to amend section 14-b to eliminate the right of states to pass "right-to-work" laws. Although he later withdrew his support of this amendment, he adamantly refused to endorse "right-to-work" movements, insisting it was a state matter. Goldwater saw Taft-Hartley differently; he believed that "Thanks to some unwise provisions and to the absence of others that should have been included, the delicate balance of power we sought to achieve between labor and management has shifted, in avalanche proportions, to labor's advantage."[7] Goldwater promoted and enthusiastically supported state efforts to pass "right-to-work" laws as one way of making up that advantage.

Eisenhower's secretary of Agriculture, Ezra Taft Benson, was in favor of eliminating price supports and restoring the free market for agricultural commodities. Under Eisenhower's influence, however, he concluded that this would have to be done gradually. In the mean time, the Department of Agriculture administered programs such as the Soil Bank to diminish farm surpluses, the root cause of the agricultural problem. Goldwater also wanted to restore the free market for agriculture, but his approach to the problem was far less pragmatic. He considered federal involvement in the agricultural sector unconstitutional and believed that to "reward people for not producing," was "absurd and self-defeating." His solution for the problem of the surplus was "prompt and final termination of the farm subsidy program," with "no equivocation." This he said would be the only way to persuade "inefficient" farmers to enter other fields of endeavor.[8] This position put him at odds with many of his fellow conservatives, particularly those from farm states.

Goldwater's position on federal legislation for the protection of the civil rights of black Americans was among his most controversial. In 1957, when Senator Paul Douglas (D-IL) and Senate Minority Leader William Knowland (R-CA) circumvented the Senate Judiciary Committee by placing civil rights legislation directly on the Senate calendar, Goldwater was one of only five Republicans who voted against the move.[9] Later, when southern Democrats introduced an amendment to what would become the Civil Rights Act of 1957, guaranteeing those charged with violating an individual's civil rights a trial by jury, Goldwater had been one of twelve Republicans who voted in favor of it. The legislation's supporters, including the president, believed this amendment would cripple the legislation.[10] Goldwater was also outspokenly against the Supreme Court's rulings on *Brown v. Board*. Since "No powers regarding education were given the federal government" in the Constitution, he argued, "the entire field was reserved to the states" by virtue of the Tenth Amendment. Since the "equal protection" clause of the Fourteenth Amendment did not grant any new power to the federal government in the area of education, he said, the Supreme Court could only arrive at its decision in *Brown v. Board* by "engrafting its own views onto the established law of the land." He was, therefore, "not impressed by the claim that the Supreme Court's decision on school integration is the law of the land." Because of this, he supported "all efforts by the States, excluding violence of course, to preserve their rightful powers over education."[11]

Many of Goldwater's views were interpreted by the press and his political opponents as being harsh and callous. This was a belief he did little to dispel. In January 1964, during an appearance on the *Today Show,* host Martin Agronsky gave Goldwater an opportunity to soften his stand. Referring to a controversial speech Goldwater had made, Agronsky asked, "You said that the attitude or the actions of the poor contributed to their own plight . . . [that] most people who have no skill, have no education for the same reason, and that is low intelligence or ambition. There has been an enormous amount of criticism of that speech; would you like to clarify it or say what you meant?" Goldwater responded, "It said what I meant."[12] On another occasion he told a New York City crowd that it was time for "a frontal attack against Santa Claus . . . the Santa Claus of . . . the free lunch, [and] the government handout."[13]

Goldwater opposed the "middle way" in foreign policy as well. Most frustrating to Eisenhower was Goldwater's belief that the mutual security program was a "give-away" program intended to win friends for the United States.[14] He recommended that Congress "eliminate all government-to-government capital assistance and encourage the substitution of private investment."[15] Other foreign and military policies that Goldwater was associated with included withdrawal from the United Nations; withdrawal of diplomatic recognition from the Soviet Union; and giving the Supreme Commander of NATO the authority to fire tactical nuclear weapons without approval from the president.[16] These views made Goldwater seem like a dangerous radical to many.

Although he avoided outright criticism of Eisenhower, Goldwater believed that, for the previous twenty years, Republican presidential candidates had offered voters little more than an "echo" of the policies of their Democratic counterparts. Goldwater suggested that, if this was what voters really wanted, they should turn to the Democratic Party, "where the liberal noise really originates." The Republican Party should offer voters a choice. "I think if we offered them a choice this year of conservatism versus so-called liberalism," Goldwater said in 1964, "the choice is going to be in the direction of conservatism."[17] This was based on Goldwater's belief that, while "Eastern Establishment" liberals had been successful in controlling presidential nominations, they were a very small minority within the party, consisting of only 10–15 percent, with conservatives making up the other 85–90 percent.[18]

Campaigning for the Republican Nomination

Rockefeller followed through on his decision to run for president despite Nixon's reluctance to support him. He formally announced his candidacy in Nashua, New Hampshire, on November 7, 1963.[19] In his campaign Rockefeller represented himself as a responsible, middle-of-the-road candidate, while portraying Goldwater as a dangerous radical whose views lay outside the mainstream of the Republican Party. "I want to help build a party that rejects the extremism of both the left and the right," he told a Portsmouth, New Hampshire, audience in the opening days of the campaign, "a party that moves forward in the broad mainstream of American political thought and instinct."[20] To the audience of *Face the Nation,* Rockefeller said, "Imagine the Republican Party presenting the American people a candidate and a platform calling for U.S. withdrawal from the U.N., granting military field commanders discretion to use nuclear weapons, cutting off all foreign aid . . . ending farm price supports, leaving the protection of human rights to the states . . . and favoring enactment of a federal right-to-work law." These were the things, he warned the viewers, that Goldwater would do if elected president.[21] Goldwater protested that Rockefeller was representing his position "as being against mother love, free beer, and wide roads."[22]

Goldwater formally announced his candidacy on January 3, 1964. He claimed that a Rockefeller nomination would not offer Americans a significant alternative to the policies of the Democratic Party. "I decided to do this," he told the crowd that gathered at his home in Paradise Valley, Arizona, to hear him announce his candidacy, "because I have not heard from any announced Republican candidate a declaration of conscience or of political position that could possibly offer the American people a clear choice in the next presidential election."[23]

Sixteen states held primaries in 1964. Of these, Goldwater and Rockefeller went head-to-head in only three: New Hampshire, Oregon, and California.[24] In New Hampshire, Goldwater made Rockefeller's tactic of painting him as an extremist easy. While the senator's prepared speeches were moderate and well received, his impromptu remarks were often inflammatory. His more controversial comments included assertions that Eisenhower had "stolen" the nomination from Taft in 1952; that people should "do what they're supposed to do" and take care of the poor on their own; that recognition of the Soviet Union had been a "dreadful" mistake; and that the United States should have used a low-yield atomic bomb on North Vietnam "ten years ago" to defoliate the jungle. Remarks such as these caused even the more conservative New Hampshire Republicans to take a closer look at Rockefeller.[25]

Despite the fact that New Hampshire voters considered him a "tax-and-spend" liberal, Rockefeller might have won the nation's first primary if it had not been for the informal candidacy of Henry Cabot Lodge. The Lodge campaign was launched by a group of political amateurs from Boston who desired an alternative to Goldwater and Rockefeller. They hoped that, if they could demonstrate Lodge had enough support, he would return from Saigon where he was serving as ambassador to South Vietnam. Lodge supporters' remarkable success shows that this group was not alone in their desire for an alternative candidate. Although Lodge's name was not on the ballot, he received 33,000 write-in votes in the March 10 primary, a convincing victory over Goldwater, who had 20,700, and Rockefeller, who came in a close third with 19,500. Goldwater and Rockefeller were disappointed with the inconclusive results of the New Hampshire primary, and both considered the possibility of dropping out of the race. Both, however, persevered. Goldwater continued because his staff told him he could still win, and Rockefeller continued because he wanted to stop Goldwater.[26]

The next direct confrontation between the two men was in the Oregon primary on May 15. In this contest, Rockefeller had the field to himself. Lodge, whose candidacy gained widespread support after his showing in New Hampshire, did not return to the country to participate in the campaign; and Goldwater chose to go directly to California, where the stakes were much bigger. This allowed Rockefeller to add, "He cares enough to come" to his main theme of portraying Goldwater as an extremist. The strategy worked. Oregon Republicans, who already had a reputation of being more liberal than their New Hampshire counterparts, gave Rockefeller the victory with 93,000 votes to Lodge's 78,000. Goldwater came in third with 50,000.[27]

Despite Rockefeller's win in Oregon, many experts believed that Goldwater already had enough delegates to win the nomination. Of the 1,308 delegates that would be present at the convention, only 540 were committed to primary results. The inconclusiveness of the head-to-head contests between the two thus far, however, led Goldwater to declare that a loss in California would rule him out as a candidate. This made California, with its eighty-four committed delegates, into a climactic showdown between the two wings of the Republican Party.[28]

Goldwater, since he skipped the Oregon campaign, had been in California longer and was better organized than Rockefeller. His legions of volunteers canvassed the state asking voters whether they wanted "an echo or a choice." Nevertheless, it appeared that Rockefeller had the edge, leading Goldwater by eleven percentage points less than two weeks before the June 2 primary.[29] Rockefeller continued to drive home the extremism theme, an issue on which Goldwater was particularly vulnerable in California. The John Birch Society, an organization whose positions Rockefeller had been using as examples of right-wing extremism, had a large membership in Southern California; and Robert Welch, the society's founder, had endorsed Goldwater for president. Goldwater wanted to distance himself from some of this group's statements (for instance their claim that Eisenhower and Dulles were "fellow travelers," a term suggesting they had ties to communists), but he never repudiated their support. Goldwater later defended his decision, saying the majority of John Birch Society members, were "patriotic, concerned, law-abiding, hard-working, and productive" citizens.[30]

One week before the primary, Rockefeller received a further boost when Eisenhower released a statement regarding his preferences for the 1964 nominee. "Many concerned people have urged me to indicate my preference among the possible Republican candidates," he began. "I do not intend to do this." What he did do, however, was list the policies upon which he believed the successful candidate should stand. He said these "responsible, forward looking" policies had been most recently spelled out in the 1960 platform. Using the expansion of Social Security benefits during his first term as an example, he said that Republicans should "not shrink from a recognition that there are national problems that require national solutions." The former president said that the biggest domestic problem facing the country was civil rights. Recalling the passage of the Civil Rights Acts of 1957 and 1960, he said, "As the party of Lincoln, Republicans have a particular obligation to be vigorous in the furtherance of Civil Rights." In the field of foreign and military affairs he said that maintaining peace and protecting freedom required the "loyal support of the United Nations," and he warned that there was no room for "impulsiveness" in nuclear-age diplomacy. The *New York Herald Tribune* ran the story under the headline "Eisenhower Outline Fits All Except Goldwater." At a San Diego news conference, Rockefeller declared, "I fall within the framework of that description. I don't think Senator Goldwater's views are compatible." Most observers—amateurs and experts alike—agreed.[31]

With just three days to go before the California primary, Rockefeller led Goldwater in the polls by 9 percent. His victory seemed all but ensured. Then the bottom dropped out. The roots of Rockefeller's defeat in California went back several years. In November 1961, Rockefeller and Mary Todhunter Clark, his wife for more than thirty years and the mother of his five children, separated. Three months later Mrs. Rockefeller filed for divorce on grounds of mental cruelty. Rockefeller's divorce had little immediate effect on his political life. He was reelected governor in November 1962 by a larger margin than in his first victory. In May 1963, Rockefeller married Margaretta "Happy" Murphy, who had, one month earlier, divorced her husband, a friend and employee of the Rockefeller family and father of her four young children.[32]

Political columnist Stewart Alsop observed at the time that Rockefeller could have remarried or become president, but he could not do both. The prediction seemed to be true. Rockefeller's ratings in the polls dropped dramatically in the weeks following the wedding. Over the next year, however, Rockefeller overcame the setback with his respectable showing in New Hampshire and his victory in Oregon. Then, just two days before the California vote, Happy Rockefeller gave birth. Rockefeller left California and flew back to New York to be with his wife and new son, Nelson Jr. The story, with help from the Goldwater campaign, reminded the California voters of the unsavory circumstances surrounding Rockefeller's divorce and remarriage. By the eve of the primary Rockefeller's lead had disappeared. The next day, June 2, Goldwater won with just under 52 percent of the vote.[33]

The "Stop Goldwater" Movement

Goldwater's victory in California threw the "stop Goldwater" forces into high gear. Since their candidate was not on the ballot in California, the Lodge forces had given their support to Rockefeller with the hope that a victory by the New York governor would deadlock the convention and lead to the selection of Lodge. Other prominent members of the moderate-liberal wing of the party had remained silent, hoping that Rockefeller would win without their help, allowing them to save their influence for the convention battle that would then ensue. This fact had not escaped Rockefeller who blamed his defeat on the silence of other prominent Republicans who opposed Goldwater.[34]

The first occasion for the anti-Goldwater forces to meet after Goldwater's victory in California was at the National Governor's Conference in Cleveland, Ohio, during the second week of June. The majority of the sixteen Republican governors were in agreement that a Goldwater nomination would be devastating for the Republican Party. They knew that if they were to prevent it, they would have to agree on who the alternative candidate should be. Rockefeller told reporters he planned to continue fighting for the nomination himself. If another situation developed, however, he said he would be happy to sacrifice his own ambitions for the sake of the party.[35]

The most likely alternative to Rockefeller as a "stop Goldwater" candidate was Pennsylvania Governor William Scranton. On June 6, the day before going to Cleveland for the governors' conference, Scranton met with Eisenhower at the former president's Gettysburg home. The two discussed their mutual belief that if Goldwater were nominated it would assure a Johnson landslide. During their discussion Scranton got the impression that if he were to run, Eisenhower would endorse him. Already scheduled to appear on *Face the Nation* from Cleveland the next day, Scranton decided to use the program to announce his belated candidacy. When he arrived in Cleveland, Scranton heard that Eisenhower had been trying to reach him. Scranton phoned Eisenhower, and the former president said that he hoped Scranton had not misinterpreted his encouragement as an endorsement, since he planned to stay neutral. Scranton's appearance on the *Face the Nation*, therefore, was anticlimactic. Deciding at the last minute not to announce without Eisenhower's support, Scranton did little more than reiterate his objections to Goldwater.[36] When the story got out, Eisenhower declared that he was "astonished to learn that my con-ference with Governor Scranton had been interpreted generally as support-ing him over the ambitions of other candidates."[37]

Since Scranton seemed to be out of the picture, the governors began looking for another possibility. Rockefeller, Governor James Rhodes of Ohio, and Richard Nixon, also in Cleveland, briefly supported Governor George Romney of Michigan who pledged to "do everything within my power to keep him [Goldwater] from becoming the party's presidential can-didate." Nixon had encouraged Romney to run but did not want his name mentioned in connection with Romney's decision. He was probably hop-ing that a Romney candidacy would deadlock the convention. If this occurred, Nixon himself might be nominated. Romney, however, told the press he had Nixon's support, probably dooming the former vice presi-dent's chances, even as a dark-horse candidate. In any event, Romney's candidacy was short-lived. Voters in Michigan vociferously reminded him of his pledge not to run for president while serving the state.[38]

Meanwhile, an issue was developing in Washington, D.C., that would make Scranton reconsider his decision not to run. Southern Democrats were filibustering the legislation that became the Civil Rights Act of 1964. On June 10, Goldwater voted against the cloture motion that succeeded in ending the filibuster. He then offered amendments to eliminate from the legislation those sections prohibiting discrimination in public accommoda-tions and mandating fair employment practices. Goldwater said these sec-tions "would force you to admit drunks, a known murderer or an insane person into your place of business" and would lead to the hiring of "incompetent" employees.[39] He argued that the federal government had no constitutional jurisdiction in this area, and it should be left to state and local governments. On June 18, 1964, he was one of twenty-seven senators to vote against the act.

On June 11, the day after Goldwater's vote against cloture, Governor Scranton announced his candidacy. He was no longer concerned with whether Eisenhower would support him. Putting a twist on Goldwater's favorite catchphrase, Scranton said, "I have come here to offer our party a real choice. I reject the echo we have thus far been handed—the echo of fear and reaction—the echo from the never-never land that puts our nation on the road backward to a lesser place in the world of free men. . . . Can we in good conscience turn our backs on the century-old progressive history of our party? You and I know we cannot." Rockefeller threw his support behind Scranton and recommended that "all like-minded Republicans who believe in the moderate, progressive position for our party should unite back of Bill Scranton for the nomination."[40]

With little more than a month before the Republican National Convention at the "Cow Palace" in San Francisco, Scranton had no chance to gather delegates in the customary way. His only hope was to win enough converts to prevent Goldwater from being nominated on the first ballot. If he was successful in this, anything could happen in the ensuing ballots. To do this, Scranton's supporters sought to focus the convention's attention on issues that might cause dissension among the delegate ranks. "What we were looking for," said one Scranton supporter, "was something that would put the nation and the rank and file of the party on alert to the fact that our leading candidate was impetuous, irresponsible, and slightly stupid."[41] Unable to agree on one specific issue, Scanton's team decided to challenge the Arizona senator to a debate. Unfortunately for Scranton, he failed to read the letter his overzealous staff members wrote to Goldwater. More an indictment than a request for a debate, the letter called "Goldwaterism" a "crazy-quilt collection of absurd and dangerous positions that would be soundly repudiated by the American people in November."[42] Goldwater released the letter to the press and refused the debate.

At the convention, Rockefeller made one final attempt to focus the convention's attention on Goldwater's weaknesses. Given ten minutes to address the delegates, Rockefeller used the time to propose an amendment to the platform on the subject of extremism. The amendment asserted that Republicans "repudiate the efforts of irresponsible, extremist groups, such as the Communists, the Ku Klux Klan, the John Birch Society and others, to discredit our Party by their efforts to infiltrate positions of responsibility in the Party, or to attach themselves to its candidates."[43] By this time, however, Goldwater supporters were in complete control of the Cow Palace. Rockefeller was unable to deliver a five-minute text in ten minutes due to the booing and chanting. He later compared the experience to being run over by a steamroller.[44]

The next night Goldwater was nominated on the first ballot, ending any chance that Scranton could broker the convention. Richard Nixon, being the party's previous nominee, was chosen to introduce him. Nixon, always playing the role of party unifier, gave Goldwater the perfect opportunity to begin bridging the deep rift between the two wings of the Republican Party. "Before this convention we were Goldwater Republicans, Rockefeller Republicans, Scranton Republicans, [and] Lodge Republicans," he told the delegates, "but now that this convention has met and made its decision, we are Republicans, period, working for Barry Goldwater for President of the United States." Goldwater ignored the opening. "Anyone who joins us in all sincerity we welcome," he responded. "Those who don't care for our cause, we don't expect to enter our ranks in any case." Nixon later recalled that he felt "physically sick" as he sat on the platform and listened to the climax of Goldwater's speech: "Extremism in the defense of liberty is no vice! . . . Moderation in the pursuit of justice is no virtue!"[45]

Goldwater's speech greatly disturbed the liberal-moderate wing of the party. Rockefeller called it "dangerous, irresponsible, and frightening."[46] Nixon, wanting to give Goldwater another chance, wrote to the candidate and asked him to clarify his convention statements, letting him know that he would release the candidate's response to the press. Goldwater wrote that if he were to paraphrase his most controversial statement, he would say that "Wholehearted devotion to liberty is unassailable and . . . half-hearted devotion to justice is indefensible." Nixon was relieved that Goldwater had at least not used the word "extremism."[47] He believed that Goldwater was ready to compromise.

Still trying to mediate the dispute, Nixon suggested to Eisenhower that he meet with Goldwater so the two men could iron out their differences. The meeting could be followed by a Republican "unity conference" where all the party leaders would get together and put on a positive front before kicking off the general election. Eisenhower agreed to both suggestions. Nixon, who sat in, reported that the meeting between Eisenhower and Goldwater was candid. The former president told Goldwater that he should stop "shooting from the hip" and begin making conciliatory speeches. The Republican nominee told Eisenhower that it was not in his nature to be cautious but that he had not meant anything personal in his statements that had been taken as critical of the Eisenhower administration.[48] On the whole, however, the meeting was a success. Afterward, Eisenhower released a statement saying, "Any uncertainties I may have felt as to the fitness, adequacy, and quality of the political program they [Goldwater and his running mate, William Miller] will offer to the U.S. in the 1964 campaign have been resolved. I fully support the Republican national ticket in the coming campaign."[49]

The "unity conference" was held in Hershey, Pennsylvania, on August 12. Among the attendees were Eisenhower, Nixon, Goldwater, Rockefeller, Scranton, and Romney. Goldwater's speech at the meeting was gracious and moderate.[50] Afterwards the Republican leaders engaged in an optimistic discussion of how the campaign should be run. The real purpose of the event, however, was to put on a good front for the press conference that followed the meeting. To Nixon's amazement, Goldwater once again blew his chance. He told reporters that he did not consider his speech conciliatory and that he had not made any concessions on issues of substance. Goldwater himself then brought up the controversial subject of giving military commanders in the field control over tactical nuclear weapons.[51]

The "unity conference" had accomplished very little. On the way back to Gettysburg, Eisenhower said, "You know, before we had this meeting I thought that Goldwater was just stubborn. Now I am convinced that he is just plain dumb."[52] The Goldwater candidacy was doomed from the start. Nixon did his best for the candidate, Eisenhower and Scranton put in half-hearted efforts on Goldwater's behalf, Rockefeller endorsed him but did not actively campaign, and Romney never even endorsed him.[53] Former Eisenhower cabinet members Oveta Culp Hobby, Arthur Flemming, and Marion Folsom all endorsed Lyndon Johnson.

Nixon said that it was frustrating for him "to see as inept a candidate as Goldwater running for president." By early evening on election day, all three networks had predicted a Johnson landslide. They proved to be correct. Johnson defeated Goldwater by 16 million votes, 43 million to 27 million, and won 486 electoral votes to Goldwater's 52. In terms of the popular vote, it was the worst defeat in presidential election history. It might have been worse without Goldwater's opposition to the Civil Rights Act of 1964, which won him the electoral votes of Louisiana, Mississippi, Alabama, Georgia, and South Carolina, the only states he carried besides his home state of Arizona. The Republicans lost thirty-seven seats in the House and two in the Senate. Goldwater blamed the "stop Goldwater" Republicans for his landslide loss, saying that they were responsible for the distortions the Democrats used throughout the general campaign.[54] On this point at least, Nixon seemed to agree; he called Rockefeller a "spoilsport and a divider."[55]

Conclusion

In 1964, conservative forces united behind Barry Goldwater as the one man who could break the hold that liberal and moderate candidates had maintained on Republican presidential nominations since 1936. The only thing that liberal and moderate Republicans were united on was that they needed to stop Goldwater from winning the nomination. Eisenhower had once told Hagerty that if the Republicans nominated an "Old Guard" conservative for president he would "go up and down this country, campaigning against them."[56] When Goldwater was nominated, however, Eisenhower did no such thing. More important, he failed to take decisive action to prevent the nomination of Goldwater in the first place. Eisenhower remained silent, even when a timely endorsement of Nelson Rockefeller or William Scranton might have prevented conservatives from taking over the convention. In fact, no member of Eisenhower's administration except Rockefeller and Nixon played an important role in the 1964 campaign. Other prominent adherents to the tenants of "modern Republicanism," such as Governors George Romney, James Rhodes, and Scranton were unable to overcome their own political ambitions long enough to promote the greater interests of their wing of the party. Their failure to act cost them not only the nomination but also control of the party.

Conclusion

On February 20, 1996, conservative presidential candidate Patrick Buchanan pulled off a remarkable upset by defeating Republican Party favorite, Senator Robert Dole, in the New Hampshire primary. The margin of victory had been slim, 28 percent to 27 percent, but Dole hoped to avoid another such embarrassment in the following week's primaries in North Dakota, South Dakota, and Arizona—all conservative strongholds. With this in mind Dole traveled to Paradise Valley, Arizona, home of the party's 1964 nominee, Barry Goldwater. Dole hoped that being seen with Goldwater would help him win the votes of conservatives who might otherwise vote for Buchanan. As television cameras looked on, Dole reminisced that he had backed Goldwater in 1964. "Now he's helping me," Dole said. The eighty-seven-year-old Goldwater pronounced Dole the true heir to the "Barry Goldwater, Ronald Reagan legacy of conservatism." Buchanan's message, Goldwater said (without intending irony) was "fearful and divisive." Dole and Goldwater concurred that the party had changed since 1964, which prompted Dole to say, "Barry and I—we've sort of become the liberals." Goldwater laughingly agreed. "We're the new liberals of the Republican Party. Can you imagine that?"[1] This brief exchange shows how far the Republican Party had shifted to the right in less than forty years. This is the very shift that, as president, Dwight D. Eisenhower had attempted to prevent.

The primary reason that Eisenhower decided to run for president in 1952 was that he disagreed with the conservative policies of the front-running candidate, Robert Taft.[2] He believed that with his enormous popularity and experienced leadership he could convince the party to abandon the conservatism of Taft and proceed along the "middle way." Eisenhower was not successful in achieving this goal. The conservative Republicans in Congress favored a complete overturn of the New Deal–internationalist policies of the previous twenty years. When Eisenhower's administration not only failed to pursue this but in fact promoted the expansion of social welfare and global commitments, the conservatives resisted. They refused to support the administration's policy initiatives in health care, education, labor, agriculture, civil rights, foreign aid, and international trade. They referred to Eisenhower's proposals in these areas as "creeping socialism" or, at best, a mere continuation of Democratic policies. By adding their votes to those of liberals who wanted more government involvement than Eisenhower did, conservatives contributed to an unwitting alliance that defeated or compromised most of the administration's proposals in these areas.

Another of Eisenhower's goals was for a number of prominent Republicans to emerge during the course of his administration, who, when the time came, would be willing and capable of continuing his pursuit of the "middle way." This goal also went unfulfilled. Eisenhower's friends and advisors persuaded him to run for a second term in 1956, claiming that there was no one to continue his legacy and the party would be taken over by conservatives if he retired. This belief even led the president to consider the possibility of "dumping" Nixon from the ticket so that he could gain maturity in another job while someone else received national exposure in the vice presidency. Little had changed by 1960. Devastating Republican losses in 1956 and 1958 left the party in a shambles, and Nixon was still the only Republican capable of winning the nomination.

Nixon's place in the Republican Party was ambiguous. He had been selected by Eisenhower, in part, because of his close ties to conservatives, but his eight-year association with Eisenhower left him beholden to the moderate policies of the president. In 1960, when Nixon capitulated to Rockefeller in the "Compact of Fifth Avenue," conservatives had finally had enough. After Nixon's defeat they began a grassroots campaign to nominate Barry Goldwater, the Arizona senator who had emerged as the leading conservative spokesman since Robert Taft's death. A strong challenge by New York Governor Nelson Rockefeller and a last-minute "stop Goldwater" movement could not prevent the senator from capturing the 1964 nomination.

Despite Goldwater's landslide defeat, his nomination marked the death of Eisenhower's "middle way." Nixon, after his reemergence as a national political figure and subsequent election to the presidency in 1968, attempted to revive some of Eisenhower's failed policies, but the Democrats' hatred for Nixon made any attempt to label his policies as liberal fall on deaf ears. For this reason Nixon's place on the political spectrum remains ambiguous. His moderate views on social welfare and his establishment of détente with the Soviet Union earned him the hatred of many conservatives, while his extreme political partisanship, his policies in Vietnam, and the scandal of Watergate earned him the hatred of most liberals. At best he is thought of as a political pragmatist, promoting what was best for Nixon rather than adhering to a strict political ideology.

Whatever return to the "middle way" may have accompanied Nixon's resurgence was, in any event, short-lived. When the Republican Party recovered from the setbacks of Vietnam and Watergate, it looked to Ronald Reagan, whose speeches in support of Goldwater in 1964 had caught the attention of conservatives. "The truth is," Reagan had said, "that outside of its legitimate function, government does nothing as well or as economically as the private sector."[3] Reagan, who had been a registered Democrat until 1962, appealed to many of the same conservatives who had responded to Goldwater's appeal. Reagan's charisma and public-speaking skills gave him a broader base of support, however, allowing him to capture more of the mainstream as well as the intellectual conservatives of the Northeast. This, combined with the growing political clout of the religious right and the increasing electoral significance of the Sunbelt, gave the Republican Party its first truly conservative president since Herbert Hoover.[4] His first inaugural address echoed the sentiments of the 1964 speech that had propelled him into political prominence. "Government," he argued "is not the solution to our problem; government is the problem."[5]

Republican presidential candidates since Reagan have been more likely to invoke his memory than Eisenhower's, despite the fact that both Republican presidents won two terms and remained popular throughout their eight years in office. Reagan's continued popularity relative to Eisenhower's is based on the Republican Party's repudiation of its liberal past. Even the word "liberal," despite its intimate connection with U.S. political history, has taken on a negative connotation among Republicans. This was apparent during the 1988 campaign when Reagan's vice president, George H. W. Bush, mocked the Democratic candidate, Massachusetts Governor Michael Dukakis, for being a "card-carrying member of the A. C. L. U."[6] By the time Barry Goldwater declared 1996 Republican presidential candidate Bob Dole to be heir to "the Barry Goldwater, Ronald Reagan legacy of conservatism," the party had clearly abandoned the "middle way." Dole's claim that he and Goldwater were "the new liberals of the Republican Party," only reinforced the point.[7]

In the early twenty-first century, with the Republican Party as a whole standing farther to the right than at any time since 1932, it is easy to forget the important role the party played in the creation of America's liberal society. This is the party that abolished slavery; enacted civil service reform; drafted the nation's first regulatory, antitrust, consumer protection, and conservation legislation; and led the United States toward a more active role in international affairs. The Republican Party of today, however, has become the party of the right, and liberals within its ranks are branded as mavericks or misfits. The current ideological division between the two parties has become so firmly established that contemporary students of political history ask why mid-twentieth-century liberal Republicans did not just become Democrats.[8]

Historians have contributed to this presentist attitude. The liberal reform movements necessitated by the rise of industrial capitalism are among the defining elements of twentieth-century U.S. history. With the exception of a few progressive-era Republicans like Theodore Roosevelt, however, historians more often identify Democrats with these reform movements. Republicans are depicted as conservatives slowing reform by desperately attempting to maintain the status quo. This depiction fails to recognize the liberal wing that existed within, and often dominated, the Republican Party throughout much of the century.

If historians have overlooked the contributions of Republicans to American liberalism, they have also cleared them of any responsibility for liberalism's failures. Historians tie the so-called crisis of liberalism in the late 1960s to the conflict within the Democratic Party created by domestic social upheaval and the trauma of Vietnam. The failure of Eisenhower's "middle way" demonstrates that the "crisis of liberalism" actually began in the Republican Party a decade earlier, with the defeat of liberals within its ranks. Since the Republican Party, after 1964, went on to win five out of the next six presidential elections, the defeat of liberalism within its own ranks had a profound effect on the future of liberalism itself.

Notes

Introduction

1. Theodore White, *The Making of the President, 1960* (New York: Harper and Row, 1961), 59.

2. Stephen Ambrose, *Eisenhower,* vol. 1, *Soldier, General of the Army, President-Elect, 1890–1952* (New York: Simon and Schuster, 1983), 515, 528; William B. Pickett, *Eisenhower Decides to Run: Presidential Politics and Cold War Strategy* (Chicago: Ivan R. Dee, 2000).

3. Robert H. Ferrell, ed., *The Diary of James C. Hagerty: Eisenhower in Mid-course, 1954–1955* (Bloomington: Indiana University Press, 1983), 3.

4. Dwight D. Eisenhower (hereafter DDE), "Radio and Television Address to the American People on the Achievements of the 83d Congress," August 23, 1954, *Public Papers of the Presidents; Containing the Public Messages, Speeches, and Statements of the President* (hereafter *PPP*) *1954* (Washington, D.C.: GPO, 1958–1961), 746–56.

5. *New York Times,* October 11, 1952, 8.

6. George H. Mayer, *The Republican Party, 1856–1964* (New York: Oxford University Press, 1964), 274–75; Nicol C. Rae, *The Decline and Fall of the Liberal Republicans from 1952 to the Present* (New York: Oxford University Press, 1989), 17.

7. Campaign speech in Wheeling, West Virginia, September 24, 1952, in Excerpts 1952 Campaign Speeches, box 1, Chronological Campaign Subseries, Campaign Series, Dwight D. Eisenhower Papers as President of the United States, 1953–61 (hereafter DDE Papers as President), Dwight D. Eisenhower Library, Abilene, Kansas (hereafter DDEL).

8. Campaign speech in Boise, Idaho, August 20, 1952, *New York Times,* August 21, 1952, 12.

1—A Floor over the Pit of Personal Disaster

1. DDE to Bradford Chynoweth, July 13, 1954, in Chynoweth, box 5, Name Series, DDE Papers as President, DDEL.

2. "Summary of Policy Statements Made by General Eisenhower; As Excerpted from Major Speeches Carried by the *New York Times* and Other Papers from June until November 4th [1952]," vol. 5, Health, Education, and Welfare (HEW), Record Group (RG) 4, Nelson A. Rockefeller (NAR) Personal, Rockefeller Archive Center, North Tarrytown, New York (RAC) (hereafter HEW).

3. President's Advisory Committee on Government Organization (PACGO), vol. 67, Washington D.C. files, RG4.NAR Personal.RAC. The committee, when first created by President-elect Eisenhower in November 1952, was known as the President's Advisory Committee on Government Organization. Executive Order 10432 on January 24, 1953, formalized the committee's status, making it the Special Committee on Government Organization (SCGO). It was later known as the Reorganization Advisory Committee (REAC).

4. Letter to President Eisenhower, March 5, 1953, in folder 439, box 49, REAC, ibid.

5. "Special Message to the Congress Transmitting Reorganization Plan 1 of 1953 Creating the Department of Health, Education, and Welfare," March 12, 1953, *PPP 1953*, 28.

6. See February 24, 1955, in February 1955 (1), box 4, Ann C. Whitman Diary Series (hereafter ACW Diary), DDE Papers as President, DDEL; Archie Robinson, *George Meany and His Times: A Biography* (New York: Simon and Schuster, 1981), 208.

7. Quoted in Cary Reich, *The Life of Nelson A. Rockefeller: Worlds to Conquer, 1908–1958* (New York: Doubleday, 1996), 511.

8. Ibid., 526. See also Joe Alex Morris, *Nelson Rockefeller: A Biography* (New York: Harper, 1960), 289.

9. *New York Times,* October 21, 1952, 24.

10. See Yonkers, New York, October 29, 1952, "Summary of Policy Statements Made by General Eisenhower," also "Aims of the Eisenhower Administration, 1952," both in HEW, vol. 5.

11. "Annual Message to the Congress on the State of the Union," February 2, 1953, *PPP 1953,* 12–34; "Special Message to the Congress Transmitting Proposed Changes in the Social Security Program," August 1, 1953, ibid., 534–36.

12. Donald Bruce Johnson and Kirk H. Porter, eds., *National Party Platforms, 1840–1972* (Urbana: University of Illinois Press, 1973), 503.

13. *Congress and the Nation, 1945–1964: A Review of Government and Politics in the Postwar Years* (Washington, D.C.: Congressional Quarterly Service, 1965), 1238.

14. Ibid., 1247.

15. Ibid.

16. Cabinet meeting, November 20, 1953, *Minutes and Documents of the Cabinet Meetings of President Eisenhower (1953–1961),* 10 microfilm reels (Washington, D.C.: University Publications of America, 1980), reel 1.

17. *Congress and the Nation,* 1246.

18. DDE to E. F. Hutton, October 7, 1953, in folder 156-C, Social Security 1953, box 848, Official File, DDE Records as President, White House Central Files, 1953–1961 (hereafter DDE Records as President), DDEL.

19. "Special Message to the Congress on Old Age and Survivors Insurance and on Federal Grants-in-Aid for Public Assistance Programs," January 14, 1954, *PPP 1954,* 62–68; "Annual Budget Message to the Congress, Fiscal Year 1955," January 21, 1954, ibid., 79–192.

20. New York City Speech, February 2, 1954, HEW, vol. 2.

21. *Congress and the Nation,* 1247; Reich, *Rockefeller,* 527.

22. "General Summary of Provisions of Old-Age and Survivors Insurance Bill," HEW, vol. 39; also Legislation, box 25, Oveta Culp Hobby Papers (hereafter Hobby Papers), DDEL; *New York Times,* September 2, 1954.

23. Under the Truman administration's compulsory health insurance proposal, employees would have contributed to a trust through a federal payroll tax. They would then have received benefits in the form of comprehensive health services, and payment for the medical services would be rendered from the trust fund through the administration of state agencies.

24. DDE quoted from "Aims of the Eisenhower Administration," 1952, HEW, vol. 5; Johnson and Porter, *National Party Platforms,* 503–4.

25. Los Angeles campaign speech, October 10, 1952, "Aims of the Eisenhower Administration," HEW, vol. 5; "Limited Federal Reinsurance Service: Fact Sheet Issued in Connection with Legislative Proposals of 1954," March 1954, HEW, vol. 59.

26. Press conference, Secretary Hobby, March 11, 1954, in ibid.

27. Health, box 7, Campaign Series, DDE Papers as President, DDEL.

28. Ibid.

29. "Principle Features of Proposed Legislation on Health Service Prepayment Plans," March 10, 1954, HEW, vol. 39.

30. Cabinet meeting, December 10, 1954, *Minutes and Documents,* reel 2.

31. "Special Message to the Congress on the Health Needs of the American People," January 18, 1954, *PPP 1954,* 69–77; DDE speech, New York City, February 2, 1954, HEW, vol. 2.

32. Cabinet meetings, February 16, 26, 1954, *Minutes and Documents,* reel 2; Reich, *Rockefeller,* 531.

33. "Reinsurance Bill Fought by A.M.A.," *New York Times,* April 6, 1954, 31.

34. Memorandum from Secretary Hobby to the president, "Luncheon with Insurance Company Executives," May 14, 1954, in Hobby (4), box 19, Administration Series, DDE Papers as President, DDEL.

35. Transcript of television speech, in folder 493 (Health 1954–1955), HEW, box 57; Meeting with AMA officials regarding reinsurance bill, July 7, 1954, in Reinsurance, box 17, Hobby Papers, DDEL.

36. Roswell B. Perkins to Secretary Hobby, "AMA Attacks on Reinsurance Bill," July 2, 1954, in Reinsurance, box 17, Hobby Papers, DDEL.

37. Meeting with AMA officials regarding reinsurance bill, July 7, 1954, ibid.

38. *Congress and the Nation,* 1153.

39. Ferrell, *Diary of James Hagerty,* 89.

40. DDE press conference, July 14, 1954, in Reinsurance, box 17, Hobby Papers, DDEL.

41. Ferrell, *Diary of James Hagerty,* 94.

42. DDE press conference, July 14, 1954, in Reinsurance, box 17, Hobby Papers, DDEL; "Special Message to the Congress Recommending a Health Program," January 31, 1955, *PPP 1955,* 216–23.

43. *Congress and the Nation,* 1204–5. The law had lapsed in 1952 because of a pocket veto by President Truman, who feared it would promote segregation.

44. Dwight D. Eisenhower, *The White House Years, a Personal Account: Waging Peace, 1956–1961* (New York: Doubleday, 1965), 139. The legislation referred to was killed in committee in the House the following year.

45. Quoted in James T. Patterson, *Mr. Republican: A Biography of Robert A. Taft* (Boston: Houghton Mifflin, 1972), 315–39 (323, 320).

46. DDE to Representative Ralph Gwinn of New York, June 7, 1949, in Education, box 7, Campaign Series, DDE Papers as President, DDEL. See also "Summary of Campaign Statements Made by General Eisenhower," HEW, vol. 5.

47. DDE quoted in Stephen Ambrose, *Eisenhower*, vol. 2, *The President* (New York: Simon and Schuster, 1984), 115.

48. *Congress and the Nation*, 1206; "The Eisenhower Administration's Education Program," March 3, 1954, HEW, vol. 68.

49. *Congress and the Nation*, 1206.

50. Ibid; Cabinet meeting, February 26, 1954, *Minutes and Documents*, reel 1; "Federal Aid for Public School Construction: Cabinet Discussion," February 26, 1954, HEW, vol. 69.

51. DDE speech, Washington, D.C., February 8, 1955, in box 22, Special Assistant to the President, Washington, D.C., files, RG4.NAR Personal.RAC (hereafter SAP).

52. Cabinet meeting, January 14, 1955, *Minutes and Documents*, reel 2.

53. Reich, *Rockefeller*, 533–36.

54. Cabinet meeting, January 14, 1955, *Minutes and Documents*, reel 2.

55. DDE speech, Washington, D.C., February 8, 1955, in box 22, SAP.

56. "Special Message to Congress Concerning Federal Assistance in School Construction," February 8, 1955, *PPP 1955*, 243–50.

57. Ibid.

58. *Congress and the Nation*, 1206.

59. Dwight D. Eisenhower, *The White House Years, a Personal Account: Mandate for Change, 1953–1956* (New York: Doubleday, 1963), 500.

60. *Congress and the Nation*, 1206.

61. Ibid.

62. January 10, 1956, in 1956 (1), box 2, Legislative Meetings Series, DDE Papers as President, DDEL.

63. *Congress and the Nation*, 1206.

64. Ibid., 1207; "Special Message to the Congress on Federal Aid to Education," January 28, 1957, *PPP 1957*, 89.

65. "Address to the Republican National Conference," June 7, 1957, ibid., 447.

66. Johnson and Porter, *National Party Platforms*, 550.

67. Legislative leadership meeting, May 1, 1957, Supplementary Notes by L. A. Minnich, Jr., in 1957 (3), box 2, Legislative Meetings Series, DDE Papers as President, DDEL.

68. Eisenhower, *Waging Peace*, 139.

69. "Address to the 1957 Governors' Conference, Williamsburg, Virginia," June 24, 1957, *PPP 1957*, 486.

70. *Congress and the Nation*, 1207.

71. Walter A. McDougall, *The Heavens and the Earth: A Political History of the Space Age* (Baltimore: Johns Hopkins University Press, 1985). The United States launched its own satellite four months later.

72. Reminiscences of Marion B. Folsom (January 10, 1968), from the Columbia University Oral History Research Office Collection (hereafter CUOHROC). Secretary Hobby resigned in August 1955.

73. Cabinet meetings, November 15, December 2, 1957, *Minutes and Documents*, reel 6.

74. DDE quoted from "Special Message to the Congress on Education," January 27, 1958, *PPP 1958*, 127–32; *Congress and the Nation*, 1208.

75. *Congress and the Nation*, 1208; Eisenhower, *Waging Peace*, 243; Entry, December 30, 1957, in December 1957, box 9, ACW Diary, DDE Papers as President, DDEL; Eisenhower, *Waging Peace*, 243.

76. "Statement by the President upon Signing the National Defense Education Act," September 2, 1958, *PPP 1958,* 671.

77. Entry, December 30, 1957, in December 1957, box 9, ACW Diary, DDE Papers as President, DDEL.

78. "Statement by the President upon Signing Bill Continuing School Construction Aid in Federally Affected Areas," August 12, 1958, *PPP 1958,* 601.

79. Cabinet meeting, January 16, 1959, *Minutes and Documents,* reel 8.

80. Benson to DDE, January 19, 1959, in Benson, Ezra 1959 (3), box 7, Administration Series, DDE Papers as President, DDEL.

81. Cabinet meeting, January 16, 1959, *Minutes and Documents,* reel 8; DDE discussion with Bryce Harlow, in April 1960 (1), box 11, ACW Diary, DDE Papers as President, DDEL; DDE in 1953 quoted in Ambrose, *Eisenhower,* 2:115.

82. "Proposed 1959 Education Program," December 29, 1958, in Flemming (3), box 15, Administration Series, DDE Papers as President, DDEL; *Congress and the Nation,* 1208–10.

83. Legislative leadership meeting, March 8, 1960, in 1960 (2), box 3, Legislative Meetings Series, DDE Papers as President, DDEL.

84. *Congress and the Nation,* 1209.

85. Cabinet meeting, April 22, 1955, *Minutes and Documents,* reel 3.

86. Robert Goldberg, *Barry Goldwater* (New Haven: Yale University Press, 1995), 105; Barry Goldwater, *With No Apologies* (New York: Berkley Books, 1979), 89.

87. Edgar Eisenhower to DDE, November 1, DDE to Edgar Eisenhower, November 8, 1954, in Edgar 1954 (2), box 11, Name Series, DDE Papers as President, DDEL. Remark to ACW, June 21, 1955, in 1953 (1), box 2, Legislative Meetings Series, DDE Papers as President, DDEL.

2—Giving Labor an Equal Voice

1. Eisenhower, *Mandate for Change,* 219.

2. Robert H. Ferrell, ed., *The Eisenhower Diaries* (New York: Norton, 1981), 269.

3. Speech to the AFL Convention, New York City, September 17, 1952, "Aims of the Eisenhower Administration 1952," HEW, vol. 5.

4. *Congress and the Nation,* 571–72.

5. Stephen Ambrose, *Nixon,* vol. 1, *The Education of a Politician, 1913–1962* (New York: Simon and Schuster, 1987), 141–42.

6. *Congress and the Nation,* 581.

7. Eisenhower, *Mandate for Change,* 90–91.

8. Ibid.

9. Taft, in *New York Times,* December 31, 1952, 1; "Washington Wire," *New Republic,* December 15, 1952, 3.

10. "Annual Message to the Congress on the State of the Union," February 2, 1953, *PPP 1953,* 6.

11. Eisenhower, *Mandate for Change,* 291.

12. "Aims of the Eisenhower Administration 1952," HEW, vol. 5; Eisenhower, *Mandate for Change,* 196.

13. "Taft-Hartley (Working Papers of Proposed Changes in Bill)," in folders 1–3, box 82, Confidential Files, DDE Records as President, DDEL.

14. R. Alton Lee, *Eisenhower and Landrum-Griffin: A Study in Labor Management Politics* (Lexington: University Press of Kentucky, 1990), 21–22; "Labor," *Fortune* (January 1953): 63.

15. Ferrell, *Eisenhower Diaries,* 227.

16. Quoted in Lee, *Eisenhower and Landrum-Griffin,* 26.

17. "Summary of White House Recommendations for Amendments to the Taft-Hartley Law and Comments Theron," 124–26, in Taft-Hartley 1953 (4), Official File, DDE Records as President, DDEL.

18. Ambrose, *Eisenhower,* 2:117; Albert Clark, "Taft-Hartley Law—Eisenhower Circulates His Ideas for Revision: They Favor Unions," *Wall Street Journal,* August 3, 1953, 1.

19. Eisenhower, *Mandate for Change,* 197.

20. Ibid., 197–98.

21. "The President's News Conference of September 30, 1953," *PPP 1953,* 624.

22. Eisenhower, *Mandate for Change,* 198–99; Ferrell, *Eisenhower Diaries,* 267.

23. Eisenhower, *Mandate for Change,* 219.

24. Ibid., 298; DDE meeting with Herbert Brownell, June 15, 1954, in June 1954 (2) folder, box 2, ACW Diary, DDE Papers as President, DDEL; Ferrell, *Eisenhower Diaries,* 269.

25. Ferrell, *Eisenhower Diaries,* 264.

26. Cabinet meeting, December 15, 1953, *Minutes and Documents,* reel 1.

27. "Message to the 72d Annual Convention of the American Federation of Labor in St. Louis," September 23, 1953, *PPP 1953,* 608–11.

28. "Annual Message to the Congress on the State of the Union," January 7, 1954, *PPP 1954,* 19.

29. "Special Message to the Congress on Labor-Management Relations," January 11, 1954, *PPP 1954,* 40.

30. Ibid.; "Summary of White House Recommendations for Amendments to the Taft-Hartley Law and Comments Theron," 124–26, in Taft-Hartley 1953 (4), Official File, DDE Records as President, DDEL.

31. "Special Message to the Congress on Labor-Management Relations," January 11, 1954, *PPP 1954,* 44.

32. *Congress and the Nation,* 579.

33. Nixon quoted in Lee, *Eisenhower and Landrum-Griffin,* 34–35.

34. *Congress and the Nation,* 597–98.

35. DDE quoted in Lee, *Eisenhower and Landrum-Griffin,* 39.

36. "Annual Message to the Congress on the State of the Union," January 6, 1955, *PPP 1955,* 7–30, and January 5, 1956, *PPP 1956,* 1–27; "Remarks to the AFL Convention," Los Angeles, September 24, 1954, *PPP 1954,* 882; Cabinet meeting, May 13, 1955, *Minutes and Documents,* reel 3; Lee, *Eisenhower and Landrum-Griffin,* 40; Eisenhower, *Mandate for Change,* 489.

37. "Annual Message to the Congress on the State of the Union," January 6, 1955, *PPP 1955,* 7–30; *Congress and the Nation,* 641–42.

38. *Congress and the Nation,* 599.

39. "Labor Legislation—Secretary Mitchell Proposals," December 4, 1957, in 1957 (5), box 2, Legislative, DDE Papers as President, DDEL; Cabinet meeting, November 8, 1957, *Minutes and Documents,* reel 6.

40. "Special Message to the Congress on Labor-Management Relations," January 23, 1958, *PPP 1958,* 118.

41. Ibid.; *Congress and the Nation,* 601–2.

42. *Congress and the Nation,* 605–7.

43. Ibid., 600.

44. Eisenhower, *Waging Peace*, 376; DDE to Knowland, September 23, 1958, Staff Notes, in September 1958, box 36, DDE Diary, DDE Papers as President, DDEL.

45. DDE to Nixon, September 29, 1955, in Nixon 1958–1961 (3), box 28, Administration Series, DDE Papers as President, DDEL.

46. Quoted in Ambrose, *Nixon*, 1:488–89.

47. Reminiscences of William F. Knowland (1967), CUOHROC.

48. "Special Message to the Congress on Labor Management Relations," January 28, 1959, *PPP 1959*, 143–46.

49. Goldwater, *No Apologies*, 74; and quoted in Goldberg, *Goldwater*, 134–35.

50. "Radio and Television Address to the American People on the Need for an Effective Labor Bill," August 6, 1959, *PPP 1959*, 567–70.

51. Ibid.

52. Lee, *Eisenhower and Landrum-Griffin*, 143.

53. *Congress and the Nation*, 609–10.

54. Ibid., 610–12; Lee, *Eisenhower and Landrum-Griffin*, 157.

55. "Statement by the President Following the Adoption by the House of Representatives of the Landrum-Griffin Labor Reform Bill," August 13, 1959, *PPP 1959*, 583.

56. Lee, *Eisenhower and Landrum-Griffin*, 151, 158–59; *Congress and the Nation*, 610.

3—A Program for All Farmers and for All America

1. Ezra Taft Benson, *Cross Fire: The Eight Years with Eisenhower* (New York: Doubleday, 1962), 4.

2. Ibid., 11.

3. Barry Goldwater, *The Conscience of a Conservative* (Shepherdsville, KY: Victor, 1960), 39–44.

4. Ezra Taft Benson oral history, recorded at DDEL, 1975.

5. *Congress and the Nation*, 682.

6. Ibid., 682, 684.

7. Ibid., 684–85.

8. Ibid., 687–89.

9. Ibid., 689–91.

10. Ibid., 690–91.

11. Ibid., 691.

12. Ibid., 695.

13. "Summary of Policy Statements Made by General Eisenhower; As Excerpted from Major Speeches Carried by the *New York Times* and Other Papers from June until November 4th [1952]," HEW, vol. 5.

14. Benson, *Cross Fire*, 38.

15. Congress, Senate, Committee on Agriculture and Forestry, *Confirmation Hearing, Ezra Taft Benson, Secretary of Agriculture-Designate*, 83d Cong., 1st sess., January 15, 1953.

16. Benson, "General Statement on Agricultural Policy," *Cross Fire*, appendix D, 602–5.

17. Benson, *Cross Fire*, 67–68.

18. Ibid., 70.

19. Ibid., 73.

20. Ibid., 152–53; Cabinet meeting, October 22, 1953, *Minutes and Documents,* reel 1; Eisenhower, *Mandate for Change,* 288–89.

21. Benson, *Cross Fire,* 162; Cabinet meeting, December 11, 1953, *Minutes and Documents,* reel 1.

22. "Special Message to the Congress on Agriculture," January 11, 1954, *PPP 1954,* 23–32; *Congress and the Nation,* 697–98; Eisenhower, *Mandate for Change,* 288–89; Benson, *Cross Fire,* 164–65, 169–70.

23. Benson, *Cross Fire,* 170–71.

24. Ibid., 185.

25. Ibid., 193–95; Cabinet meeting, May 21, 1954, *Minutes and Documents,* reel 1.

26. Benson, *Cross Fire,* 195.

27. Ibid.

28. *Congress and the Nation,* 698; Martin quoted from Benson, *Cross Fire,* 205.

29. Benson, *Cross Fire,* 185–86.

30. *Congress and the Nation,* 698.

31. Ibid., 698–99; "Statement by the President upon Signing the Agricultural Act of 1954," August 28, 1954, *PPP 1954,* 220–22.

32. *Congress and the Nation,* 700.

33. Benson, *Cross Fire,* 258–59.

34. Cabinet meeting, October 7, 1955, *Minutes and Documents,* reel 3; Benson, *Cross Fire,* 272, 276.

35. Quoted in Ambrose, *Eisenhower,* 2:277.

36. Ibid., 277–78.

37. Cabinet meeting, December 9, 1955, *Minutes and Documents,* reel 4.

38. Ibid.; Benson, *Cross Fire,* 291–92.

39. "Special Message to the Congress on Agriculture," January 9, 1956, *PPP 1956,* 45–48; Benson, *Cross Fire,* 291–92.

40. "Special Message to the Congress on Agriculture," January 9, 1956, *PPP 1956,* 40; DDE to Senator Aiken, February 8, 1956, in folder 106-J, Soil Bank (1), box 505, Official File, DDE Records as President, DDEL.

41. *Congress and the Nation,* 702.

42. Benson, *Cross Fire,* 294.

43. Cabinet meeting, April 22, 1955, *Minutes and Documents,* reel 3; *Congress and the Nation,* 700.

44. *Congress and the Nation,* 702.

45. Eisenhower, *Mandate for Change,* 559–60.

46. Ferrell, *Eisenhower Diaries,* 317; Benson, *Cross Fire,* 313.

47. Benson, *Cross Fire,* 316.

48. Legislative leadership meeting, April 9, 1956, in Legislative, box 2, ACW Diary, DDE Papers as President, DDEL.

49. Ezra Taft Benson oral history, DDEL.

50. January 10, 1956, in 1956 (1), Legislative, box 2, ACW Diary, DDE Papers as President, DDEL.

51. Benson, *Cross Fire,* 317–18.

52. Ibid., 318 (emphasis in original).

53. "Veto of the Farm Bill," April 16, 1956, *PPP 1956,* 385–90.

54. "Radio and Television Address to the American People on the Farm Bill Veto, April 16, 1956," ibid., 391–99; Cabinet meeting, April 27, 1956, *Minutes and Documents,* reel 4.

55. *Congress and the Nation,* 702; "Statement by the President upon Signing the Agricultural Act of 1956," May 28, 1956, *PPP 1956,* 538; *Congress and the Nation,* 704.

56. Benson, *Cross Fire,* 351–52.

57. Cabinet meeting, April 12, 1957, *Minutes and Documents,* reel 5.

58. Cabinet meeting, June 17, 1957, ibid., reel 6.

59. *Congress and the Nation,* 703.

60. "Special Message to the Congress on Agriculture," January 16, 1958, *PPP 1958,* 100–107.

61. Benson, *Cross Fire,* 386–87.

62. Ibid., 388.

63. Ibid., 388–89.

64. *Congress and the Nation,* 705.

65. DDE to Ezra Taft Benson, March 20, 1958, reel 9, Ezra Taft Benson Papers, DDEL (emphasis in original).

66. "Veto of the Farm Freeze Bill," March 31, 1958, *PPP 1958,* 250–56.

67. Benson, *Cross Fire,* 399–401.

68. Ibid, 402–3; *Congress and the Nation,* 706.

69. *Congress and the Nation,* 706–7; Benson, *Cross Fire,* 404–5.

70. The year 1958 was the first that Alaska elected senators and a representative.

71. "Special Message to the Congress on Agriculture," January 29, 1959, *PPP 1959,* 146–51; *Congress and the Nation,* 708.

72. "Veto of Bill Relating to the Wheat Program," June 25, 1959, *PPP 1959,* 476–77; "Veto of Tobacco Price Support Bill," June 25, 1959, ibid., 140–41.

73. "Special Message to the Congress on Agriculture," February 9, 1960, *PPP 1960,* 162–65.

74. *Congress and the Nation,* 710.

75. Benson, *Cross Fire,* 525; "Accomplishments of the Department of Agriculture, 1953–1960," reel 9, Ezra Taft Benson Papers, DDEL.

4—Civil Rights, States' Rights, and Federal Responsibilities

1. E. Frederic Morrow oral history, recorded at DDEL, 1977; E. Frederic Morrow, *Black Man in the White House: A Diary of the Eisenhower Years by the Administrative Officer for Special Projects, the White House, 1955–1961* (New York: Coward-McCann, 1963), 218.

2. Eisenhower, *Waging Peace,* 149.

3. DDE to Chynoweth, July 13, 1954, in Chynoweth, box 5, Name Series, DDE Papers as President, DDEL.

4. "Annual Message to the Congress on the State of the Union," February 2, 1953, *PPP 1953,* 30.

5. Robert F. Burk, *The Eisenhower Administration and Black Civil Rights* (Knoxville: University of Tennessee Press, 1984), 49–50.

6. Eisenhower, *Waging Peace,* 148–49.

7. Burk, *Black Civil Rights,* 50–52; Eisenhower, *Waging Peace,* 234–36.

8. Morrow, *Black Man in the White House,* 11–14; Morrow oral history, DDEL.

9. Morrow, *Black Man in the White House,* 11–14; Morrow oral history, DDEL.

10. Morrow oral history, DDEL.

11. DDE quoted in Burk, *Black Civil Rights,* 28.

12. *Congress and the Nation,* 1617.

13. Burk, *Black Civil Rights,* 25–26.

14. Ibid., 35–37; Eisenhower, *Waging Peace,* 234–36.

15. Burk, *Black Civil Rights,* 28–33.

16. "Memorandum Concerning Segregation in Schools on Army Posts," March 25, 1953, *PPP 1953,* 127.

17. Burk, *Black Civil Rights,* 30.

18. *New York Times,* June 4, 11, 1953.

19. Burk, *Black Civil Rights,* 31–32.

20. *Brown v. Board of Education of Topeka, Kansas,* 347 U.S. 483 (1954), and 349 U.S. 294 (1955).

21. One recent example of this is Gayle B. Montgomery and James W. Johnson, *One Step from the White House: The Rise and Fall of Senator William F. Knowland* (Berkeley and Los Angeles: University of California Press, 1998).

22. Goldwater, *No Apologies,* 64.

23. Herbert Brownell, *Advising Ike: The Memoirs of Attorney General Herbert Brownell* (Lawrence: University Press of Kansas, 1993), 164–65.

24. Eisenhower, *Mandate for Change,* 226–29.

25. Brownell, *Advising Ike,* 165–67; Eisenhower, *Mandate for Change,* 226–29.

26. Brownell, *Advising Ike,* 165–67.

27. Edgar Eisenhower to DDE, September 28, 1953, DDE to Edgar Eisenhower, October 1, 1953, in Edgar 1953 (1), box 11, Name Series, DDE Papers as President, DDEL.

28. DDE quoted in Ambrose, *Eisenhower,* 2:129.

29. Brownell, *Advising Ike,* 173; Herbert Brownell oral history, recorded at DDEL, 1977.

30. "Press Conference," January 25, 1956, *PPP 1956,* 182.

31. Entry, January 30, 1956, in Ferrell, *Eisenhower Diaries,* 313–14.

32. These were the southern states of Texas, Florida, Tennessee, and Virginia, and the border states of Oklahoma, Missouri, and Maryland.

33. E. Frederic Morrow to Dr. Gabriel Hauge, March 21, 1956, in March 1956 Misc. (2), box 24, DDE Diaries Series, DDE Papers as President, DDEL.

34. Folder on Civil Rights, 1954, Papers of the Republican National Committee Chair, DDEL. See also James C. Duram, *A Moderate among Extremists: Dwight D. Eisenhower and the School Desegregation Crisis* (Chicago: Nelson-Hall, 1981), 113–15.

35. DDE, phone conversation with Oveta Culp Hobby, March 21, 1956, in March 1956 Diary Ann Whitman (1), box 8, ACW Diary, DDE Papers as President, DDEL.

36. Memorandum for the record, August 19, 1953, Brownell 1952–1954 (c), Administration Series, DDE Papers as President, DDEL.

37. DDE to Governor James F. Byrnes, December 1, 1953, DDE Diary, in December 1953 (2), box 4, DDE Diaries Series, DDE Papers as President, DDEL.

38. Eisenhower, *Waging Peace,* 150.

39. Telegram from DDE to Walter White, June 29, 1954, for delivery at the Forty-fifth Annual Meeting of the NAACP, in box 47, President's Personal Files, DDE Records as President, DDEL; Duram, *Moderate among Extremists,* 116.

40. DDE to Swede Hazlett, October 23, 1954, in Robert Griffith, ed., *Ike's Letters to a Friend, 1941–1958* (Lawrence: University Press of Kansas, 1984), 134–35.

41. "Press Conference," November 23, 1954, *PPP 1954,* 1060.

42. Herbert Brownell, "Brief for the United States on the Further Argument of the Question of Relief," November 24, 1954, in *Transcripts of Records and File Copies of Briefs*, Supreme Court of the United States, 1954, 11:3–4 (quote); Duram, *Moderate among Extremists*, 118–19.

43. *Brown v. Board of Education of Topeka, Kansas*, 349 U.S. 294 (1955).

44. August 14, 1956, in August 1956 Diary-ACW (1), box 8, ACW Diary, DDE Papers as President, DDEL.

45. DDE to Swede Hazlett, July 22, 1957, in Griffith, *Ike's Letters*, 186.

46. Cabinet meeting, March 9, 1956, *Minutes and Documents*, reel 4.

47. Brownell, *Advising Ike*, 183, 179–80.

48. "Annual Message to the Congress on the State of the Union," January 5, 1956, *PPP 1956*, 1–27.

49. Brownell, *Advising Ike*, 218–19.

50. Cabinet meeting, December 2, 1955, *Minutes and Documents*, reel 4 (DDE was not present at this meeting).

51. Brownell, *Advising Ike*, 218–19; Cabinet meeting, March 9, 1956, *Minutes and Documents*, reel 4; *Congress and the Nation*, 1620.

52. Brownell, *Advising Ike*, 219; Cabinet meeting, March 23, 1956, *Minutes and Documents*, reel 4; Eisenhower, *Waging Peace*, 153–54, 158.

53. Legislative leaders meeting, April 17, 1956, in 1956 (2), box 2, Legislative Meetings Series, DDE Papers as President, DDEL.

54. *Congress and the Nation*, 1620.

55. Eisenhower, *Waging Peace*, 154.

56. "Annual Message to the Congress on the State of the Union," January 10, 1957, *PPP 1957*, 23.

57. *Congress and the Nation*, 1621; Montgomery and Johnson, *One Step from the White House*. Also among the thirty-nine were several Democrats who would later be considered champions of civil rights: J. William Fullbright, Albert Gore, Lyndon Johnson, Estes Kefauver, and John Kennedy.

58. "Statement by the President on the Objectives of the Civil Rights Bill," July 16, 1957, *PPP 1957*, 545.

59. *Congress and the Nation*, 1621–24.

60. Ibid., 1623.

61. Ibid.; DDE to Robert Woodruff, August 6, 1957, in Woodruff, R.W. (2), box 34, Name Series, DDE Papers as President, DDEL.

62. "Legislative Leadership Meeting, July 30, 1957, Supplementary Notes," in 1957 (3–4), box 2, Legislative Meetings Series, DDE Papers as President, DDEL.

63. *Congress and the Nation*, 1624. The twelve Republicans were Hugh Butler (NE), Homer Capehart (IN), Francis Case (SD), Carl Curtis (NE), Barry Goldwater (AZ), George Malone (NV), Karl Mundt (SD), Chapman Revercomb (WV), Andrew Schoeppel (KS), Margaret Chase Smith (ME), John Williams (DE), and Clifton Young (NV). DDE quoted from Cabinet meeting, August 2, 1957, *Minutes and Documents*, reel 6.

64. "Statement by the President on the Civil Rights Bill," August 2, 1957, *PPP 1957*, 587.

65. *Congress and the Nation*, 1621–22, 1624.

66. "Legislative Leadership Meeting, August 13, 1957, Supplementary Notes," in 1957 (4), box 2, Legislative Meetings Series, DDE Papers as President, DDEL; Eisenhower, *Waging Peace*, 160.

67. "Legislative Leadership Meeting, August 13, 1957, Supplementary Notes," in 1957 (4), box 2, Legislative Meetings Series, DDE Papers as President, DDEL.

68. Martin Luther King to Richard Nixon, August 30, 1957, in Nixon-VS. Correspondence (7) January–October 1957, box 50, William Rogers Papers, DDEL.

69. "Legislative Leadership Meeting, August 13, 1957, Supplementary Notes," in 1957 (4), box 2, Legislative Meetings Series, DDE Papers as President, DDEL.

70. Brownell, *Advising Ike*, 205–6.

71. Duram, *Moderate among Extremists*, 144–45.

72. Ibid., 145–46.

73. Ibid., 146–48.

74. "Telegram to the Governor of Arkansas in Response to His Request for a Meeting," September 11, 1957, *PPP 1957*, 673–74.

75. "Notes dictated by the President on October 8, 1957 concerning visit of Governor Orval Faubus of Arkansas to Newport on September 14, 1957," in Little Rock, Arkansas (1), box 23, Administration Series, DDE Papers as President, DDEL; "Statement by the President Following a Meeting with the Governor of Arkansas," September 14, 1957, *PPP 1957*, 674–75.

76. Brownell, *Advising Ike*, 210.

77. "Statement by the President on the Developments at Little Rock," September 21, 1957, *PPP 1957*, 678–79.

78. Brownell, *Advising Ike*, 211; "Statement by the President Regarding Occurrences at Central High School in Little Rock," September 23, 1957, *PPP 1957*, 689.

79. Eisenhower, *Waging Peace*, 170.

80. DDE to General Alfred M. Gruenther, September 24, 1957, in September 1957, box 9, ACW Diary, DDE Papers as President, DDEL.

81. "Radio and Television Address to the American People on the Situation in Little Rock," September 24, 1957, *PPP 1957*, 689–94.

82. Ibid., 690.

83. "Telegram to Senator Russell of Georgia Regarding the Use of Federal Troops at Little Rock," September 28, 1957, *PPP 1957*, 695–96.

84. Duram, *Moderate among Extremists*, 161–63. The four southern governors were Frank G. Clement (TN), LeRoy Collins (FL), Luther Hodges (NC), and Theodore McKeldin (MD).

85. "Statement by the President Concerning the Removal of the Soldiers Stationed at Little Rock," May 8, 1958, *PPP 1958*, 387.

86. Eisenhower, *Waging Peace*, 175.

87. Notes on legislative meeting, February 3, 1959, in 1959 (2), box 3, Legislative Meetings Series, DDE Papers as President, DDEL.

88. "Special Message to the Congress on Civil Rights," February 5, 1959, *PPP 1959*, 164–67.

89. *Congress and the Nation*, 1628; "Statement by the President upon Signing the Civil Rights Act of 1960," May 6, 1960, *PPP 1960*, 398.

5—Republican Internationalism

1. Eisenhower, *Mandate for Change*, 213.

2. Richard M. Nixon, *RN: The Memoirs of Richard Nixon* (New York: Simon and Schuster, 1978), 139; DDE quoted from Ferrell, *Eisenhower Diaries*, 234.

3. Ambrose, *Eisenhower*, 2:55; Goldwater, *No Apologies*, 52–53.

4. DDE quoted from Ferrell, *Eisenhower Diaries*, 234; DDE to Harry Bullis, May 18, 1953, in 99-R McCarthy, Joseph, box 368, Official File, DDE Records as President, DDEL; Eisenhower to Bill Robinson of the *New York Herald Tribune*, July 27, 1953, in December 1952–July 1953 (1), box 3, DDE Diaries Series, DDE Papers as President, DDEL. See also Eisenhower, *Mandate for Change*, 316–31.

5. DDE quoted in Ambrose, *Eisenhower*, 2:57; Nixon, *Memoirs*, 139.

6. Johnson and Porter, *National Party Platforms*, 499; "Annual Message to the Congress on the State of the Union," February 2, 1953, *PPP 1953*, 14.

7. Eisenhower, *Mandate for Change*, 211; "Letter to the President of the Senate and to the Speaker of the House of Representatives Transmitting a Proposed Resolution on Subjugated Peoples," February 20, 1953, *PPP 1953*, 81–83 (quote).

8. Eisenhower, *Mandate for Change*, 211.

9. See Dave Tananbaum, *The Bricker Amendment Controversy: A Test of Eisenhower's Political Leadership* (Ithaca: Cornell University Press, 1988).

10. Bricker Amendment, 83d Cong., 1st sess., *Congressional Record* 99 (June 18, 1953): 6777.

11. DDE quoted in Ambrose, *Eisenhower*, 2:69.

12. Eisenhower, *Mandate for Change*, 278–79.

13. Cabinet meeting, February 20, 1953, *Minutes and Documents*, reel 1.

14. "Memo on the Bricker Amendment for the President from John Foster Dulles," March 31, 1953, in Bricker Amendment, box 10, Confidential File, DDE Records as President, DDEL.

15. Eisenhower, *Mandate for Change*, 279–80.

16. Edgar Eisenhower to DDE, March 27, and DDE to Edgar, April 7, 1953, in Edgar 1953 (2), box 11, Name Series, DDE Papers as President, DDEL.

17. Eisenhower, *Mandate for Change*, 281; Sherman Adams, *Firsthand Report: The Story of the Eisenhower Administration* (New York: Harper, 1961), 104.

18. Cabinet meeting, February 25, 1953, *Minutes and Documents*, reel 1.

19. Cabinet meetings, March 13, 20, 27, 1953, ibid.. See also Ferrell, *Eisenhower Diaries*, 248.

20. Cabinet meeting, April 3, 1953, *Minutes and Documents*, reel 1; *Congress and the Nation*, 111; Edgar Eisenhower cited from reminiscences of John Bricker (1968), CUOHROC.

21. Cabinet meetings, June 5, July 17, 1953, *Minutes and Documents*, reel 1; Memo of phone conversation between DDE and Brownell, June 23, 1953, in Phone Calls, February–June 1953 (1), box 4, DDE Diaries Series, DDE Papers as President, DDEL.

22. Eisenhower, *Mandate for Change*, 595 (quotes), 282.

23. "Statement by the President on a Proposed Amendment to the Constitution Relating to Treaties," July 22, 1953, *PPP 1953*, 509.

24. Eisenhower, *Mandate for Change*, 283.

25. *Congress and the Nation*, 112.

26. Ibid.

27. Entry, February 2, 1954, in Ferrell, *Diary of James Hagerty*, 14.

28. Eisenhower, *Mandate for Change*, 208.

29. Burton Ira Kaufman, *Trade and Aid: Eisenhower's Foreign Economic Policy, 1953–1961* (Baltimore: Johns Hopkins University Press, 1982).

30. *Congress and the Nation*, 187.

31. Ibid., 187, 193–96.

32. Speech to the *New York Herald Tribune* Forum, New York City, October 21, 1952, and Speech at Springfield, Massachusetts, October 22, 1952, in "Aims of the Eisenhower Administration, 1952," HEW, vol. 5.

33. Johnson and Porter, *National Party Platforms*, 499.

34. "Annual Message to the Congress on the State of the Union," February 2, 1953, *PPP 1953*, 15.

35. Cabinet meeting, January 23, 1953, *Minutes and Documents*, reel 1.

36. Eisenhower, *Mandate for Change*, 209; "Special Message to the Congress Recommending the Renewal of the Reciprocal Trade Agreements Act," April 7, 1953, *PPP 1953*, 163–65; Cabinet meeting, April 3, 1953, *Minutes and Documents*, reel 1.

37. Eisenhower, *Mandate for Change*, 209; *Congress and the Nation*, 197, 188–89.

38. Eisenhower, *Mandate for Change*, 208–9; Ferrell, *Eisenhower Diaries*, 228–29. See also Cabinet meetings, March 27, April 10, 1953, *Minutes and Documents*, reel 1.

39. Eisenhower, *Mandate for Change*, 210.

40. Entry, July 2, 1953, in Ferrell, *Eisenhower Diaries*, 244.

41. *Congress and the Nation*, 197.

42. Ibid.; "Statement by the President upon Signing the Trade Agreements Extension Act of 1953," August 7, 1953, *PPP 1953*, 558.

43. *Congress and the Nation*, 197.

44. "Letter to the President of the Senate and to the Speaker of the House of Representatives Recommending Establishment of a Commission on Foreign Economic Policy," May 2, 1953, *PPP 1953*, 252.

45. Kaufman, *Trade and Aid*, 19.

46. Commission on Foreign Economic Policy, *Report to the President and Congress* (Washington, D.C.: GPO, 1954).

47. Ibid.; Kaufman, *Trade and Aid*, 17–26.

48. "Special Message to Congress on Foreign Economic Policy," March 30, 1954, *PPP 1954*, 352–64.

49. Ferrell, *Diary of James Hagerty*, 9.

50. *Congress and the Nation*, 198.

51. "Annual Message to the Congress on the State of the Union," January 6, 1955, *PPP 1955*, 11–12; "Special Message to the Congress on the Foreign Economic Policy of the United States," January 10, 1955, *PPP 1955*, 33–40.

52. *Congress and the Nation*, 198–99.

53. Ibid; Eisenhower, *Mandate for Change*, 498.

54. Campaign speech, New York City, October 21, 1952, HEW, vol. 5.

55. Dwight D. Eisenhower, *Crusade in Europe* (New York: Doubleday, 1948), 476–77.

56. Cabinet meeting, March 6, 1953, *Minutes and Documents*, reel 1.

57. DDE quoted from "Aims of the Eisenhower Administration," 1952, HEW, vol. 5; *Congress and the Nation*, 171.

58. Eisenhower, *Mandate for Change*, 215–16.

59. "Letter to the Chairman, Senate Appropriations Committee, on the Mutual Security Program," July 23, 1953, *PPP 1953*, 511–13.

60. *Congress and the Nation*, 173–74.

61. Ibid., 173; "Special Message to the Congress on the Mutual Security Program," June 23, 1954, *PPP 1954*, 590–94.

62. *Congress and the Nation*, 172–73; "Special Message to the Congress Requesting General Legislation Authorizing the Use of Agricultural Commodities for Emergency Relief," June 30, 1953, *PPP 1953*, 125; "Statement by the President upon Signing the Agricultural Trade Development and Assistance Act of 1954," July 7, 1954, *PPP 1954*, 626.

63. Kaufman, *Trade and Aid*.

64. International Development Advisory Board (IDAB) Report, March 1, 1951, in IDAB, box 31, Washington D.C. Files, RG4.NAR Personal.RAC.

65. "Special Message to the Congress on the Foreign Economic Policy of the United States," January 10, 1955, *PPP 1955*, 32.

66. "Special Message to the Congress on the Mutual Security Program," April 20, 1955, ibid., 404–11.

67. Ibid.; *Congress and the Nation*, 174; Cabinet meeting, April 22, 1955, *Minutes and Documents*, reel 3; "Statement by the President upon Signing the Mutual Security Appropriations Act," August 2, 1955, *PPP 1955*, 753.

68. *Congress and the Nation*, 174; "Statement by the President upon Signing Bill Amending the Agricultural Trade Development Assistance Act," August 12, 1955, *PPP 1955*, 791.

69. "Special Message to the Congress on the Mutual Security Program," March 19, 1956, *PPP 1956*, 314–24.

70. Kaufman, *Trade and Aid*, 63–65.

71. "Special Message to the Congress on the Mutual Security Program," March 19, 1956, *PPP 1956*, 319.

72. Legislative leaders meeting, December 12, 1955, in December 1955 (4), box 7, ACW Diary, DDE Papers as President, DDEL; Kaufman, *Trade and Aid*, 70.

73. *Congress and the Nation*, 175.

74. Report-Summary, in box 2, U.S. President's Citizen Advisors on the Mutual Security Program (Fairless Committee), DDEL.

75. Ibid.; "Report of the President's Citizen Advisors on the Mutual Security Program," March 1, 1957, in Mutual Security Program, box 27, Administration Series, DDE Papers as President, DDEL.

76. "Special Message to the Congress on the Mutual Security Programs," May 21, 1957, *PPP 1957*, 372–85.

77. Eisenhower, *Waging Peace*, 133.

78. "Radio and Television Address to the American People on the Need for Mutual Security in Waging the Peace," May 21, 1957, *PPP 1957*, 385–96.

79. "Conversation between the President and Senator Styles Bridges," May 21, 1957, in May 1957 Misc. (2), box 24, DDE Diaries Series, DDE Papers as President, DDEL.

80. Ibid.

81. Eisenhower, *Waging Peace*, 145.

82. "Statement by the President on the Mutual Security Bill," July 17, 1957, *PPP 1957*, 560–61; *Congress and the Nation*, 176.

83. *Congress and the Nation*, 176; "Statement by the President on Senate Restoration of Mutual Security Funds," August 27, 1957, *PPP 1957*, 634–35; "Statement by the President upon Signing the Mutual Security Appropriation Bill," September 3, 1957, *PPP 1957*, 655.

84. "Annual Message to the Congress on the State of the Union," January 9, 1958, *PPP 1958*, 2–15.

85. "Special Message to the Congress on the Mutual Security Program," February 19, 1958, *PPP 1958*, 160–68.

86. "Remarks and Address at Dinner of the National Conference on the Foreign Aspects of National Security," February 25, 1958, *PPP 1958,* 176.

87. "Statement by the President on the House Appropriations Committee Cut in Mutual Security Funds," June 27, 1958, *PPP 1958,* 508; *Congress and the Nation,* 176–78.

88. "Special Message to the Congress on the Reciprocal Trade Agreements Program," January 30, 1958, *PPP 1958,* 132. See also Adams, *Firsthand Report,* 393–94.

89. *Congress and the Nation,* 200–201.

90. Ibid., 178–79; "Special Message to the Congress on the Mutual Security Program," March 13, 1959, *PPP 1959, 255.*

91. "Special Message to the Congress on the Mutual Security Program," February 16, 1960, *PPP 1960,* 177; "Statement by the President Concerning Mutual Security Appropriations," August 26, 1960, ibid., 659–60; "Letter to the Majority and Minority Leaders of the Senate on Mutual Security Appropriations," August 26, 1960, ibid., 600; "Letter to the Speaker of the House of Representatives on Mutual Security Appropriations," August 26, 1960, ibid., 661; *Congress and the Nation,* 179–80.

92. DDE quoted in Robert Griffith, *The Politics of Fear: Joseph R. McCarthy and the Senate* (Rochelle Park, NJ: Hayden, 1976), 137–38.

6—The Politics of Modern Republicanism

1. Ferrell, *Diary of James Hagerty,* 129.

2. Ferrell, *Eisenhower Diaries,* 288–89.

3. Ferrell, *Diary of James Hagerty,* 129.

4. DDE to Gabriel Hauge, September 30, 1954, DDE Diaries, in September 1954 (1), box 8, DDE Diaries Series, DDE Papers as President, DDEL.

5. Adams, *Firsthand Report,* 28.

6. Ambrose, *Eisenhower,* 2:152.

7. Ferrell, *Eisenhower Diaries,* 289.

8. DDE to Edgar Eisenhower, May 2, 1956, in Edgar 1956 (2), box 11, Name Series, DDE Papers as President, DDEL.

9. Paul Hoffman visit, June 1, 1955, in June 1955 (6), box 6, ACW Diary, DDE Papers as President, DDEL.

10. Ferrell, *Diary of James Hagerty,* 53, 106. See also Cabinet meeting, December 15, 1953, *Minutes and Documents,* reel 1.

11. Entry, February 13, 1956, in February 1956, box 8, ACW Diary, DDE Papers as President, DDEL. Henry Cabot Lodge encouraged these views; see Lodge to DDE, October 15, 1953, in Brownell, Herbert, Jr. 1952–1954 (5), Administration Series, ibid. See also Ambrose, *Nixon,* 1:386; Ambrose, *Eisenhower,* 2:294.

12. Interview with Merriman Smith, November 23, 1954, in November 1954 (2), box 3, ACW Diary, DDE Papers as President, DDEL.

13. Meeting with Paul Hoffman, December 1, 1954, in December 1954 (5), ibid. See also Ambrose, *Eisenhower,* 2:281–82.

14. Eisenhower, *Mandate for Change,* 566–75.

15. Nixon, *Memoirs,* 176–77.

16. DDE to Richard Nixon, September 29, 1954, in Nixon, Richard M. (4), box 28, Administration Series, DDE Papers as President, DDEL; Nixon, *Memoirs,* 163.

17. Eisenhower, *Waging Peace,* 7–8.

18. Ibid., 7; Nixon, *Memoirs,* 167.

19. Entry, February 9, 1956, in February 1956 Diary, box 8, ACW Diary, DDE Papers as President, DDEL; Eisenhower, *Waging Peace,* 8. Eisenhower had suffered a heart attack several months earlier.

20. Eisenhower, *Waging Peace,* 9.

21. George Whitney to DDE, March 9, 1956, in Whitney, George [GOP Politics], box 34, Name Series, DDE Papers as President, DDEL.

22. Entry, March 13, 1956, in March 1956 Diary (2), box 8, ACW Diary, ibid.

23. Nixon, *Memoirs,* 167–68.

24. Entry, February 9, 1956, in February 1956 Diary, box 8, ACW Diary, DDE Papers as President, DDEL.

25. Nixon, *Memoirs,* 169–71.

26. Ibid., 171–72.

27. Nixon Meeting with DDE, April 26, 1956, in Nixon, Richard M. (2), box 28, Administration Series, DDE Papers as President, DDEL.

28. Memorandum to the President from Harold Stassen, July 19, 1956, in Stassen 1956 (2), box 34, ibid.

29. Eisenhower, *Waging Peace,* 10.

30. Ibid.

31. Nixon, *Memoirs,* 175.

32. Acceptance Speech at the Republican National Convention, August 23, 1956, in box 16, Speech Series, DDE Papers as President, DDEL.

33. Campaign meeting, September 2, 1955, in September 1955 (6), box 6, ACW Diary, ibid.; Meeting in press office, July 25, 1956, in Campaign 1956 (2), box 3, Campaign Series, ibid.; Cabinet meetings, July 27, September 28, 1956, *Minutes and Documents,* reel 5.

34. Summary Report 1956 Elections, in box 4, Campaign Series, DDE Papers as President, DDEL; Nixon, *Memoirs,* 180.

35. Remarks of the President at the Sheraton Park Hotel, Washington D.C. on his election victory, November 7, 1956, in box 7, Speech Series, ibid.

36. Statement given extemporaneously to reporters on November 14, 1956, in Modern Republicanism, box 717, Official File, DDE Records as President, DDEL.

37. Harold Stassen to Sherman Adams, November 29, 1956, in Political Affairs (2), box 50, Confidential Files, White, ibid.

38. Nixon, *Memoirs,* 180–81.

39. Bricker quoted in Goldberg, *Goldwater,* 112.

40. Goldwater on Modern Republicanism, 86th Cong., 1st sess., *Congressional Record* 105 (April 8, 1957): 5258–65.

41. Barry Goldwater to DDE, April 9, 1957, in box 514, Official File, DDE Records as President, DDEL.

42. Jack Anderson to Ann Whitman, April 13, 1957, in April 1957 Diary—Staff Memos (2), box 23, and press conference briefing, May 15, 1957, in May 1957 Misc. (3), box 24, both in DDE Diaries Series, DDE Papers as President, DDEL.

43. Lunch with Meade Alcorn, March 13, 1958, Ann Whitman Diary in March 1958 (1), box 9, ACW Diary, ibid.

44. Entry, November 13, 1956, in November 1956 Diary—Ann Whitman (2), ibid.

45. Nixon, *Memoirs,* 200.

46. *Congress and the Nation,* 28–30.

47. Nixon, *Memoirs,* 200.

48. *Wall Street Journal,* January 4, 1960.

49. Rockefeller quoted in Morris, *Nelson Rockefeller,* 305. See also White, *Making of the President, 1960,* 67.

50. Morris, *Nelson Rockefeller,* 310; White, *Making of the President, 1960,* 67, 69.

51. Reich, *Rockefeller,* 688–89, author's interview with Pat Weaver.

52. Collected in *Prospect for America: The Rockefeller Panel Reports* (New York: Doubleday, 1961).

53. *U.S. News and World Report,* January 17, 1958.

54. *Post* quoted in Morris, *Nelson Rockefeller,* 348.

55. White, *Making of the President, 1960,* 70–75.

56. *New York Times,* December 27, 1959.

57. Eisenhower, *Waging Peace,* 590.

58. *New York Times,* June 9, 1960.

59. Eisenhower, *Waging Peace,* 592–93; legislative leaders meeting, June 9, 1960, in 1960 (3), box 3, Legislative Meetings Series, DDE Papers as President, DDEL. For more on the strained Eisenhower-Rockefeller relationship, see DDE to Sherman Adams, in Adams, Sherman (1), box 1, Administration Series; DDE to William E. Robinson, February 9, 1959, in DDE Dictation, February 1959, box 39, DDE Diaries Series; DDE to Nelson Rockefeller, May 5, 1960, in NAR 1960, box 31, Administration Series; all in DDE Papers as President, DDEL.

60. Eisenhower, *Waging Peace,* 593.

61. White, *Making of the President, 1960,* 186–87.

62. Joseph E. Persico, *The Imperial Rockefeller: A Biography of Nelson A. Rockefeller* (New York: Simon and Schuster, 1982), 40–41.

63. Rockefeller quoted in White, *Making of the President, 1960,* 70.

64. Ibid., 195, 197.

65. Nixon, *Memoirs,* 215.

66. Text of a statement released by Governor Rockefeller in New York, Saturday, July 23, 1960, in White, *Making of the President, 1960,* Appendix B, 388–90.

67. Ibid.

68. Nelson Rockefeller oral history (1967), Columbia University Oral History Project, read at Rockefeller Archive Center, North Tarrytown, New York (RAC).

69. Eisenhower, *Waging Peace,* 596, 595.

70. Goldwater, *No Apologies,* 109, 92.

71. Eisenhower, *Waging Peace,* 596. See also telephone call from Senator Cooper, July 24, 1960, in Telephone Calls, July 1960, box 51, DDE Diaries Series, DDE Papers as President, DDEL.

72. Eisenhower, *Waging Peace,* 596.

73. Johnson and Porter, *National Party Platforms,* 604–21.

74. "Address at the Republican National Convention in Chicago," July 26, 1960, *PPP 1960,* 589; "Remarks at the Republican National Committee Breakfast, Chicago, Illinois, July 27, 1960," ibid., 602.

75. Nixon, *Memoirs,* 216.

76. Goldwater, *No Apologies,* 106.

77. Ibid., 111–12.

78. Summary Report 1960 Elections, in box 4, Campaign Series, DDE Papers as President, DDEL.

79. Goldwater, *No Apologies,* 123.

80. Goldwater quoted in *Time,* November 21, 1960, 21.

81. Goldwater quoted in *New York Times,* November 10, 1960, 23.

82. Eisenhower, *Waging Peace,* 652.

7—An Echo or a Choice?

1. Nixon, *Memoirs,* 251.

2. "Public Record of Barry Goldwater," *Congressional Quarterly* 21, September 20, 1963, 1622.

3. "Barry Goldwater, the U.S. Senate—and the 1960 Republican Platform," in Kutchel, Thomas H., box 42, Principal files, 1964, Dwight D. Eisenhower Postpresidential Papers, 1961–1969 (hereafter DDE Postpresidential Papers, DDEL).

4. *New York Times Magazine,* November 24, 1963. See also *U.S. News and World Report,* September 2, 1963.

5. Goldwater on Education, 87th Cong., 1st sess., *Congressional Record* 107 (June 21, 1961): 10,187.

6. Goldwater, *Conscience of a Conservative,* 78–87.

7. Ibid., 48.

8. Ibid., 39–44.

9. *Congress and the Nation,* 1621. The other four were George Malone (NV), Karl Mundt (SD), John Williams (DE), and Milton Young (ND).

10. *Congress and the Nation,* 1624. The twelve Republicans were Hugh Butler (NE), Homer Capehart (IN), Francis Case (SD), Carl Curtis (NE), Barry Goldwater (AZ), George Malone (NV), Karl Mundt (SD), Chapman Revercomb (WV), Andrew Schoeppel (KS), Margaret Chase Smith (ME), John Williams (DE), and Clifton Young (NV).

11. Goldwater, *Conscience of a Conservative,* 32–38.

12. Goldwater on the *Today Show,* January 24, 1964, in folder 797, box 10, Subseries 2, Campaign for the 1964 Republican Presidential Nomination, March 1963–June 1964 (1964 Campaign), Series 22, New York Office, RG15.NAR Gubernatorial.RAC.

13. Goldwater speech, New York City, January 15, 1964, in folder 789, ibid.

14. Goldwater speech, St. Anselm's, New Hampshire, in folder 783, ibid.

15. Goldwater, *Conscience of a Conservative,* 101.

16. Ibid., 88–127. See also Barry Goldwater, *Why Not Victory? A Fresh Look at American Foreign Policy* (New York: McGraw, Hill, 1962), 141–42; *U.S. News and World Report,* September 2, 1963.

17. Goldwater speech, January 22, 1964, in folder 795, box 10, Subseries 2, 1964 Campaign, Series 22, New York Office, RG15.NAR Gubernatorial.RAC.

18. Barry Goldwater oral history (1967), Columbia University Oral History Project, read at DDEL. See also Goldwater press conference, January 7, 1964, Concord, New Hampshire, in folder 782, box 10, Subseries 2, 1964 Campaign, Series 22, New York Office, RG15.NAR Gubernatorial.RAC.

19. Rockefeller speech, Nashua, New Hampshire, November 7, 1963, in box 12, Subseries 3, Special Assistant to the Governor for Radio and Television, 1961–1965 (Radio and TV), Series 22, New York Office, RG15.NAR Gubernatorial.RAC.

20. Rockefeller speech, Portsmouth, New Hampshire, December 31, 1963, in folder 1007, box 12, ibid.

21. Rockefeller appearance on *Face the Nation,* November 17, 1963, in folder 988, ibid.

22. Goldwater press conference, Portland, Oregon, February 7, 1964, in folder 505, box 8, Subseries 1, Appointments Office, 1959–1965, ibid.

23. Goldwater press conference, Paradise Valley, Arizona, January 3, 1964, in folder 779, box 10, Subseries 2, 1964 Campaign, ibid.

24. The other primary states were Wisconsin, Illinois, New Jersey, Massachusetts, Pennsylvania, Indiana, Ohio, Nebraska, West Virginia, Maryland, Florida, South Dakota, and Texas. The District of Columbia also had a primary.

25. Theodore White, *The Making of the President, 1964* (New York: Harper and Row, 1965), 131–33.

26. Ibid., 135–38. Nixon, also a write-in candidate, received 15,600.

27. Ibid., 142–43. Lodge and Nixon were both on the ballot in Oregon.

28. Ibid., 149, 161. The story of how Goldwater's team captured the delegates that were not committed to primaries is, in itself, an interesting story. In addition to *The Making of the President,* see F. Clifton White, *Suite 3505: The Story of the Draft Goldwater Movement* (New Rochelle, NY: Arlington House, 1967).

29. White, *Making of the President, 1964,* 151.

30. Robert Welch, *The Blue Book of the John Birch Society* (Belmont, MA: Western Islands, 1961), 119–20; Robert Welch, *The Politician* (Belmont, MA: Western Islands, 1963); Goldwater, *No Apologies,* 116.

31. "Ike Describes Ideal Candidate for Party," *New York Herald Tribune,* May 25, 1964, 1; Rockefeller News Conference, San Diego, May 25, 1964, in box 30, Graham Molitor Papers, RAC.

32. Peter Collier and David Horowitz, *The Rockefellers: An American Dynasty* (New York: Holt, Rinehart and Winston, 1976), 345–49.

33. Ibid., 350–53; White, *Making of the President, 1964,* 151.

34. Governors' Conference, Cleveland, Ohio, June 7, 1964, in NAR News Conferences, box 30, Molitor Papers, RAC.

35. Ibid.

36. White, *Making of the President, 1964,* 149–50, 153–54; Scranton interview for *Face the Nation,* June 7, 1964, in Transcripts, Speeches, box 31, Molitor Papers, RAC; Scranton interview for NBC-TV *Today,* New York City, June 8, 1964, in folder 922, box 11, Subseries 2, 1964 Campaign, Series 22, New York Office, RG15.NAR Gubernatorial.RAC; Scranton interview for *Issues and Answers,* June 14, 1964, in Transcripts, Speeches, box 31, Molitor Papers, RAC.

37. DDE Statement, June 11, 1964, in ST-2 Statement—Made by DDE (2), box 22, Principle Files, 1964, DDE Postpresidential Papers, DDEL.

38. Goldberg, *Goldwater,* 196; White, *Making of the President, 1964,* 181–88; Stephen Ambrose, *Nixon,* vol. 2, *The Triumph of a Politician, 1962–1972* (New York: Simon and Schuster, 1989), 51.

39. Goldwater quoted in *New York Times,* February 15, 1964, 11. See also Goldberg, *Goldwater,* 196–97.

40. Scranton quoted in *Time,* June 19, 1964, 14; Rockefeller News Conference, New York City, June 16, 1964, in box 30, Molitor Papers, RAC.

41. White, *Making of the President, 1964,* 238.

42. Scranton to Goldwater, July 12, 1964, in Scranton Convention Material, box 31, Molitor Papers, RAC.

43. Rockefeller speech, July 14, 1964, in San Francisco, 1964 Republican Convention, box 29, Speech Series, RG15.NAR Gubernatorial.RAC.

44. Rockefeller on the *Today Show,* July 15, 1964, in ibid.

45. Nixon, *Memoirs,* 260.

46. Rockefeller press release, July 17, 1964, in box 29, Speech Series, RG15.NAR Gubernatorial.RAC.

47. Nixon, *Memoirs,* 261.

48. Ibid.

49. DDE Statement, August 11, 1964, in Hershey, Pennsylvania, box 22, Principle Files, 1964, DDE Postpresidential Papers, DDEL.

50. Goldwater speech, August 12, 1964, ibid.

51. Nixon, *Memoirs,* 262.

52. DDE quoted in ibid.

53. Ibid., 262–63; Rockefeller speech, September 25, 1964, in Albany, New York City, box 29, Speech Series, RG15.NAR Gubernatorial.RAC.

54. Goldwater, *No Apologies,* 168–69, 173, 183.

55. Nixon, *Memoirs,* 263–64.

56. Ferrell, *Diary of James Hagerty,* 129.

Conclusion

1. *New York Times,* February 26, 1996, 7.

2. Pickett, *Eisenhower Decides to Run.*

3. Ronald Reagan, "A Time for Choosing, October 27, 1964," televised address for the Goldwater presidential campaign, Ronald Reagan Presidential Library (RRPL), <http://www.reagan.utexas.edu/archives/reference/timechoosing.html> (accessed November 6, 2005).

4. Mary C. Brennan, *Turning Right in the Sixties: The Conservative Capture of the GOP* (Chapel Hill: University of North Carolina Press, 1995).

5. Ronald Reagan, "Inaugural Address, January 20, 1981," Public Papers of President Ronald W. Reagan, RRPL, <http://www.reagan.utexas.edu/archives/speeches/1981/12081a.htm> (accessed November 6, 2005).

6. "The First Bush-Dukakis Presidential Debate, September 25, 1988," Commission on Presidential Debates, <http://www.debates.org/pages/trans88a.html> (accessed November 6, 2005).

7. *New York Times,* February 26, 1996, 7.

8. At least students in my Modern America course do.

Works Cited

Primary Sources

Manuscript Collections

Dwight D. Eisenhower Library, Abilene, Kansas (DDEL):
   Benson, Ezra Taft
   Eisenhower, Dwight D., Papers as President of the United States, 1953–1961 (Ann
      Whitman File)
      Administration Series
      Ann Whitman Diary Series
      Campaign Series
      DDE Diaries Series
      Legislative Meetings Series
      Name Series
      Speech Series
   Eisenhower, Dwight D., Papers, Postpresidential, 1961–69
   Eisenhower, Dwight D., Records as President, White House Central Files, 1953–1961
      Confidential File
      Official File
      President's Personal Files
   Fairless Committee
   Hobby, Oveta Culp
   Republican National Committee
   Rogers, William
   Republican National Committee, Office of the Chairman

Rockefeller Archive Center, North Tarrytown, New York:
   Molitor, Graham
   Rockefeller, Nelson A.
      Gubernatorial Files, 1959–1973
      Personal, Washington, D.C., Files, 1944–1958

Oral Histories

Columbia University Oral History Research Office:
   Bricker, John

Folsom, Marion B.
Goldwater, Barry
Knowland, William F.
Rockefeller, Nelson

Dwight D. Eisenhower Presidential Library:
Benson, Ezra Taft
Brownell, Herbert
Morrow, E. Frederic

Periodicals

Congressional Quarterly
Congressional Record
Fortune
New Republic
New York Herald Tribune
New York Times
New York Times Magazine
Time
Transcripts of Records and File Copies of Briefs (Supreme Court of the United States)
U.S. News and World Report
U.S. Supreme Court Reports
Wall Street Journal

Diaries, Memoirs, and Published Works

Adams, Sherman. *Firsthand Report: The Story of the Eisenhower Administration.* New York: Harper, 1961.

Benson, Ezra Taft. *Cross Fire: The Eight Years with Eisenhower.* New York: Doubleday, 1962.

Brownell, Herbert. *Advising Ike: The Memoirs of Attorney General Herbert Brownell.* Lawrence: University Press of Kansas, 1993.

Commission on Foreign Economic Policy. *Report to the President and Congress.* Washington, D.C.: GPO, 1954.

Eisenhower, Dwight D. *Crusade in Europe.* New York: Doubleday, 1948.

———. *The White House Years, a Personal Account: Mandate for Change, 1953–1956.* New York: Doubleday, 1963.

———. *The White House Years, a Personal Account: Waging Peace, 1956–1961.* New York: Doubleday, 1965.

Ferrell, Robert H., ed. *The Diary of James C. Hagerty: Eisenhower in Mid-course, 1954–1955.* Bloomington: Indiana University Press, 1983.

———. *The Eisenhower Diaries.* New York: Norton, 1981.

Goldwater, Barry. *Conscience of a Conservative.* Shepherdsville, Ky.: Victor, 1960.

———. *Goldwater.* New York: St. Martin's Press, 1988.

———. *Why Not Victory? A Fresh Look at American Foreign Policy.* New York: McGraw, Hill, 1962.

———. *With No Apologies.* New York: Berkley Books, 1979.

Griffith, Robert, ed. *Ike's Letters to a Friend, 1941–1958.* Lawrence: University Press of Kansas, 1984.

Johnson, Donald Bruce, and Kirk H. Porter, eds. *National Party Platforms, 1840–1972.* Urbana: University of Illinois Press, 1973.

Minutes and Documents of the Cabinet Meetings of President Eisenhower, 1953–1961. Microfilm. Ed. Paul Kesaris and Joan Gibson. Washington, D.C.: University Publications of America, 1980.

Morrow, E. Frederic. *Black Man in the White House: A Diary of the Eisenhower Years by the Administrative Officer for Special Projects, the White House, 1955–1961.* New York: Coward-McCann, 1963.

Nixon, Richard. *RN: The Memoirs of Richard Nixon.* New York: Simon and Schuster, 1978.

Prospect for America: The Rockefeller Panel Reports. New York: Doubleday, 1961.

Public Papers of the Presidents; Containing the Public Messages, Speeches, and Statements of the President, 1953–1961. 8 volumes. Washington, D.C.: GPO, 1958–1961.

U.S. Congress. Senate. Committee on Agriculture and Forestry. *Confirmation Hearing. Ezra Taft Benson, Secretary of Agriculture-Designate.* 83d Cong., 1st sess. January 15, 1953.

White, F. Clifton. *Suite 3505: The Story of the Draft Goldwater Movement.* New Rochelle, N.Y.: Arlington House, 1967.

Secondary Sources

Books

Alexander, Charles C. *Holding the Line: The Eisenhower Era, 1952–1961.* Bloomington: Indiana University Press, 1975.

Ambrose, Stephen. *Eisenhower.* Vol. 1, *Soldier, General of the Army, President-Elect, 1890–1952.* New York: Simon and Schuster, 1983.

———. *Eisenhower.* Vol. 2, *The President.* New York: Simon and Schuster, 1984.

———. *Nixon.* Vol. 1, *The Education of a Politician, 1913–1962.* New York: Simon and Schuster, 1987.

———. *Nixon.* Vol. 2, *The Triumph of a Politician, 1962–1972.* New York: Simon and Schuster, 1989.

Brennan, Mary C. *Turning Right in the Sixties: The Conservative Capture of the GOP.* Chapel Hill: University of North Carolina Press, 1995.

Burk, Robert F. *The Eisenhower Administration and Black Civil Rights.* Knoxville: University of Tennessee Press, 1984.

Collier, Peter, and David Horowitz. *The Rockefellers: An American Dynasty.* New York: Holt, Rinehart and Winston, 1976.

Congress and the Nation, 1945–1964: A Review of Government and Politics in the Postwar Years. Washington, D.C.: Congressional Quarterly Service, 1965.

Duram, James C. *A Moderate among Extremists: Dwight D. Eisenhower and the School Desegregation Crisis.* Chicago: Nelson-Hall, 1981.

Goldberg, Robert. *Barry Goldwater.* New Haven: Yale University Press, 1995.

Griffith, Robert. *The Politics of Fear: Joseph R. McCarthy and the Senate.* Rochelle Park, N.J.: Hayden, 1976.

Kaufman, Burton Ira. *Trade and Aid: Eisenhower's Foreign Economic Policy, 1953–1961.* Baltimore: Johns Hopkins University Press, 1982.

Lee, R. Alton. *Eisenhower and Landrum-Griffin: A Study in Labor Management Politics.* Lexington: University Press of Kentucky, 1990.

Mayer, George H. *The Republican Party, 1856–1964*. New York: Oxford University Press, 1964.

McDougall, Walter A. *The Heavens and the Earth: A Political History of the Space Age*. Baltimore: Johns Hopkins University Press, 1985.

Montgomery, Gayle B., and James W. Johnson. *One Step from the White House: The Rise and Fall of Senator William F. Knowland*. Berkeley and Los Angeles: University of California Press, 1998.

Morris, Joe Alex. *Nelson Rockefeller: A Biography*. New York: Harper, 1960.

Patterson, James T. *Mr. Republican: A Biography of Robert A. Taft*. Boston: Houghton Mifflin, 1972.

Persico, Joseph E. *The Imperial Rockefeller: A Biography of Nelson A. Rockefeller*. New York: Simon and Schuster, 1982.

Pickett, William B. *Eisenhower Decides to Run: Presidential Politics and Cold War Strategy*. Chicago: Ivan R. Dee, 2000.

Rae, Nicol C. *The Decline and Fall of the Liberal Republicans from 1952 to the Present*. New York: Oxford University Press, 1989.

Reich, Cary. *The Life of Nelson A. Rockefeller: Worlds to Conquer, 1908–1958*. New York: Doubleday, 1996.

Robinson, Archie. *George Meany and His Times: A Biography*. New York: Simon and Schuster, 1981.

Tananbaum, Dave. *The Bricker Amendment Controversy: A Test of Eisenhower's Political Leadership*. Ithaca: Cornell University Press, 1988.

Welch, Robert. *The Blue Book of the John Birch Society*. Belmont, Mass.: Western Islands, 1961.

———. *The Politician*. Belmont, Mass.: Western Islands, 1963.

White, Theodore. *The Making of the President, 1960*. New York: Harper and Row, 1961.

———. *The Making of the President, 1964*. New York: Harper and Row, 1965.

Web Sites

Commission on Presidential Debates
Dwight D. Eisenhower Presidential Library
Rockefeller Archive Center
Ronald Reagan Presidential Library

Index

Acheson, Dean, 89
Adams, Sherman, 56, 66, 82, 94, 115, 116, 117, 120, 122, 123
Agriculture, Department of, 50, 53, 56, 58
agricultural legislation: 1938, 44, 45; 1949, 47, 49; 1954, 52, 58; 1956, 57; 1958, 61
Aid to Education Act, 17
Aid to Impacted Areas (AIA), 16, 23
Aiken, George, 46, 52, 55
Alsop, Stewart, 139
American Federation of Labor–Congress of Industrial Organizations (AFL-CIO), 20, 28, 36, 37, 41
American Medical Association (AMA), 15, 16
Americans for Democratic Action (ADA), 15
Anderson, Clinton, 47, 55
Anderson, Robert, 67, 116

baby boom, 17
Benson, Ezra Taft: on agriculture policy, 50, 51, 52, 53, 58; on federal aid for education, 24; general views of, 43, 48, 49, 135; on meeting Eisenhower, 43; on Soil Bank, 54, 55
Bently, Alvin M., 109
Bohlen, Charles E. "Chip," 89, 91, 112
Brannan, Charles, 46
Brennan, William J., 75
Bricker, John, 17, 29, 90, 112–13, 122, 124; and Bricker amendment, 91–96
Bridges, Styles, 90, 106, 109
Brown, Clarence J., 21
Brownell, Herbert, 34, 116, 117; on appointment of Earl Warren, 70–71; and Bricker amendment, 93, 94, 95;

and *Brown v. Board,* 72, 73, 74; and civil rights legislation, 76; and desegregation of Little Rock Central High School, 81, 82
Brown v. Board, 16, 20, 22, 69–75, 76, 77, 81, 84, 135–36
Buchanan, Patrick, 145
Budget Bureau, 15
Bunche, Ralph, 80
Burton, Herald, 70
Bush, George H. W., 147
Byrd, Harry, 122
Byrnes, James F., 72

campaigns and elections: 1946, 29; 1952, 8, 27, 97; 1954, 34, 100–101, 114, 116; 1956, 76, 77, 114, 116, 119, 121, 146; 1958, 24, 61, 123–24, 146; 1960, 123, 124–31, 146; 1964, 133–34, 137–44
Chamber of Commerce, 10, 36, 38
Chynowith, Bradford G., 7, 65
civil rights legislation: 1957, 81, 85; 1960, 86; 1964, 141, 144
"Civil Rights Manifesto," 77
Clark, Mary Todhunter, 139
Columbia Broadcasting System (CBS), 66
Commerce, Department of, 30, 32, 66
Curtis, Carl T., 11, 12

Darden, Colgate W., 107
Davies, Ronald N., 81, 83
Defense, Department of, 107, 108
Defense Production Acts, 47, 49, 50, 51
Deupress, Richard R., 107
Dewey, Thomas, 3, 116, 123, 124, 125
Dingell, John D., 11